REFLECTING ON OUR WORK

NSF Teacher Enhancement in K-6 Mathematics

Edited by

Susan N. Friel
George W. Bright

This project was supported, in part,
by the

National Science Foundation
Opinions expressed are those of the authors
and not necessarily those of the Foundation

University Press of America, Inc.
Lanham • New York • London

Copyright © 1997 by
University Press of America,® Inc.
4720 Boston Way
Lanham, Maryland 20706

12 Hid's Copse Rd.
Cummor Hill, Oxford OX 2 9JJ

Library of Congress Cataloging-in-Publication Data

Reflecting on our work : NSF teacher enhancement in K-6 mathematics
/ edited by Susan N. Friel and George W. Bright.
p.   cm.
l. Mathematics--Study and teaching (Elementary)--United States--
Congresses. I. Friel, Susan N. II. Bright, George W.
QA135.5.R425   1997   372.7--dc21   96-39396 CIP

ISBN 0-7618-0633-4 (cloth: alk.: ppr.)
ISBN 0-7618-0634-2 (pbk: alk. ppr.)

™ The paper used in this publication meets the minimum
requirements of American National Standard for information
Sciences—Permanence of Paper for Printed Library Materials,
ANSI Z39.48—1984

Table of Contents

CHAPTER I: Overview of the Conference

> *Mathematics teachers develop professionally in the same ways all other teachers do but with a specific focus of applying professional knowledge within a meaningful and relevant mathematical context for the improvement of the mathematical understanding of children and youth.*
>
> *Professional development takes many forms, but true professional development, in the sense of resulting in meaningful and long-lasting qualitative change in a teacher's thinking and approaches to educating, is an autonomous activity chosen by a teacher in search of better ways of knowing and teaching mathematics.*
>
> Castle and Aichele, 1994, p. 3.

In November 1994, with funding provided from the National Science Foundation (NSF), a small, informal conference was held that focused on teacher enhancement in elementary mathematics education. Conference attendees included recognized experts in professional development and teacher change for K–6 teacher enhancement, primarily in mathematics. They were convened in order to organize, summarize, and discuss what is known about models of effective teacher enhancement. Representatives from a few science programs were also included so that the perspectives of both mathematics and science would be addressed. (See Appendix C for final conference agenda.)

Rationale for the Conference

For a number of years, there has been general agreement that K–12 mathematics and science teaching in the United States is in critical need of major reform. This belief is driven by a number of factors: the changing demography of the student population, demands for equity with respect to underrepresented groups, increasing availability of technology in the schools, changes in what are appropriate knowledge and skills for the workplace, and international competitiveness.

In response to this identified need, the National Science Foundation has supported a wide variety of Teacher Enhancement Projects with a view to learning what strategies are effective in bringing about genuine, long-term teacher change (i.e., improved teaching and learning in mathematics or science) and, ultimately, long-term systemic change in schools. These projects have served as "pilot" or "experimental" programs, allowing NSF and the Principal Investigators to explore a variety of strategies for working with teachers to promote changes in the ways they teach and facilitate student learning of mathematics and science.

In Spring, 1994, NSF was in the midst of planning efforts directed toward moving teacher enhancement for mathematics, science, and technology from the experimental or piloting phase to a large-scale implementation phase with national impact. As a first important step in this direction, Congress asked for a federally supported initiative to reach 600,000 K–12 teachers (with at least half being at the K–6 level) with a minimum of 100 hours of intensive professional development. (See Appendix D.)

Given NSF's history of support for pilot teacher enhancement efforts and plans for large-scale implementation, it seemed to be a good time to take stock of what has been learned through NSF-funded Teacher Enhancement Projects. NSF has supported the identification and development of a number of promising practices, and documentation of both successes and cautions seemed a reasonable expectation. Further, given the emphasis on K–6 education, it seemed clear that there needed to be a synthesis of current understanding of the impact of particular efforts in mathematics and science teacher enhancement at these levels.

Purpose of the Conference

The conference addressed the following central question:

> *As a result of research and experience, what do we know about teacher enhancement programs K–6 in mathematics that can inform the design of large-scale teacher enhancement programs with optimal impact?*

In particular, it was hoped we could identify several kinds of information:

1. Generic principles to guide development of teacher enhancement programs.
2. Common components across current teacher enhancement programs.
3. Capabilities of current teacher enhancement programs to respond to scaling up their work.
4. Alternative strategies and options that may be different from what is occurring in current teacher-enhancement programs.

Participants included Principal Investigators from selected NSF-funded Teacher Enhancement Projects and curriculum supervisors, principals, and teachers who had participated or were participating in the projects represented at the conference. The projects were selected to exemplify diversity in terms of professional development models. Selected other participants included experts on teacher change, staff development, sociology of school change, assessment, and policy development. (See Appendix E for list of participants.)

One emphasis of the conference was on the sharing among the Teacher Enhancement Projects. Some science projects were included so that the Principal Investigators from these projects could articulate the major themes that have emerged from science-based Teacher Enhancement Projects and address the relationship of mathematics reform to concurrent science reform.

Pre-Conference Work

Representatives from the Teacher Enhancement Projects represented at the conference prepared descriptions of those projects which were received and read by participants prior to the conference (See Appendix B). In their descriptions, Principal Investigators were asked to respond to several questions:

1. Provide a one-page overview about how your project works or worked.
2. Based on your experiences, what have you learned (and/or now hypothesize) about helping elementary teachers improve mathematics instruction, including the delivery of instruction to all students? If possible, cite or briefly describe evidence that supports your comments.
3. Based on what you have learned, what advice might you give to someone who is thinking about planning for large-scale teacher change in mathematics instruction that has optimal impact? As a particular, how can we address the need to reach diverse teacher populations?

4. Based on your experiences, how would you suggest that people monitor and/or evaluate both teacher change and student change in such large-scale projects?

Four issues identification papers were also developed either prior to or as a follow-up to the conference (See Appendix A). Pre-conference drafts of three of these papers were distributed to participants addressing issues related to teacher change in mathematics education (Ball), reform efforts in mathematics education (Ferrini-Mundy), and systemic change, teacher change, and staff development (Loucks-Horsley). Authors of these pre-conference papers were asked to consider specific sub-questions (detailed below), identifying, clarifying, and/or emphasizing issues that should be considered, given the purpose of the conference.

1. What do we know about effecting changes in *teachers*? (e.g., what are the salient characteristics of effective programs; what can be achieved in a given length of time; how is that time best distributed; does grade level matter; does mathematics content matter?)
2. What do we know about effecting changes in *schools and school districts*? (e.g., how are the various stakeholders best involved; what kinds of commitments are necessary; what kinds of networking and partnerships work best; what kinds of models are best suited to different kinds of schools [e.g., inner city, rural]; what is the relationship of mathematics reform to concurrent science reform; how should the community be involved?)
3. What do we know about how changes in teachers and schools effect changes in *children*? (e.g., what kinds of support do children need, [e.g., parental, peer]; what changes in children's understanding of mathematics result from changing teachers and schools; instructional materials/resources; assessment practices?)
4. What *resources* (i.e., human, institutional, monetary) are available for this teacher enhancement effort? How can they best be marshaled and organized?
5. What do we know about *assessing impact* of teacher enhancement programs? (e.g., how do we document and/or measure changes in teachers, schools, and students?)
6. What are other related issues that must be considered and are not addressed by the above five sub-questions? (e.g., how much "start-up" time do projects need; how can community resources [museums] be integrated; what role do business/school partnerships have; what is the role of teacher-leader models vs. direct delivery of inservice to teachers?)

An additional post-conference paper was commissioned as one of the outcomes of the conference. This paper addressed issues related to evaluation of Teacher Enhancement Projects (Hein).

Structure of the Conference

In initial plans, the authors of the issues identification were to present short sessions that expanded their discussion of issues related to the sub-questions, incorporating what they had gained by reading the project descriptions. The goal for their presentations was to look for contradictions, in a sense "hunting for the truth" in order to sharpen the issues in relation to what they had read in the project descriptions and to provoke conference participants' thinking in anticipation of the tasks to be addressed in working groups.

Working groups were to be formed and, in a variety of break-out sessions, were expected to respond to issues pertinent to the NSF initiative, making recommendations relating to:

1. What does "scaling up" mean? What are the units of transformation we want to consider? (e.g., whole school; individual teachers; lead teachers; enhancing content knowledge; enhancing pedagogy; changing cultures in schools; implementing new curriculum?) Are there existing models or combinations of models that are good candidates for expanding to large-scale projects? Are there alternative models that need to be piloted as part of the "scaling-up" efforts?

2. What goals are reasonable to set under various conditions? (e.g., length of time, money, current situation of targeted schools, and so on).

3. What should the tie-ins be with large projects like Goals 2000, Statewide Systemic Initiatives, Urban Systemic Initiatives, and so on?

4. What factors need to be in place to ensure that momentum continues after NSF funding ceases?

5. How can available resources for teacher enhancement be effectively distributed for maximum benefit?

6. What data do we need to collect to accurately assess the impact of the project?

7. What partnerships should we form in order to provide adequate resources—human and financial?

8. Should mathematics and science teacher enhancement be done together? Under what circumstances is this viable? What are the pros and cons?

Monograph

This monograph reports the outcomes of the conference and includes the papers written as part of the conference. The conference itself very quickly took on a life and shape of its own; agenda and tasks were modified and redefined. Many of the original questions and/or issues were not addressed directly, yet many other questions and/or issues were raised and addressed that stimulated all participants to creative work not anticipated when we first began our endeavor together.

Reference

Castle, K., & Aichele, D. B. (1994). Professional development and teacher autonomy. In D. B. Aichele & A. F. Coxford (Eds.) *Professional development for teachers of mathematics* (pp. 1–8). Reston, VA: National Council of Teachers of Mathematics.

CHAPTER II: Common Components and Guiding Principles for Teacher Enhancement Programs

> *Quilts are designed very differently. You have crazy quilts, you have sampler quilts in which every section is different, you have ones that have real designs in them. And you can also have combinations of those. You can have a centerpiece that is a crazy quilt and then build more specialized designs around the outside. But quilting takes a lot of time and it takes attention to detail. That's exactly what we need to be able to do. If you cut a piece slightly wrong, it doesn't fit and then you have to start over again. If you try to put certain colors together even though intuitively they look like they are going to work, you find that they don't so you start over again.*
>
> Margaret Cozzens, conference transcript[1]

Drawing an analogy with quilt making is one way to describe both the process and the products of the conference. By making adjustments and modifications throughout the process of working together, pieces were created that indeed did fit well together. The number of working groups that formed and re-formed attests to the patterns that seemed to work well as people made choices for where to spend their energies. What is the quilt that has been crafted? It is a combination quilt that involves many different elements but, when we step back, we find that it is a quilt with a real design.

At the center of the design are pieces which represent common principles that may be used to guide development of teacher enhancement programs. The three issues papers provide the major points from which we compare, contrast, and generalize principles about professional development as it relates to teacher enhancement in K–6 mathematics. Each of the authors wrote from a slightly different

---

[1] The main sessions of the conference were audiotaped; written transcriptions of these sessions were used in preparation of this manuscript. For the most part, the participants quoted are not named; it was not always possible to idenify who was speaking during the discussions.

perspective, and while they give voice to a number of common principles, the conference participants supplemented and clarified understandings that need to be considered with respect to professional development (See Figure 1, p. 15).

Teacher Beliefs

The authors stress the importance of teacher beliefs. Ball[2] points to the impact these beliefs have on what teachers learn. Loucks-Horsley notes that working to change teacher beliefs (as opposed to attitudes and behaviors) is the first and primary work of professional development. Many of the project discussion papers also highlight the importance of addressing teacher beliefs. Beliefs may be explicit (stated) or implicit (not at the level of awareness on the part of the believer); indeed stated beliefs may not always appear to be consistent with practice.

Strategies to support changes in teachers' beliefs are not clearly defined. As Ferrini-Mundy notes, experimenting with practice may change beliefs. "It is clear that teachers' beliefs about the value of certain reformist tenets shift as a result of their tentative experimentation with practice" (p. 123). This results from teachers seeing evidence of student success in their classrooms during such experimentation. Nelson notes that changes in beliefs and changes in practice are an interactive process. As teachers' conceptions of learning and mathematics change, they begin to see their classrooms through different eyes and want to interact differently with their students. Corwin comments on the potential for videotapes of one's own classrooms or cases written about the dilemmas of teaching to impact beliefs and practice. The first step in change is becoming aware of the beliefs that are shaping practice. The next step may well be creating tension between what is currently believed and "evidence" that challenges those beliefs. Clearly, practice is unlikely to change without changes in beliefs.

Time for Change

The need for time is addressed by the three authors. Ball emphasizes that learning to create the kinds of teaching envisioned by mathematics

---

[2] Both issues papers and project descriptions are cited throughout the manuscript by referring to the author(s) in the manner shown. Papers are not referenced at the end of a chapter as they are included in the appendices of this monograph.

reform takes a *long time* and is hard. Loucks-Horsley supports the claim that change takes a long time and provides a developmental perspective within which to view change as a process. She reviews the Concerns-Based Adoption Model for describing teacher change.

> *People undergoing change evolve in the kinds of questions they ask and in their use of the change. In general, early questions are more self-oriented (what is it? how will it affect me?); when these questions are resolved, questions emerge that are more task-oriented (how do I do it? how can I use these materials efficiently? how can I organize myself? why is it taking so much time?). Finally, when self and task concerns are largely resolved, the individual can focus on impact: is this change working for my students? is there something that will work even better?* (Loucks-Horsley, p. 135)

Such a developmental perspective has implications for professional development. Loucks-Horsley further notes that it is important: (a) to attend to where people are and to address the questions they are asking when they are asking them, (b) to pay attention to implementation over several years because of the transitions people need to make between resolving earlier concerns and moving forward with newer concerns, and (c) to create realistic expectations in the system for change. It is likely to take one to two years (at minimum) for teachers to become comfortable and routine in using a new practice or program, so expecting student achievement to change in the same time frame is not realistic. Loucks-Horsley emphasizes that change is a process not an event. This perspective makes sense in the context of the model for change that she discusses.

In a similar vein, Ferrini-Mundy highlights vision as a process, not a product. Visions happen at many different levels. Vision statements are written for school systems and for schools; however, each teacher has a vision of mathematics learning and teaching (tied to beliefs) as well. Loucks-Horsley's work suggests that as teachers change, their visions of the teaching and learning also change. Schools and systems are made up of people; it is probably not surprising to consider that visioning and goal-setting on a macro level may operate in a manner similar to that at a micro level.

Implicit within the context of time and change is the need to address ways to find time for teachers to collaborate and/or reflect. In addition, as suggested in some of the project discussions, time to plan for teaching and learning needs to be addressed. Data from international studies suggests that American teachers spend more time teaching during a school day than their counterparts (Shanker, 1995). Further, evidence suggests that limiting the time to teach is not synonymous with "working less," either here or abroad. Rather, time not spent in direct teaching with students is used for instructional planning and for providing additional academic support for individuals or groups of students. The need for adequate time to teach and time to learn (plan, collaborate, reflect) appears at the top of most teachers' lists of roadblocks.

Reflection, Collaboration, and Inquiry

Reflection, collaboration, and inquiry may be viewed as *three* sides of the same coin. Teachers need to reflect; often this may be more productive if there can be interactions among teachers with respect to that reflection. There are a number of questions that surface as we consider the role of reflection:

1. What do we mean by reflection? Is there a difference between reflection and sharing?
2. Are teachers naturally reflective? What motivates teachers to want to reflect?
3. With whom do teachers need to reflect? Other teachers? ...parents? ...administrators? ...students?
4. Who else needs to reflect and, again, with whom? Administrators? ...parents?
5. What is the substance of reflection? ...teaching practice? ...children's learning? ...mathematics?
6. Does reflection have to be done with others? All of the time? ...some of the time?
7. Are there constraints that make reflection harder to do in this job than in other jobs?

Collaboration points to the issue of isolation that exists among teachers. Working collaboratively often supports teachers' inquiry into their practice as they seek to change practice and to reflect on these efforts to change. As Schifter notes, the kind of teaching that is now proposed necessitates a greater investment in the instructional responsibility of the teacher which, concomitantly, entails a greater need for collegial cooperation. The project discussions also provide insights into strategies that may be used for promoting reflection, collaboration, and inquiry.

Teacher Participation in Planning

The importance of teachers' role in making choices and planning agendas surfaces across papers. Ball's statement that teacher development is especially productive when the teachers are in charge of the agenda raises issues that may be characterized simplistically as the "blind leading the blind." During the conference, participants struggled with the role of teachers (and other school personnel) and the place of "experts" in making decisions about the nature and content of professional development. Loucks-Horsley tempers the dictate "teachers must be in charge" by noting that effective professional development programs need to involve participants in decisions about as many aspects as possible. Ferrini-Mundy characterizes this consideration under a broader heading of congruence and fit, noting that there is often a match between how a site chooses to interpret a reform and the critical contextual features at the site. Her comments point to the influence of the context as an additional factor in determining the agenda. Various project discussions also address this issue.

In order to help teacher leaders understand new directions in mathematics education, one project (Bright, et al.) held "visioning" sessions prior to the teachers' conducting needs assessments of the mathematics programs at their respect schools. The purpose was to expose teachers to such change efforts as those initiated by the NCTM *Standards* (NCTM, 1989, 1991) and to provide them with one or more situations in which they experienced mathematics in a way that modeled the directions espoused in the *Standards*. The intent was to begin to broaden teachers' views of what is good mathematics instruction so that they could better assess their programs and their needs. Following these visioning sessions, teacher leaders spent a considerable amount of time assessing their needs at the school level with respect to mathematics education and, using their needs assessments, developing school improvement plans. The school improvement plans were used in planning summer workshops. The receptivity of teacher leaders in this project (Bright, et al.) to the content of the summer workshops appeared to be related to the fact that they felt that they had influenced this content through their school improvement plans.

In other projects, the role of outside experts is addressed directly.

Ongoing involvement of nationally recognized experts strengthens and enriches every aspect of reform projects. Consultants ... have the capacity to be objective about local conditions which impact the success of reform. Outside change agents are free to challenge ideas and practices and offer constructive suggestions from a national perspective. (Gregg, p. 219)

Parker also points to the impact of outside change agents when district-level mathematics restructuring efforts are at issue. Such change agents, while working with district decision makers, are removed from internal politics; they may be able to more easily challenge existing structures and practices.

Contexts in which Teachers Work

Both the context of the school/school district and the community's involvement are raised as important components. As Ball notes, context includes space and resources and, more importantly, students, parents, administrators, testing practices and policies, and district and state curricular objectives and guidelines. Loucks-Horsley addresses the issue of context as a "systems concern," that is, the success of professional development depends on simultaneous attention to changing the system within which teachers work. She notes that a major premise of systems thinking is that it is not the individuals who are responsible for the problems, rather the systems in which they live and work must be aligned and strengthened if change is to happen. Ferrini-Mundy addresses context and community in two points. She notes that systematic attention to community involvement is important. This ranges from notes home and parents' nights to formal committees involving parents in making decisions about the goals of a mathematics program. In addition, her broader characterization of "congruence and fit" points to the impact of critical contextual features at a site which must be taken into account when seeking to make changes of any magnitude.

The importance of the school functioning as an involved and informed community surfaced during discussions at the conference. Large-scale teacher change occurs by school, not by individual(s). Being a member of a community matters, and attention to the culture of the school is important. "Empowered" teachers returning to "unempowered" environments run into trouble. Teacher learning is both an individual and collective community activity. Isolation makes growth and change very difficult.

The role of the principal and the importance of parent involvement and understanding with respect to the changes being made cannot be minimized. Various project discussions address this component to a greater or lesser extent. Many clearly specify the important role that the principal plays as instructional leader.

Active participation is necessary if principals are to be knowledgeable of mathematics reform goals, able to distinguish between classroom practices consistent with and inconsistent with those goals, understanding of the change process, prepared to support teachers' risk taking and growth through periods of confusion and discouragement, and able to effectively communicate the necessity and goals of mathematics reform efforts to parents and to teachers. (Parker, p. 239)

It is clear that better articulation of what needs to be done and how to do it in the context of systemic attention to school and community involvement remains to be done.

Teacher Leadership

Specialists of many sorts seem to be key to successful efforts in schools (Ferrini-Mundy). Their roles include spreading ideas, facilitating communications among teachers, planning and initiating staff development, and addressing political problems with administrators and community members. Loucks-Horsley includes leadership and sustained effort as attributes of effective professional development programs. She notes that leadership may come from administrators but it can also come from teacher leadership teams.

A number of participants at the conference were involved in projects in which the development of teacher leadership was the major focus. Both Gregg and Parker caution against identifying teacher leadership candidates too early, noting that teacher leaders often "emerge" as part of a process of professional development. Such teachers have credibility with their staffs and also are willing to take risks and push for deep-level mathematics restructuring in their own classrooms. The importance of classroom experiences is further highlighted by Friel and Danielson. Classroom experiences provide leaders with "personal memory tapes" of the practical, as well as the pedagogical, issues related to implementation.

Bush notes that the support facilitated by teacher leaders appears to be more successful than actually offering short workshops. Support groups which meet regularly to share ideas and concerns seem to have greater impact on classroom practice. Friel and Danielson point out that teachers who become workshop leaders may need specialized assistance in conceptualizing effective staff development. Such leaders progress through their own stages of growth with respect to readiness and potential to serve as workshop leaders. Further, as Gregg notes, teachers do not automatically make connections between facilitating the learning of children and facilitating the learning of adults. Grady also notes that specialized training is needed to support lead teachers' efforts to move beyond their own classrooms to work with colleagues who are seeking to reform their own mathematics teaching. Serving in a support capacity for other teachers may be part of a developmental process that leads eventually to conducting workshops and institutes.

Bright, et al., identify factors that help teachers carry out leadership roles, including cooperative work with principals, close networking among the lead teachers, and explicit attention during inservice to helping lead teachers understand factors that inhibit change. Joyner comments on the need to set expectations for leadership. The teachers with whom she worked agreed prior to participation that they would carry out a variety of leadership tasks including conducting inservice programs for other teachers.

Several of the leadership projects highlight the importance of teacher teams.

> *There are two major reasons why change agents should work in teams. First, while many mathematics reform issues relate directly to all levels (primary, intermediate, middle school, and high school), the way the issues play out in specific day-to-day classroom practices varies significantly at those levels. Expertise must be provided at each level while assuring that consistent and compatible practices are promoted overall. Articulation between grade levels and between school levels will become important as districts work to institutionalize powerful mathematics programs. Second, restructuring efforts that result in classrooms, schools and districts aligned with the NCTM Standards are long-term, involve many unanticipated surprises, and can often be messy, uncomfortable, and frustrating for both participants and change agents. Change agents will need the support that comes form working in teams as they work to understand and communicate with their constituents about the complex dynamics involved in change efforts of this magnitude. (Parker, p. 244)*

At a building level, Bright, et al., comment that it seems important to have two teachers working together to provide support for each other. In hindsight, teams of two teachers from primary grades or from intermediate grades rather than primary/intermediate teams may prove to be more beneficial when considering teacher leadership development.

Underhill notes that change agents need strong support mechanisms and that focusing on teams of teachers offers greater strength if both are trained in leadership, integration, and content. Both Friel and Danielson and Joyner emphasize the importance of teacher teams serving as presenters for workshops, reflecting an awareness of the differing strengths of teacher leaders and the importance of collegial planning.

Long-Term, Ongoing Support

Ball and Loucks-Horsley emphasize the role of follow-up as part of most effective staff development models. This usually takes the form of long-term support. Indeed, many now consider this a part of the professional development program, not as follow-up but rather as an integral part of an on-going program.

There are a variety of reasons to plan for follow-up support. These include helping teachers reflect on their practice, building networks so that teachers can learn from each other, keeping the focus on staff development for a long enough time so that teachers can internalize the change, helping teachers overcome conditions that may work against the continued development of the focus of the staff development, facilitating dialogue and communication among teachers, providing time for someone to monitor what is going in the school, and providing a sounding board for problems. On-site support seems to be a critical aspect of follow up. This may be provided by someone in the building, a team partner who might be at another school, electronic teaming, and so on.

There continues to be a lack of clarity, however, about what constitutes "effective follow-up." Although many projects engage in long-term support, it may be difficult to capture its essence from the words written in this manuscript. It would seem that the events that begin a project often meld into the building of a community that both gives and needs support which may be provided in a variety of ways. Bush offers the guideline that a successful teacher enhancement project should use professional development models which include mentoring, peer coaching, team teaching, and reflection. He highlights what many now believe: professional development activities for teachers must be more sustained that a series of workshops. Schifter points out that regular school-year support is an indispensable catalyst for the change process. Visions of possibility may be created in inservice courses or institutes; realities of implementation happen in teachers' classrooms with their own students. As teachers begin to make changes in practice, they are confronted with innumerable issues and ideas that could not be predicted, much less addressed, in earlier inservice work. Rather, on-site and immediate mechanisms are needed to help teachers address questions and challenges that arise and receive support for their continued efforts to make change.

Subject Matter Knowledge

Ball highlights the importance of subject matter knowledge in learning to teach for understanding. As Schifter notes, teachers themselves must become mathematics learners. Not only must inservice programs provide opportunities for teachers to explore their own mathematics content knowledge, they must also help teachers learn how to learn mathematics in the context of their own teaching. In her project, Corwin involved teachers first in the doing of mathematics.

> *We are now confident that doing mathematics and reflecting on it make a major contribution to a paradigm shift for many teachers in a long-term staff development program. Shifting the focus from their teaching helps some teachers pursue their own mathematical identities. Subsequently they develop more mathematical confidence.... Too often in inservice meetings teachers' own mathematics is not being enhanced because the mathematics in teacher enhancement seminars is done for the children.* (Corwin, p. 188-9)

Grady found that one of the factors needed to help teachers change their practice focused on content, specifically, the need to provide strong mathematics content sessions given by a mathematician who has a practicing experience of the elementary classroom. Bush talks about developing sufficient pedagogical knowledge in mathematics— mathematics that elementary teachers need to understand in order to challenge their students. Parker notes, too, that the practice of addressing mathematics for teachers as learners is not always popular with teachers. Teachers involved in doing mathematics often argue that they can't afford the time. Their preference is to have new activities for their classrooms. However, over time, teachers do come to value this process and their own mathematical empowerment.

To teach mathematics well, a teacher needs to know mathematics— specifically, the nature and structure of school mathematics. The *Teaching Standards* (NCTM, 1991) make a point of highlighting the importance of having teachers revisit school mathematics, this time from a perspective quite different than the one they held as students.

> *Central to the preparation for teaching mathematics is the development of a deep understanding of the mathematics of the school curriculum and how it fits within the discipline of mathematics. Too often, it is taken for granted that teachers' knowledge of the content of school mathematics is in place by the time they complete their own K–12 learning experiences. Teachers need opportunities to revisit school mathematics topics in ways that will allow them to develop deeper understandings of the subtle ideas and relationships that are involved between and among concepts.* (NCTM, 1991, p. 134)

There are a variety of ways to address the issue of learning mathematics content, including engaging teachers in adult-relevant mathematical activities, studying rich problems with students so that students' thinking is exposed, exploring adult-level tasks but with content that is generally relevant to the mathematics content that teachers are expected to teach, and inquiring into classroom situations that raise the need for deeper understanding of mathematical thinking.

Children's Thinking

Teachers' knowledge of content interacts with their knowledge of children. Ball indicates that knowledge of children and their mathematics is crucial to teaching for understanding. Nelson concurs, noting that the changes in mathematics instruction proposed by the NCTM *Standards* require the development of a professional and school culture that supports ongoing inquiry into how students' mathematical thinking develops.

Fennema, et al., have investigated how learning about children's thinking in addition and subtraction and in whole-number arithmetic influences primary grades teachers' instruction, beliefs, and the learning of their children.

> *Knowledge of their own children's thinking enables teachers to make instructional decisions so that children's learning of mathematics improves.* (Fennema, et al., p. 195)

The structure of the professional development experiences in this project has teachers engaged in doing activities which enable them to consider the research-based model in relationship to children. Central to this, they view videotapes of children solving problems and identify relationships between the solution strategies and the problem types, and how the solution strategies they see can be used to predict how other problems can be solved. Eventually, they interact with their own students in similar ways in order to make their students' thinking visible in ways the can be used to direct instruction.

Campbell, et al., also interpret research addressing children's learning of mathematical topics that are critical to a given grade level. The expectation is that teachers reflect on the needs of their children and work with others to determine the activities, problems, or resources they should access. Three approaches to do this are utilized.

> *One scheme is to make time available to examine and discuss examples of commercial materials that address mathematical topics appropriate for children. The second venue is to offer examples of activities or tasks, but always with another purpose in mind ... a third approach is to follow an adult-level mathematics session with the challenge to the teachers to define a task that would address that same mathematical topic at a level appropriate for their students.* (Campbell et al., p. 184)

Gregg discusses the value of structuring interview sessions with small groups of children. In this format, one teacher interviews students to probe their thinking about a specific mathematical idea while a second teacher records responses. As educators learn about the conceptions children hold and how children think, they increasingly are willing to restructure learning experiences in their own classrooms, engage in dialogue about the results, and continue to work to improve instructional practice. At the same time, they may well deepen their own understanding of mathematics.

Role of Curriculum

Ferrini-Mundy comments on the dilemma that reform sites experience in coming to grips with the role of curriculum. Decisions about mathematical content emphasis, pedagogical strategies, and so on may be quite dependent on the nature of the curricular stance. Indeed, as was voiced during the conference, the choice of curriculum may well set the context for what is valued as mathematics and mathematics pedagogy. Do reform sites look to adopting and adapting reform curriculum that are now available with some widespread commitment across a district? Do they attempt to "create their own" curriculum—a practice that may prove to be more limiting to reform in the long run? Or do they find some place "in the middle" and if so, what is that place?

Russell addresses the role of curriculum as a tool for professional development. She presents several views of mathematics curriculum, highlighting the view that the best mathematics teaching environment is a partnership between teacher and curriculum.

> *The link between curriculum and teacher decision-making is a focus on mathematical reasoning. Neither curriculum nor teacher can fully anticipate the complex and idiosyncratic nature of the mathematical thinking that might go on among thirty students in a single classroom during any one mathematics class. However, both teacher and curriculum contribute to a repertoire of knowledge about student thinking that leads to better mathematics teaching and learning.* (Russell, p. 248-9)

Russell emphasizes that the best use of good curriculum materials is in the context of a long-term staff development program in which teachers are engaged in ongoing reflections about students' mathematical thinking and about their own continued work with their peers on mathematics content. Schifter makes the point that teacher development and curriculum reform go hand-in-hand. Curricular materials must become a vehicle for ongoing teacher development in order to help teachers deepen their knowledge of mathematics content, children's mathematical thinking, and pedagogical approaches.

Modeling Pedagogical Approaches

"Teachers teach the way they are taught" and "professional development experiences must model appropriate pedagogy" go hand-in-hand and have surfaced as common rhetoric, often supported by infrequent action.

> *Mathematics and mathematics education instruction should enable all learners to experience mathematics as a dynamic engagement in solving problems. These experiences should be designed deliberately to help teachers rethink their conceptions of what mathematics is, what a mathematics class is like, and how mathematics is learned.* (NCTM, 1991, p. 128)

As Ball notes, teacher educators and staff developers should model the approaches which they are promoting. This becomes more problematic as the directions for teaching shift to a constructivist view of learning. What does it mean to create a constructivist environment of teachers' learning?

> *Just as we need literate teachers ... we need numerate teachers who enjoy finding patterns and exploring relationships—teachers who are open to the rhythms and balances of spatial and numerical relationships, interested in questions of "what if" in mathematics. Keeping an exploratory frame of mind alive in staff development experiences is essential if we want teachers to replicate that mindset in their classrooms. A challenge for large programs, it is still necessary to find ways of retaining tentativeness, serendipity, and spontaneity.* (Corwin, p. 189)

> *It is increasingly evident that tenets of constructivism apply to adult learners. Learning is a meaning-making process which is personally constructed and impacted by experience, context, and the environment. Teachers need to continuously experience learning through problem solving and inquiry before they can own the process.* (Gregg, p. 217)

> *Just as mathematics instruction must be organized to facilitate construction of mathematical concepts, so should in-service instruction facilitate construction of a new pedagogical theory and practice.* (Schifter, et al., p. 256)

Constructivist pedagogy extends well beyond the workshop.

> *Sharing personal experiences and particular struggles and triumphs in the process of change provided acknowledgment that this hard work is an important part of the process of change and helped teachers see that the process of learning something new has ups and downs for everyone—themselves, their colleagues, and their students. Summer institutes and Inquiry Groups where teachers worked collegially provided a context in which they could be learning to listen to another person's mathematical thinking and asking the question that helps that person stretch their thinking just a bit.* (Nelson, p. 231)

Tensions of Change

Ferrini-Mundy raises a set of issues that might be characterized as the "emotional" tensions of change. The disequilibrium and disagreement that are an inevitable part of reform exist in tension with high levels of caring and respect for individuals' feelings and points of views. Similar tensions emerge when confronted with deeply held philosophical differences about the commitment to development of "basic skills" and development of understanding. Additional "insiders" tensions arise because of the presence of both "nay-sayers" and the "anointed" within the context of reform in a school or school district as teachers move on different paths toward reform in mathematics education. Equally as challenging are tensions experienced by "outsiders"—those who observe with intention of seeing images that promise reform only to find more superficial embodiments of what was anticipated. Acknowledging all of these tensions is a first step toward considering the ways that they may be addressed within the larger context of reform.

Summary

There are a dozen pieces at the center of our quilt. Perhaps these pieces fit together as a crazy quilt in the sense that we may be unable to characterize all the nature of interactions that occur among them. Placing the pieces becomes more a matter of identification and not of design. Or perhaps these pieces fit together as a sampler quilt in the sense that we may not know if we have identified all the components that need to be considered. Placing the pieces is a matter of design but we may have holes for pieces as yet unnamed. Very possibly, our quilt is the start of a real design. The additions we make in the next two chapters will fill it out, providing a richness of color and fabric that reflects the additional attention to detail.

Reflecting on Our Work

References

National Council of Teachers of Mathematics (1989). *Curriculum and evaluation standards for school mathematics*. Reston, VA: Author.

National Council of Teachers of Mathematics (1991). *Professional standards for teaching mathematics*. Reston, VA: Author.

Shanker, A. (1995). Less is more, *The Developer*. (National Staff Development Council), October, p. 3.

Figure 1:   Summary of Points from Pre-Conference Issues Papers

Widely Held Beliefs about Teacher Learning (Ball)	*Principles of Change and Staff Development* (Loucks-Horsley)	*Reoccurring Themes that Seem Important* (Ferrini-Mundy)
1. What teachers bring to learning to teach—prior belief and experience—affects what they learn.	1. Fundamental change (learning) occurs over time, through active engagement with new ideas, understandings, and real life experiences. (Working to change teacher beliefs is the first and primary work of professional development.)	1. *Specialists of many sorts* Specialists seem to be the key to the efforts in the school: they were involved in helping to spread ideas, to facilitate communications among teachers, to plan and initiate staff development, and to address political problems with administrators and community members.
2. Learning to create the kinds of teaching envisioned by the mathematics reforms takes a long time and is hard.[1]	2. As individuals change their practice over time, they go through predictable stages in how they feel about the change and how knowledgeable and sophisticated they are in using it.	2. *Community involvement* Systematic attention to community involvement was important; this ranged from the usual parent nights and notes of explanation sent home, to formal committees including parents, charged with determining goals for the mathematics program.
3. Often, the most effective staff development model involves follow-up, usually in the form of long-term support (e.g., opportunities to meet with others engaged in the same process) and coaching in teachers' classrooms.	3. Effective professional development programs have many attributes in common with effective teaching. They: • foster collegiality and collaboration • promote experimentation and risk taking • draw their content from available knowledge bases • involve participants in decisions about as many aspects as possible • provide time to participate, reflect on, and practice what is learned	3. *Mathematics reform centered in the school* Although every site in the study did have specific connections to outside resources, both in the form of funding and personnel, the school itself, with its teachers, administrators, and community context, was the identified center of the reform activity.
4. Teacher educators and staff developers should model the approaches which they are promoting.		
5. Subject matter knowledge matters in learning to teach for understanding.		
6. Knowledge of children and their mathematics is crucial to teaching for understanding.		

[1] What actually makes it hard does not seem to be well understood nor finely articulated.

Widely Held Beliefs about Teacher Learning (Ball)
[continued]

7. The contexts in which teachers work affect what they can do. (Included in "context" are students, parents, administrators, tests, district and state objectives and curricular guidelines.)

8. Reflection is central to learning to teach.

9. Teacher development is especially productive when teachers are in charge of the agenda, determining the focus, nature, and kind of programming or opportunities.

Principles of Change and Staff Development (Loucks-Horsley)
[continued]

- provide leadership and sustained support.
- supply appropriate rewards and incentives.
- are designed based on knowledge of adult learning and change.
- integrate individual, school, and district goals.
- integrate both organizationally and instructionally with other staff development and change efforts.

4. There are other ways to learn than through workshops, courses and institutes. Sparks and Loucks-Horsley (1989) identify four general models in addition to training.
- Individually-guided staff development
- Observation and assessment
- Involvement in a development or improvement process
- Inquiry in to practice

5. Professional development can only succeed with simultaneous attention to changing the system within which educators work.

Reoccurring Themes that Seem Important (Ferrini-Mundy)
[continued]

4. *Collaborative communities*
Perhaps the most striking commonality across the sites was the visibility of close, collegial communities of practitioners engaged in inquiry of various sorts.

5. *Congruence and fit*
There is often a match, or congruence and fit, between the interpretation of reform that a site chooses, and some critical contextual features in the site.administrators, and community context, was the identified center of the reform activity.

6. *Experimenting with practice can change beliefs*
This is linked with observations that teachers' classrooms serve as their laboratories and their motivations for experimentation are inspired (in part) by evidence of student success.

7. *Vision is a process, not a product*
Traditional literature contends that vision and goal-setting are a first step; observations indicate that there is an interaction between vision and goal-setting and experience and evidence from practice that supports increasing articulation and definition over time.

8. *Issues that surface*
- Caring and the tension of reform
- The basic skills vs. understanding dilemma
- Being stalled: the trappings of reform
- Accommodating everyone
- Coming to grips with curriculum

CHAPTER III: Draft RFPs to Provide Directions for Teacher Enhancement

> *You can have a centerpiece that is a crazy quilt and then build more specialized designs around the outside.*
> Margaret Cozzens, conference transcript

Initial work at the conference involved consideration of widely held beliefs about teacher learning; this in turn led to discussion of a number of the common components and guiding principles that are addressed in the previous chapter. A decision was made to produce more than the set of recommendations originally targeted as the product of our work. Rather, participants chose to develop prototype Requests for Proposals (RFPs) for submission to NSF that addressed three major areas:

1. Building large-scale inservice from existing models.
2. Building capacity for providing opportunities and support for teacher learning.
3. Developing resources to support professional development.

Each of the three working groups was asked to develop an outline for an RFP along with a rationale, a description of how scaling up may be possible, and a discussion of what is essential, what is desirable, and what is variable with respect to the RFP. This chapter is a report of the work of each of the groups, as well as a presentation of each of the RFPs that the working groups produced. The discussion, as well as the RFPs themselves, addresses the more specialized concerns of scaling-up, capacity building, and developing resources with respect to professional development.

Scaling Up

> *What might it mean to "scale up" current or emerging professional development programs we believe have worked on a smaller scale to support more teachers' learning?*

The guiding question for this working group focused attention on identifying the needs of current teacher enhancement programs to respond to requests to scale up their work. Prior to the conference, participants were asked to address this question in their respective papers. What quickly emerged at the conference was that this type of approach aimed at "reaching" hundreds of times as many teachers seemed unlikely to be successful. Rather, a different perspective on what it means to scale up quickly surfaced—one that was not focused necessarily on making a small project "bigger."

The conference working group that focused on the issues of scaling up existing models for professional development quickly moved beyond labeling and naming models (i.e., models are not independent, rather there is overlap among models) as they sought to understand the various projects. The emphasis was one of conceptual, rather than model-oriented, scale up. The group members identified several points that they found to be applicable across models:

1. Purposes and the mechanisms for carrying out long-term teacher support need to be clarified and understood in greater depth. For example, are there different ways to understand what is fundamentally important about such support and to make conjectures about other ways such support may be provided?

2. How teachers gain knowledge of mathematics needs to be connected to how they gain knowledge about children's learning of mathematics. The extent to which teachers' attitudes and beliefs about mathematics influence what they can or will learn about mathematics also needs to be considered.

3. Large-scale inservice needs to address the possible distinction between the goal of developing "the ideal teacher" and/or the goal of moving large groups of "average teachers" in "appropriate" directions.

4. Ways to determine how teachers internalize the notion of mathematics reform are needed. For example, the way(s) teachers implement assessment may indicate something about how deeply they have internalized reform.

The draft RFP proposes projects that increase both teachers' content and pedagogical knowledge with respect to teaching mathematics. These projects would involve "moving" current models of inservice education from experimental to implementation status. There are a large number of successful models already in place. However, it was acknowledged that the knowledge base was insufficient for making clear choices of components; thus, a study of proposed large-scale projects is an essential part of implementation. The goal of large-scale inservice projects is to build on these proven models by combining components in new ways that will impact large numbers of teachers.

The assumptions of what is important that are found in the RFP reflect the earlier work that addressed common components and guiding principles.

1. Reflection on practice and on perceptions of how students make sense of mathematics ideas is essential.
2. Both content and pedagogical knowledge must be addressed, helping teachers make connections among the two areas.
3. While the effects of ongoing support are not well researched, there is little question that follow-up is important.
4. Teachers need a clear understanding of what "diversity" means and assistance in dealing more effectively with diversity.
5. Teachers need to be included as collaborative partners in defining not only the substance of the inservice but also the mechanisms for delivery of that inservice. Leadership development activities may need to be a part of a project as well.
6. Inservice projects need to include a variety of stakeholders within and outside the schools (e.g., parents, principals, superintendents).
7. Scaling up needs to be "large enough"; projects that are too large cannot be effective for the participants that are involved.

The RFP (see Figure 2 at the end of this chapter) provides several examples of sample projects and includes evaluation criteria.

Building Capacity

> *What might it mean to build capacity for delivering professional development to support more teachers' learning?*

During the course of the conference, an alternative perspective, which focused on building capacity, emerged. It was based on the premise that scale up cannot be accomplished if the capacity to carry out the scaling up is not there. A working group chose to focus on the issue of building capacity for professional development.

Capacity may be viewed as a general term that refers to the power or ability to do some particular thing, in this case, to provide high-quality professional development opportunities for [all] teachers in order to deepen their subject matter knowledge of mathematics and support their continual examination and modification of their teaching practices. (Conference notes)

As the working group thought about professional development for elementary teachers, they observed that, even if millions of dollars were available, we lack the capacity to provide high-quality opportunities for teachers to deepen their subject matter knowledge and to continually examine and modify their teaching practices. The group struggled with the task of distinguishing between a project that develops capacity for professional development and a project which builds professional development on a large scale. As can be seen from the final RFP (Figure 3 at the end of this chapter), eventually the group reached a consensus that was couched in outcomes. By capacity for professional development, we mean the following:

1. People who can work with teachers in supporting their own learning.
2. Support systems for professional development providers.
3. A knowledge base of professional development theory and practice.
4. Supported subcultures in which professional development flourishes.
5. Policies, resources, and structures that make professional development a central rather than marginal activity.

The development of projects that focus on building capacity and strengthening the infrastructure, rather than on projects that primarily focus on providing professional development for teachers, was a central consideration. For example, we know that the central role of professional development in educational reform has become abundantly clear. Equally clear is the limit on the number of professionals who can provide the leadership for professional development in mathematics education. Traditionally, most of the individuals responsible for staff development or inservice have been found in higher education or in mid-level school district administration. The current view of professional development calls for a much broader range of individuals who can facilitate and lead professional development work. These include teachers themselves in leadership positions, mathematics resource teachers, staff developers within school systems, and principals, among others. Building capacity for mathematics reform means developing and supporting a wide range of opportunities for individuals in all of these roles to deepen their existing professional knowledge and build the skills and knowledge needed to work with teachers to facilitate learning.

The development of a larger cadre of professional development providers is viewed to be of critical importance to the reform movement. However, short-term professional development is just as inappropriate for staff development providers as it is for teachers or any other professional group. These new providers need opportunities for support, for continued growth, and to contribute to the field. Building capacity for mathematics reform means developing and maintaining a diverse array of support structures.

Increasing capacity for supporting the continuous learning and growth of teachers need not be limited to increasing programs in which teachers participate for specific lengths of time. It may include providing contexts available to teachers on an ongoing basis in which they can "join" a network (e.g., through the internet) or a subculture of other teachers as part of a support structure in which continuous questioning and learning about teaching are encouraged. Without such dynamic networks or vibrant subcultures, it will be necessary to continue to mount professional development projects on a regular basis.

In addition to adding a variety of structures and activities to the currently available menu, it is clear that certain current state and local policies and financial arrangements constrain the degree to which teachers can participate thoughtfully in whatever professional development opportunities are available. Improving sufficient capacity will require increasing what is available to teachers and increasing the capacity of teachers and schools to take advantage of what is available. As long as structures and financial policies marginalize professional development, whatever capacity we can build will be underutilized. In this vein, anything that limits participation must also be addressed; for example, teachers' schedules, which make professional development during the school day virtually impossible; lack of opportunity for teachers to work together; and lack of long-term and consistent priorities within school systems, so that teachers' learning can accumulate.

The group noted that there ought not to be *just* an initiative that deals with building capacity. We should think about inserting capacity-building "pieces" in all projects that come through NSF. Questions to be asked of any project funded through NSF include: "What is the potential for capacity building within your project? Is there something you can do with your project as you are proposing it that will also address the question of building capacity?"

Further, one might ask what are the critical focal points (e.g., curriculum, pedagogy, assessment) that would serve to "ramp up" our capacity for professional development? In one response to such a question, Cozzens and Robinson (1994) focus on curriculum.

> *The most difficult component of mathematics and science education is the implementation of challenging, standards-based curriculum at all levels. All other components of mathematics and science education are needed to effectively implement curriculum. For example, to succeed, implementation of standards-based curriculum materials requires:*
> - *Appropriate professional development of teachers in both content and pedagogy.*
> - *Strengthened competencies of the educators of teachers.*
> - *Effective linkages with new methods of assessing student learning.*
> - *Buy-in of parents and community.*
> - *Appropriate attention to gender, racial, and ethnic issues.*
>
> (Cozzens & Robinson, pp. 1, 2)

Given curriculum as a focal point, policies, resources and structures are still needed to support large-scale implementation. There are no simple solutions to the question of capacity. However, implementation of the strategies described in the RFP and serious consideration of the question of critical focus will help maximize efforts to build capacity for reform.

Providing Resources

> *How might we use the demand for scaling up to experiment with the development of alternative materials for professional development?*

One outcome of the conference was to identify alternative strategies and options that are different from what is occurring in current teacher enhancement programs. Two different initial avenues—the use of curriculum and the development of alternative resources—were explored. The working group on resources considered the results from both earlier subgroups as exemplars related to the development of resources to support professional development.

Initially, one subgroup of participants considered the use of curriculum as a vehicle for teacher development. They characterized the role of curriculum and the structures needed for making use of curriculum, first making an assumption that a uniform curriculum is in use (specifically, materials in common, not just a framework or a set of principles). How does this change the professional development strategy for the school system, or at least in some "chunk" of schools? Clearly, the issue of how such a curriculum is selected (e.g., chosen by teachers or mandated for teachers' use) has implications for professional development plans, as does the "cycle" of professional development and the stage of implementation (e.g., first year, second year). A curriculum helps provide coherence with respect to instructional model(s), ensure some equity in instruction, and provide a common vehicle from which teachers can talk.

Developing a professional development program around a common core of curriculum materials suggested a number of different options to the working group. During the first two years, teachers' focus is on how best to use the materials; after this, teachers may begin to think about deeper issues such as mathematical content in children's thinking. At this point, teachers may meet together on a regular basis and focus on what's happening in their classrooms with respect to the mathematics they are teaching. Inservice might be designed around student work and assessment with a body of student work collected over the years around certain topics or across certain grade levels. Curriculum modules (as exemplified by several new curricula) themselves might also become texts for teachers as a way to look at mathematics content or to consider children's mathematical thinking. The use of curriculum may well have the potential for promoting both student and teacher change.

Another subgroup discussed the three vehicles of literature on teaching, video, and networking as having the potential to serve as tools both to foster reflective habits of mind and a sense of professional community and to provide a richer set of visual and mental images of teaching and learning that are reflective of mathematics reform. Much of their discussion centered on the use of literature about practice written by practitioners (broadly defined), including teachers writing about teaching. This writing could take may forms, including both books and articles about teaching, and possibly even giving rise to a journal to be read by a variety of people interested in practice. There are opportunities for professional learning through the experience of authoring such writing, as well as for readers to learn from having access to such literature. Even more provocative is the potential for such literature to become a source of learning when used within a context in which group discussions are possible.

Video and writing are different mediums and provide different images of practice. An author's craft allows him or her greater control over what the reader "sees." Video, in and of itself, requires more thought;

this includes consideration of "messy video" and "less messy video;" for example, how problematic are the interactions with the mathematics that appear on the video. Other considerations include the design of the video (e.g., what makes the right length) and in relation to viewers, what is "good" to see and what is the role of a facilitator in using video. The use of video suggests the emergence of a different paradigm of teaching practice. The person(s) shown on a video generally are not the focus of study. Rather, the person(s) form the context of an example of teaching in order to provide an opportunity to investigate an instance of teaching and/or to think more generally about a set of issues that the video's context might prompt. The issue of guided (e.g., group viewing with a facilitator) vs. unguided (e.g., individual viewing) use of such resources was raised.

The RFP that was developed is centered in the need for the creation of professional development resources as a critical factor for building capacity. The goal concentrates on lending "transportable" support to the professional education of teachers.

> *It is no more reasonable to expect that individual teacher educators should each invent the [professional development] curriculum materials of their projects than it is to expect teachers each to invent the curriculum of their mathematics instruction.* (RFP, p. 48)

As can be seen from the final RFP (Figure 4 at the end of this chapter), the focus is on the design of primary source materials for practice that can be used by teachers for professional learning. These include classroom video, collections of students' work, teachers' writing about their practice, as well as new student curricula that include professional development material intended for teachers.

A process of developmental research (Gravemeijer, 1994) is embedded in the description of the process of materials development. The rationale and/or theory both for the kind and content of the material to be developed is necessary. Plans for pilot experiments are needed that involve integrating practice with theory in order to make necessary modifications. Finally, as in the process of design of student curricula, there is a need to address the ways to support the use of the professional development materials by non-developers. The RFP provides a number of examples of kinds of materials that are possible; the three-part phase of development, experiment, and dissemination/support for use is considered. Also included is a detailed list of evaluation criteria for such projects.

Summary

Surrounding the center of our quilt are three more specialized designs. Each (scaling up, building capacity, developing resources) relies on and accents the detail provided at the centerpiece. The common components and guiding principles found in Chapter I provide the foundation for the topics addressed in this chapter. If carefully reviewed, the RFPs provide more than a set of recommendations for possible action. Rather, they provide both definition and discussion of three themes that are central to a consideration of long-term, systemic reform in mathematics education.

References

Cozzens, M. B., & Robinson, E. (1994, Fall). Implementation of standards-based curricula. *ESIE Access*, pp. 1–2.

Gravemeijer, K. (1994) Educational development and developmental research in mathematics education. *Journal for Research in Mathematics Education, 25*, 443–71.

Figure 2: Request for Proposals
Building Large-Scale Inservice from Existing Models

Need

In order for the U. S. to reach the goal of world-class mathematics instruction, teachers of mathematics at all levels must be assisted in improving the quality of instruction they deliver. Since students' attitudes and dispositions about mathematics often seem to deteriorate during the elementary schools years, there is a special need for elementary school mathematics instruction to improve. Too, since elementary school mathematics is typically taught in self-contained classrooms by teachers who may not have special expertise about mathematics pedagogy, inservice for elementary school teachers is a critical priority.

Goals

Large-scale inservice funded through this RFP should increase teachers' content and pedagogical knowledge while also improving the quality of mathematics instruction provided to elementary school children. Projects funded through the RFP should attempt to move models of inservice education from experimental status to implementation status.

Many models of teacher inservice have been developed for improving the teaching of elementary school mathematics. Some of these models come from the work of funded projects, but some come from innovations developed by school-district-supported staff development programs. Large-scale inservice should build on these models by combining components from the most successful models in ways that will impact large numbers of teachers. While the knowledge base is insufficient to allow clear choices of components to be made, further study should be made of the components that seem most likely to be successful.

Project Characteristics

1. Helping teachers become more reflective

Teachers need to reflect not only on their own practices but also on their perceptions of how their students make sense of the mathematical ideas in the curriculum. Reflection on practice may take place through discussion with peers or with other people outside the school structure, through analysis of video tapes of teaching, through reading of case studies or research, and so on. Knowing how to reflect on practice intelligently must be learned and should be continually developed. Reflection on perceptions of children's understanding requires that teachers become active observers of behaviors and active listeners to children's verbalizations. It is important for teachers to hear perceptions of many different people and to test those perceptions against students' actual performance on mathematical tasks.

Projects should also help teachers develop self-evaluation techniques so that they can continue to grow as professionals after the end of the project. Establishing networks among teachers would be one technique for enabling teachers to continue to share their knowledge.

2. Improving the knowledge base of teachers

Content knowledge and pedagogical knowledge are both important components of being an effective teacher. All teachers have room to grow in both areas. However, projects that focus on either content or pedagogical knowledge alone should not be funded. Projects need to help teachers connect content and pedagogical knowledge.

It seems especially critical for elementary school teachers to understand the connection between mathematical knowledge and children's interpretation of that knowledge. Children's knowledge develops so rapidly during elementary school, that teachers need to be attuned to the ways that changes in children's thinking might reflect increasing sophistication of mathematical understanding. In the typical project then, it may be helpful to include interactions with children as part of the inservice program.

3. On-going support for teachers

Change is difficult and takes time. Teachers need continuing support in order to make substantive changes. Projects should request funding for a long enough period of time to be able to effect true and lasting change. Although support is needed during the times when teachers are developing their personal knowledge, it seems more critical to provide support for teachers as they try to incorporate their increased knowledge into instruction.

Unfortunately, the effects of various types of follow-up support are not well researched. Thus, proposals must clearly outline the nature of the support they will provide and provide a believable rationale for why those types of support seem likely to be helpful for teachers. Projects should carefully consider how networks of teachers might be effectively used to provide some of the on-going support.

4. Implementation of equity in instruction

Because student demographics are changing rapidly throughout the US, teachers need help in struggling with how to adapt mathematics instruction to adapt to those changing demographics. Proposals should demonstrate that the staff have a clear understanding of what "diversity" means and how teachers can be helped to more effectively deal with diversity.

5. Respect for teachers as professionals

Mathematics inservice should be developed only when teachers are collaborative partners in defining not only the substance of the inservice but also the mechanisms for delivery of that inservice. Change is more likely to be sustained when those who are expected to change have input to the nature of the change.

Teachers may need assistance, however, in clearly defining both their needs and the existing attributes of instruction that might encourage or inhibit change. Projects may need to help teachers to self-assess beliefs and attitudes about mathematics and mathematics instruction, to clarify needed changes in instruction, or to accurately assess the characteristics of their current instructional practices.

In addition, teachers should be supported for participation in professional experiences outside the district and project; for example, attending professional conferences. It is probably desirable that projects allow for (and support) the possibility that some participants will become true inservice leaders who could further disseminate the inservice after the end of funding. Leadership development activities may need to be part of a project in order to help teachers self-identify their skills and attributes as future inservice leaders.

6. Inclusion of all stakeholders

Mathematics inservice should not be carried out in isolation from school administrators, school boards, and parents. Support from all these groups is critical for sustaining change. Projects may help teachers learn to obtain support from these (and other) groups and/or may work directly with these groups to elicit needed support.

7. Scale of projects

Projects should be "large" but not so large that they cannot be effective for the participants who are involved. That is, participants should feel they are integral to the project rather than feeling merely as a "cog in the wheel of change." Funding should be adequate to allow for the development of an effective program for whatever number of teachers are to be reached. Direct contact between project staff and individual teachers is critical, but mechanisms must be developed for reaching "large numbers" of teachers.

Brief Descriptions of Sample Projects

1. Expanding a proven inservice program

Numerous inservice programs (e.g., cognitively-guided instruction) have been shown to be effective when they are delivered to relatively small numbers of teachers. A project could choose to disseminate one of these programs directly to a large geographic area (e.g., a state).

2. Developing inservice leaders for a specific program

A project could develop inservice leaders who would be supported to disseminate a proven inservice program to other teachers. These leaders might be classroom teachers, university faculty, mathematics coordinators, and so on.

3. Developing building-level specialists

A project could develop building-level mathematics specialists who would serve in that one building as a resource teacher and model teacher for a particular instructional approach (e.g., an innovative curriculum) or for a particular group of approaches. These specialists might be called on to deliver long-term inservice to the teachers in the building or to act as consultants for teachers who wanted to learn how to use the particular instructional approaches.

4. Reaching the "reluctant" teacher

A project might develop a plan for very intensive inservice that would reach virtually all teachers in a district (or consortium of districts). Special attention might have to be given to developing incentives for attracting and sustaining teachers' participation. Such projects would seem to require very extensive on-going support for participants.

Proposal Evaluation Guidelines

1. Clear goals and rationale.

2. Clearly defined substance for the inservice.
   a. evidence that teachers' content and pedagogical knowledge will increase as well as their understanding of the connection between content and pedagogical knowledge
   b. evidence that teachers will better understand children's thinking and can adapt curriculum to meet the needs of increasingly diverse populations of children
   c. clear definition of ways that teachers will become more reflective
   d. evidence of sensitivity to the social and cultural contexts of classrooms
   e. evidence of attention to under-standing teachers' beliefs and attitudes and to ways for supporting teachers as those beliefs and attitudes change

3. Clearly defined and justified delivery system for the inservice.

   a. clear description of the plan for inservice activities, with rationale provided for that plan
   b. time line that reflects understanding of the difficulty of substantive change
   c. clear and equitable plan for selection of participants
   d. appropriate level of involvement of principals, parents, and so on
   e. clear level of school commitment

4. On-going support.
   a. description of plan for continuing support for teachers, with rationale for the plan
   b. development of support from local community
   c. development of networking that will extend beyond the end of funding
   d. plan for support of emerging leaders from among project participants

5. Evaluation.
   a. description of plan for gathering information that will inform the project in process as well as provide opportunities for better understanding staff development in general
   b. should address how the changes in instruction impact various groups of children
   c. documentation of changes in teachers' knowledge, beliefs, instruction, and so on

Figure 3: Request for Proposals
Building Capacity for Providing Opportunities and Support for Teacher Learning

The Need

Even if millions of dollars were available for professional development, the nation would lack the capacity to provide high-quality opportunities for teachers to deepen their subject-matter knowledge and continually examine and modify their teaching practice.

By capacity we mean:

- people who can work with teachers in supporting their own learning;
- support systems for professional development providers;
- a knowledge base of professional development theory and practice;
- supported subcultures in which professional development flourishes;
- policies, resources and structures that make professional development a central rather than marginal activity.

These are all elements of what one might call an infrastructure for professional development, nationwide.

Lacking a strong infrastructure we will see professional development that is of uneven quality, of insufficient quantity, is not cost effective, that comes in the form of projects that are not sustainable, and that too often is inaccessible and non-inclusive.

Goals

The primary goal of this initiative is to support projects that focus on building capacity and strengthening infrastructure, rather than primarily providing professional development for teachers. It also focuses on projects that are likely to have enduring national significance rather than primarily local impact. We seek innovative, creative strategies for building capacities at all levels (national, regional, state, district, school) and that contribute to the field's knowledge about professional development and capacity-building.

Successful proposals will be able to demonstrate that they contribute to:

* enhanced quality of available opportunities for teacher learning;
* increased quantity of available opportunities for teacher learning;
* increased the sustainability of teacher learning;
* increased the accessibility and inclusiveness of opportunities for teacher learning;
* cost-effective opportunities for teacher learning.

Proposals should present an argument about how one or more of the above will be achieved.

Overview of RFP

Subsequent sections of this RFP will discuss essential, desirable and variable project characteristics; examples of projects that might be funded; and evaluation and review criteria.

Project Characteristics

Projects that address different aspects of the capacity problem are likely to have characteristics particular to the needs of thatproblem. Therefore, projects submitted to this initiative are likely to have many different kinds of characteristics. Below, we elaborate the definitions of each kind of capacity need, and offer suggestions about desirable project characteristics for each.

1. People who can work with teachers in supporting their own learning.

The central role of professional development in educational reform has become abundantly clear. Equally clear is the dearth of skilled professionals who can provide the leadership for professional development in science and mathematics. Traditionally, most of the individuals responsible for staff development or in-service have been found in higher education and mid-level school district administration. The current view of professional development calls for a much broader range of individuals who can facilitate and lead professional development work. These include teachers themselves in leadership positions, science and mathematics resource teachers, staff developers within school systems, and principals, among others. Building capacity for mathematics and science reform means developing a wide range of opportunities for individuals in all of these roles to deepen their existing professional knowledge and build the skills and knowledge to work with teachers in facilitating learning. Following are three examples of programs to achieve this goal:

a. Provide multi-year support in professional development for those people in SSIs and USIs who are designing and implementing professional development activities for teachers.

b. Create state-level (or regional) professional development centers which provide professional development for teacher leaders, teacher educators, school administrators, and others. This creates more people who can work with teachers and supports them in that process.

c. Develop a graduate program that attracts high quality students from the mathematics, sciences and education and supports them in becoming leaders in professional development.

2. *Support systems for professional development providers.*

The development of a larger cadre of professional development providers is of critical importance to the reform movement. However, short-term professional development is just as inappropriate for staff development providers as it is for teachers or any other professional group. These new providers will need opportunities for support, for continued growth, and to contribute to the field. Building capacity for mathematics and science reform means developing and maintaining a diverse array of support structures. The following example is one such support structure:

Create a national center on mathematics inquiry, at which mathematicians, mathematics educators, teacher leaders, and others would be in residence for varying amounts of time, engaging in mathematical inquiry. Provide a support system and a subculture that increases professional developers' deep knowledge of mathematics and mathematical inquiry and their skills in supporting others. (Read "science" as well as "mathematics" in the above description.)

3. A knowledge base of professional development theory and practice.

There is an emergent knowledge base for professional development theory and practice that covers a wide range of contexts in which professional development occurs and kinds of professional development encounters. This knowledge base includes psychological studies of teachers in the process of changing their beliefs, mathematics and scientific knowledge, and their classroom practice; research by teacher educators on the process of teacher education itself; studies of teachers in subject-matter collaboratives and networks; studies of action research as a mode of professional development; analyses of "teacher-as-researcher" as a mode of professional development; teachers' own writing about their practice and about changed classrooms and so on. There are few comprehensive review articles covering this literature, virtually no meta-analyses, and no comprehensive attempt to synthesize this literature for professional development practitioners or to comprehensively document and assess the many extant professional development programs in a sufficiently coherent way as to cumulatively add to this knowledge base. In the absence of vehicles for cumulating knowledge and making it widely accessible, the field of professional development is segmented into small schools of thought and practice that are relatively isolated and individual practitioners doing the best they can, but largely inventing from scratch.

Further, there are a number of important questions to which we do not yet have appropriate answers. For example, what is the nature of mathematics instruction that would provide experienced teachers with the opportunity to deepen their mathematics knowledge to support teaching for understanding? Are there individual pathways of teacher change and, if so, can we use knowledge about them to design more effective professional development?

In sum, the field needs the capacity to identify, analyze and use research knowledge; identify and make available the knowledge that comes from the practice of professional development; and opportunities for all members of the professional development community to contribute to this growing knowledge base. Projects that would address this capacity need might include such activities as:

a. Development of a refereed journal on professional

development in mathematics and science.

b. Development of a journal for the publication of teachers' writing about their instructional practice and about the process of change.

c. Development of state or regional "professional development centers" whose task would be to assemble knowledge of "best practices" and engage people in their states/regions in reflection on current professional development practice.

d. Development of curricula to be used in professional development institutes.

e. Support of doctoral students, post-doctorates and others doing research on professional development to increase the amount of scholarly work done and published.

Projects submitted to address this need for capacity would need to demonstrate:

a. Broad and deep knowledge of the state of the art of our knowledge of professional development, nationally and internationally, including awareness of the questions about which we need to know more, and where work on them is being done.

b. A well-thought out theory of how knowledge is taken up by others, that guides the design of activities.

c. Appropriate plans for reaching the chosen public—national, state or regional.

d. Plans to stay up-to-date as the state of our knowledge grows.

4. Supported subcultures in which professional development flourishes.

Increasing the nation's capacity for supporting the continuous learning and growth of teachers is not limited to increasing programs in which teachers can participate for specific lengths of time. It also includes providing contexts available to teachers on an ongoing basis, in which they can "join" a subculture that embodies the values of high quality teaching and inquiry about teaching. Such subcultures would serve the function of providing ongoing support for teachers who had been in a particular program, and might join one again, but for the moment choose a different form of engagement. They also would provide rampways in for teachers who have not previously been engaged in intensive professional development but would like to try it out on a limited basis. Finally, they provide contexts that can sustain teachers over the long term, providing the context in which continuous questioning and learning about teaching is encouraged. Without such vibrant sub-cultures, it will be necessary to continue to mount professional development projects on a regular basis.

While we have spoken of the need to create subcultures for high-quality professional development in instrumental terms, there really is a deeper significance to the need to which they speak. The nature of the reform movement that is embodied in the mathematics and science standards will require not only change and learning on the part of a large number of teachers, but it also implies a different intellectual culture for schools than that which typically obtains. Therefore, we need to be providing the capacity not only for each teacher to reflect upon and examine his/her own teaching, but for the culture of teaching and schooling, itself, to change. Viewing reform as a cultural matter, as well as an individual psychological one, opens new avenues. The deliberate creation of supportive subcultures in different parts of the system would begin the process of cultural change and

give us the opportunity to understand the nature of such cultures.

Examples of subcultures that could be created include the following:

a. Create a national center of mathematical inquiry, at which mathematicians, mathematics educators, teachers and others would be in residence for varying amounts of time, engaging in mathematical inquiry.

b. Examine school-based efforts to change the culture of schooling. Professional Development Schools and schools in the Coalition of Essential Schools had the vision of a new subculture as part of their purpose. What can we learn from them?

c. Support the development of on-going groups for teachers—mathematics and science collaboratives, action research groups, and so on.

5. Policies, resources and structures that make professional development a central rather than marginal activity.

In addition to adding a variety of structures and activities to the currently available menu, it is clear that certain current state and local policies and financial arrangements constrain the degree to which teachers can participate thoughtfully in whatever professional development opportunities are available. That is, improving sufficient capacity will require not only increasing what is available to teachers, but also increasing the capacity of teachers and schools to take advantage of what is available. As long as structures and financial policies marginalize professional development, whatever capacity we can build will be underutilized. In this vein, we think of things like teachers' schedules, which make professional development during the school day virtually impossible; lack of opportunity for teachers to work in teams, to work together; insufficient financial resources to staff schools in such way that teachers could have the opportunity to do professional development during the school day; and lack of long-term and consistent priorities within school systems, so that teachers' learning can cumulate.

An example of a project that might address this capacity need is the following:

Create and study the effects of financing mechanisms at the district level that permit teachers to have 1/5 of their time available for professional development activities. This experiment would help to generate knowledge about how to make professional development more accessible and inclusive.

Evaluation Criteria

1. Project Design: What is the quality of the intervention?
   a. Is the project doing the right kind of work for the particular audience?
   b. Does it embody the principles of effective _____ (professional development, curriculum development, etc.)?
   c. Does the plan improve participation of underrepresented groups?

2. Impact: What is the likelihood that the project will lead to one or more of the following criteria for increased national capacity to provide professional development?
   a. Enhances the quality of available professional development;

b. Increases the quantity of available, high-quality professional development;

c. Increases the sustainability of teacher learning;

d. Provides cost-effective opportunities for teacher learning;

e. Increases the inclusiveness and accessibility of high-quality professional development.

3. National Significance: Is the project likely to contribute to national capacity? What is the argument that is made that the project will contribute to increased national capacity? Is that argument plausible?

4. Staffing
   a. Is the background/ expertise of staff appropriate?
   b. Is the staff diverse, or is there a plan for creating a diverse staff?

c. Is the commitment of each individual staff person commensurate with their responsibility?

5. Evaluation
   a. Does the evaluation component include mechanisms for ongoing project improvement as well as adding to the knowledge base in the field?
   b. Does the project have appropriate interim indicators so that progress can be assessed?

6. Cost-Effectiveness: Is the project cost-effective?

7. Appropriate Linkages
   a. Does the project link with other projects that are involved with capacity building?
   b. Does the project leverage resources to eliminate gaps and overlaps among reform efforts?

Figure 4: Request for Proposals
Developing Resources to Support Professional Development

The Need

The development of resources for professional development is a critical factor in building capacity to reach more teachers. When we invest in intensive programs of professional development, what we gain often does not extend beyond local effects. Too often a charismatic leader or a conducive support structure affords power to the experience that is difficult to transport, duplicate, or "scale up" to reach more teachers.

Although considerable effort is devoted to the professional development of mathematics teachers, there has been little concerted attention given to the development of resources that can provide contexts and means for teachers' learning. This stands in contrast to the education of *students*, where the materials of instruction have been a focal area for research and development: curriculum development, and students' engagement with and learning from particular problems, materials, texts, and classroom structures. As with students, what *teachers* engage with can substantially shape their opportunities for learning. Although most staff developers gather and create materials for their programs, they often lack resources for this task. It is no more reasonable to expect that individual teacher educators should each invent the curriculum materials of their projects than it is to expect teachers to each invent the curriculum of their mathematics instruction.

Goals

The primary goal for proposals solicited in this program is to develop resources for the professional development of mathematics teachers, with concrete attention given to the development of specific materials, pilot field testing in their use, and dissemination. It focuses on encouraging and supporting the development of high-quality shareable resources for professional education that can support teacher learning in a variety of contexts and structures.

Overview of RFP

This RFP supports the design of *primary source materials of practice* that can be used for exploration, experimentation, and investigation by individuals and groups of teachers. Examples of such primary source materials include classroom video, collections of students' work, teachers' writing about their practice (books, reflective journals, articles or chapters, cases), as well as new curriculum materials for students that include material intended for professional development of teachers. These materials offer close views on teaching, learning, and mathematics that can provide opportunities for discussion and analysis, generating ideas and images. In a very real sense, they provide resources for practice—the intellectual and practical nourishment of the work of teaching. They offer teachers common contexts for conversation; ideas to take and experiment with in their own classrooms, challenges by contrast to their own assumptions and current practices. And they provide opportunities to learn to take advantage of practice itself as a source of professional development—for example, to learn from close examination a set of children's papers, or from watching a videotaped classroom lesson and discussing it with other teachers.

Project Characteristics

Projects funded under this initiative must address three dimensions:

1. the design, collection, and organization of the material itself;

2. the development—including piloting and redesign—of structures for implementation of the use of the particular material for teacher development;

3. the design of means for disseminating the material and pedagogy as a resource for professional development in a variety settings.

Projects must have a vision of a kind of material that they want to design and develop and a rationale for why the particular kind of material is promising as a resource for supporting teachers' learning. For example, the use of classroom episodes written by teachers may help teachers focus on classroom dilemmas that they face. Use of videotaped lessons might be used as an opportunity to consider deeply the big ideas of mathematical content with which students are grappling in ways that are different from what is possible in the context of daily practice. Innovative curriculum materials might be used as a medium through which teachers learn more about mathematics and about the development of children's mathematical thinking.

Project plans must entail experiments with the use of the materials, focused both on improving the quality of the materials themselves and on developing concrete images of their use in professional development contexts. Like the design work of curriculum developers, this work involves thinking about ways to support the use of the materials in the spirit and with the purposes envisioned by the project.

Consequently, a major component of any project will be development of ways to make the resources usable in a variety of contexts. This entails attention to the quality and packaging of the resources themselves, but, more importantly, to the supports needed for teacher educators who will be guiding the use of the material in teacher development settings. Just as curricular materials must be designed to allow teachers to learn and grow along with their students, so teacher development materials must target the professional growth of the teacher educator. Further, any project of this sort will need to consider what experiences teacher educators will need in order to use the professional development materials successfully in their own settings.

RFP: Resources for Professional Development

IDEAS ABOUT PROTOTYPES FOR RESOURCES

DEVELOPMENT OF MATERIALS	EXPERIMENTS WITH THE USE OF SUCH MATERIALS	DISSEMINATION OF THE MATERIALS AND THEIR USES
classroom-based resources for learning about teaching and learning mathematics: episodes from classrooms, reflections by teachers about their efforts		
materials for an instructor to use in helping teachers learn mathematics (e.g., a mathematics course for teachers, a summer workshop)	examples of how the materials are used in a mathematics course for teachers	commitment of a publisher to make these materials available to a wide audience
investigations or other materials (e.g., the replacement units in California as a resource for learning about mathematics and student thinking)	development work with teachers using new materials and student work as teachers use new materials	detailing what teacher educators might need in order to carry out this kind of work
a database on teaching and learning	creating a database of particular activities, lessons, or units and discussions/articles of the mathematics, as well as stories of the use of these activities in a classroom setting— not just examples of use, but also a repository for classroom teachers who are engaging in inquiry in their classrooms	• CD-ROM • on the Internet • written collections
collection of primary material and tools for accessing it	images, models, frameworks, and tools of use	making the materials and models available

collection of resources about important issues and dilemmas (e.g., the dilemma of "following" the curriculum and "following" the kids; developing skills and understanding): might be videos, stories, journal entries by teachers	how can experienced and student or beginning teachers work together with these resources?	conferences for teacher educators about materials and ways to use them—perhaps a consortium of linked but very different institutes
case books or syllabi or other materials for graduate programs on professional development and teacher education	ways to learn about professional education, teacher education for the preparation of future teacher educators	workshops for graduate students in mathematics and science education
materials to support teachers' communication about teaching and learning, mathematics, classrooms, assessment, goals, etc. with parents, school board members, administrators—these could be actual materials to use, could be cases or simulations to help discuss challenges of such communication, particularly considering community and cultural diversity	images and ideas for communicating with other stakeholders	
materials for learning about new assessments, using new assessments as a context for teacher development		

Evaluation Criteria

Good proposals will:

1. Demonstrate explicitly what need they address.

2. State clearly the criteria by which materials will be selected for inclusion.

3. State clearly the target audience(s) and the manner(s) in which the proposer envisions them being used.

4. Provide one or two examples of pieces illustrative of the sort of material, and an explanation of their specific qualities or dimensions and how they deal with the criteria below.

5. Give a clear statement of the kinds of teacher enhancement the materials are intended to effect. How does the proposer think these materials will help teachers develop? What roles will the materials play and how will their availability and use make a difference?

  * NOTE: This is not intended to discourage bold and imaginative proposals with interesting and well-founded hypotheses about teacher development.

6. Provide a reasoned estimate of the amount of time that the project would take, a reasonable plan, informed by related work in other projects, and makes defensible choices about managing the trade-offs between depth and thoroughness and timeliness.

7. Be potentially scale-up-able—should have attended explicitly to being able to be scaled up and made more widely accessible and usable—both the materials themselves and the insights and guidance about contexts and pedagogies of use.

8. Demonstrate that there will be a demand for the materials for what it will cost

9. Provide a reasoned estimate of the impact this project would have in terms of scope and numbers.

10. Explain the "production partnerships" that this proposal would involve and require, and how these would strengthen the project.

11. Include plans for both the development of materials *and* how those materials would be used.

12. Attend to ethical issues of making public teachers' practice, students' work, etc. and provision for multiple voices and perspectives.

13. Provide resources for groups of people from among the following stakeholders in reform: practicing teachers, pre-service teachers, teacher educators, other educators, parents, administrators, school board members.

14. Include opportunities for investigating diversity/ equity issues (embedded in the teaching and learning of mathematics).

15. Include opportunities for learning mathematics .

16. Include opportunities for investigating "learning" and "understanding"

17. Include opportunities for learning about students' mathematical understanding.

18. Attend to supporting teachers' communication about teaching and learning, mathematics, classrooms, assessment, goals, etc., with parents, school board members, administrators—this could include actual materials to use, or could be cases or simulations to help discuss challenges of such communication, particularly considering community and cultural diversity in relation to the reform of mathematics education.

19. Plan to analyze and communicate about knowledge generated to the field about development, use of resources; the problem of developing and using resources in ways that promote change and reform. Proposals will have specific plans for contributing to our understanding of questions such as: What are we learning about the development and use of video? What are we learning about the development and use materials for teacher courses or workshops? What are we learning about the pedagogies and contexts of professional development?

20. Take a stance of inquiry: The materials will help teachers to consider

dilemmas and alternatives, to inquire into and develop their practice. The pedagogy of the work will not emphasize providing definite answers or approaches.

CHAPTER IV: Emerging Issues

> *If you cut a piece slightly wrong, it doesn't fit and then you have to start over again. If you try to put certain colors together even though intuitively they look like they are going to work, you find that they don't so you start over again.*
>
> Margaret Cozzens, conference transcript

The preceding chapters have identified common principles for teacher enhancement. Three alternative teacher enhancement strategies that address issues of scaling-up also have been detailed. While there is much we do not know, these summaries serve as catalysts for future efforts and for further research related to teacher enhancement.

There are other issues that emerged as the conference proceeded that reflect the "much we do not know about" category with respect to teacher enhancement. Five are described here: equity, evaluation, school culture, preservice teacher preparation, and the role of technology.

Equity

As part of the conference work, a working group focused its attention on issues related to the social, cultural, and community aspects of professional development. The community provides the context for the school; within the school community there is an infrastructure that defines goals, establishes what is rewarded and sanctioned, identifies school norms, and so on. The issue of equity (i.e., respect for diversity) was addressed within this context.

The culture for the school very much reflects the social and academic experiences of the students. Are we teaching the mathematics in a way that children themselves are feeling the impact of instruction based on who they are and what they represent from their various communities? Society separates us by color. Is it any wonder that children internalize this as a norm? What are we doing in our mathematics program to reflect this [diversity] as a value rather than devaluation? What

*is the way for mostly white mainstream teachers to think
about the education of minority children? Some children need
some special attention, not in a stereotypical sense, but rather
in a way that gives them value and does not devalue them or
their work with mathematics. How do we restructure classroom
practice so that it will be inclusive, consciously considering
cultural and social differences as we teach all students?* (edited
transcript)

Clearly, staff development needs to be continuous and relevant to the
needs of the school community. For both inservice and preservice work,
we need to focus on ways to support equity, including encouraging
appropriate expectations for all students.

The value of constructivism as a vehicle for thinking about
instruction for all students also was raised. The discussion of equity
seemed to center on whether our understanding of equity was deep
enough for us to know whether constructivism can work across a
variety of cultural settings. Two perspectives surfaced.

The first, an historical perspective, provided a view of pedagogy that
emerges, in part, from the history of segregated schools. Minority
students *did* learn mathematics in segregated schools. At that time,
successful instruction was more didactic in nature. One dilemma that
was raised concerned whether historical instructional styles reflect
current beliefs about how people come to know.

*In particular communities, the introduction of constructivist
teaching can be highly problematic because it doesn't fit with
an expectation that a teacher will be an authority figure, that
the teacher is the one with all the wisdom, that the teacher is
conveying that to students and students should be getting it
[mathematics] in a factual and more traditional, conventional
way. And so for many members of communities, culturally
distinct communities, that have those expectations for
teachers, the unexpected introduction of constructivist teaching
can be a problem. Where does this [constructivism] match or
not match with community norms? How should we be
thinking about this as part of the issue of equity?* (edited
transcript)

A second perspective considered documentation of the success of
various projects with different students. Widely argued was the "we're
doing it, so that means that it is possible" perspective. Further, concern
was raised as to whether it is possible to sort out what it is about these

projects—projects that are in the "constructivist tradition"—that makes it possible for such success to occur.

> *It seems to me that if we know that these projects [represented by conference participants] have been successful with minority children in many cases, we want to ask what is there different about these projects, or what is there rich about these projects, that will allow them to be used in situations where cultures are different? Is there enough room within a particular project framework for it to be adapted to address different cultural norms?* (edited transcript)

Of course, part of the concern about constructivism may be that we are unclear about what constructivism is. Two views were articulated:

> *I am using constructivist teaching to refer to a set of norms which I think are implicit in these projects [represented at this conference]. I think that some characteristics of this approach, which talk about teachers as being facilitators and guides and students being engaged in their own learning, and those kinds of things, conflict with the norms of some communities in which teachers are supposed to be authority figures, students are supposed to be rather passive as learners, and that because of the difference in norms, there are going to be problems implementing the kinds of things that I see people talking about wanting to implement in these projects.* (edited transcript)

> *My perception of constructivism is that it's a belief system about how people come to know and the nature of learning. As we talk about it, we are referring to children and not referring to ourselves and to the parents and to the teachers and the whole community.* (edited transcript)

On one level, constructivism may well be seen as pedagogy. On a deeper level, as a belief about how people come to know, constructivism addresses the question of who's responsible for the learning and how this responsibility may be conveyed in an instructional setting.

Yet another perspective (as part of a number of other voices) may be heard within the wider community seeking to understand issues related to equity and culture, that is, how cultural differences among children and their communities "match" with various classroom cultures. This voice did not surface during the conference. Perhaps, in our struggles to understand the issues, we may have been talking past each other. What are the cultural norms that we need to take into account as we seek to help all children attain their own power in creating their own knowledge?

Mathematics educators have little knowledge of how African-American students perceive themselves as mathematics students, how they approach mathematics, or the role of culture in their perception and mathematics performance. Questions, such as the following still remain: How do we proactively include African-American students in the mathematics community? What changes in teaching could make a difference in their understanding and achievement? Are we teaching them from their vantage point or from where we think their vantage point should be? (Malloy, in press, p. 1)

What are the interactions between cultural norms and instructional style related to ethnicity, race, gender, and so on? In Appendix B of *Women's Ways of Knowing* (Belenky, et al., 1986), eleven pairs of educational dialectics are listed; two examples are included here:

Discovery .... **Didacticism**
Constructed Knowledge   Received knowledge
How is knowledge viewed? How is the act of becoming a "knower" explained?

Being with Others...................... **Being Alone or on Own**
Collaborative, Cooperative   Solitary, Competitive
What arrangements for learning are preferred? Have been experienced?
(Belenky, et al., p. 237)

Those on the left side are said to be characteristic of ways women come to know and to learn. Writers about the learning preferences of African-American students (Hale-Benson, 1989; Shade, 1989; Solomon, 1992; Stiff, 1990; Willis, 1992) have implied a series of educational dialectics as well, with many similarities in nature and form to those identified by Belenky, et al. For example, the African-American community tends to focus on people and their activities. The interdependence of people and their environment is respected and encouraged. An instructional application of interdependence is cooperative learning which has been shown to be instrumental in the improved achievement of most students (including women), but especially minority students (Malloy, in press).

Do such learning preferences, which are perhaps part of the grist we are after, suggest that constructivism is an inappropriate stance with respect to how students come to know and learn? Perhaps we have not been asking the right questions.

Many African-American students appear to have been enculturated in ways that are different from the pervasive culture of the schools. Differences pose obstacles to the adjustment and achievement of students and could result from the curriculum and teaching practices in the schools that do not recognize or modify pedagogy to respond to the way African-American students learn. (Malloy, in press, p. 7)

Irvine (1992) indicates that effective teachers of minority students do share some characteristics and teaching behaviors with all other effective teachers. Effective teachers (a) are competent in subject matter, (b) provide all students with high-level knowledge regardless of previous categorization or labeling, and (c) have appropriately high standards and expectations for their students. Additionally effective teachers of African-American students need to be more than effective teachers, they need to be culturally responsive teachers who contextualize teaching by giving attention to immediate needs and cultural experiences of their students. (Malloy, in press, p. 9)

The impression is that constructivism is synonymous with pedagogy. However, constructivism as a belief system about how people learn does not dictate a specific set of techniques or instructional methodologies. It is true that constructivist philosophy and supporting pedagogy have been tried out and refined in middle-class settings. How this work adapts to other settings (e.g., working with inner city students, working within a culture of poverty, working within an African-American culture) is a important question. Some projects (e.g., Fennema, Campbell) are providing clues to what it means to make such adaptations when constructivism is the guiding belief system with respect to learning.

A final issue that was raised during the conference involves taking into account the very nature of the mathematics content that is taught. Separate from the classroom culture, we need to ask whether mathematics is taught as a body of ideas that can be explored or as a collection of facts and procedures to be memorized. Does the teaching help students come to find their own power of mathematical thought?

Does the teaching help students know that they can approach problems that are new to them and find ways to solve them? Is the argument for traditional classroom structures also an argument for structures that preclude access to powerful mathematical ideas?

Addressing equity within the domain of teacher enhancement requires re-thinking and re-formulating instructional practices in order to be inclusive rather than exclusive. While the literature is limited, it is beginning to be developed and needs to be considered in terms of providing direction for how such learning environments—ones in which all students can make meaning and create knowledge—may be supported.

Evaluation

During the conference, the tension between evaluation of programs and assessing improvements in student learning was acknowledged. While the content of professional development should have promise for effects on students' learning, the evaluation of such programs needs to be viewed as a process of inquiry in which questions about the extent to which the intentions of the planned program have been met occur long before questions about student outcomes are considered.

> *The purpose of public schools is to educate children. Any change—any scheme to reform schools—must be judged by the extent to which it helps children become fully functioning, competent, educated adults.... The truism above does not immediately translate into the conclusion that evaluation of educational programs must necessarily involve an assessment of the extent to which a program has resulted in increased learning by children.* (Hein, p. 151)

Hein provides an overview of an argument for what should be the role (responsibilities) for evaluation in a teacher enhancement project. The central issue involves the debate around "evaluation of what."

> *It is important to make the distinction between the capacity of project evaluators to provide information about implementation efforts—and to assist in improving these through formative evaluation—and studies that attempt to link teacher behavior with student outcomes.* (Hein, p. 161)

Further, when considering the evaluation of school reform, basic questions concerning any school intervention can be formulated:

1. *At what level(s) is the intervention targeted?*
2. *What is the strategy for influencing this level?*
3. *To what extent does the program influence the targeted level?*
4. *What is the logical argument that an intervention at the targeted level will influence the education of children?*
5. *Is there a strategy for influencing all levels?* (Hein, p. 154)

From an evaluator's perspective not every step in the logic of the argument that is intended to result in improved education for children is a component of the evaluation of a specific program targeted at a particular audience.

> *Program evaluators have two major concerns. One is a need to understand the logic of the program being evaluated. What is intended, how is it supposed to work? Although there have been suggestions that evaluation should be goal free and that evaluators might even intentionally be ignorant of program goals, most of us believe that unless we understand a program's basic assumptions, we cannot adequately evaluate it. The rationale for a program is embodied in the answers to questions 1, 2, 4 and 5 above. The second concern of the evaluator is to document and evaluate the actual program activities and consequences. In order to carry out the evaluation, the evaluator needs to understand the logic behind the program, but the evaluation work itself focuses on the activities of the program and the outcomes associated with those activities. In carrying out the evaluation, the evaluator will address primarily question 3 above.* (Hein, pp. 154-5)

For a project, there may be an additional research question: What is the evidence that changing teacher behavior changes student outcomes? However, this is a different question from that of evaluating the intervention as planned. There is a distinction to be drawn between evaluation of a project and research directed toward impact of the project on student outcomes.

Hein notes that there may be a literature about the way what teachers do impact on children. A summary of that literature, if it exists, would be enormously useful to everyone. Clearly, there are a large number of teacher enhancement projects, each with its evaluation and final report;

a meta-analysis of this material would be a good first step in a larger area of research directed toward looking at student outcomes.

One of the big stumbling blocks is not just the connection to finding out how what teachers do affects the children, but it's documenting children's growth. And it's our ability to describe that in reasonable terms that can be at least partially generalized or to tease out at least some of the main components that is inadequate. (edited transcript)

Such monitoring of children's growth is linked to the use of assessment strategies. Current assessment practices continue to be a big stumbling block with respect to achieving the reforms.

Unless one is clear about goals, the tension between program evaluation and assessment of student learning will surface. Given the implications of time needed for change to occur, monitoring the implementation of reform efforts in terms of collecting data on an ongoing basis seems imperative in order to assess progress toward targeted goals and to identify obstacles. Evaluation of any one program is part of this process of monitoring change and needs to address the expected outcomes of the program and not the expected outcomes of the total reform effort.

School Culture

The dilemma is that, once the project is over, teachers stop thinking about teaching mathematics. They're onto another project with another focus. Sometimes the tenets of the new project counter the views about teaching that were promoted in the earlier mathematics project. Teachers don't seem to question these shifts and whether they want such shifts to happen. (Mathematics teacher educator, 1995, NCTM and SIG/RME, Research Presession[1])

Elementary teachers are responsible for much more than teaching mathematics. They, and their schools/school systems, often get involved in multiple programs; often each program may be focused on a different curricular area or on some broad topic such as developing critical thinking skills. There is a need for a coherent framework that

---

[1] Preliminary results of the Conference were presented at the 1995 Research Presession, jointly sponsored by NCTM and SIG/RME. Several mathematics educators attended and participated in small group discussions about a number of issues.

spans "doing" mathematics, science, reading, social studies, and so on—a coherent view of pedagogical knowledge and reflective thinking that extends across teachers' work. With such a framework in place, we can talk about the nature of long-term support that transcends programs and projects. How do we promote building an educational community that is always looking across programs and projects with the perspective of a school-based culture that has articulated a vision about children's learning and teachers' teaching?

Loucks-Horsley addresses this issue from the perspective of implications for teacher enhancement projects.

If schools are indeed to become professional learning settings for teachers, they will need a strong infrastructure to help them "reculture" and to maintain that new culture. Given where they are starting, they will need a lot of help in doing so. How could teacher enhancement projects become that infrastructure or part of it? What could they do beyond carrying out their own projects? What would it be like if they had a common set of beliefs and ways of working with teachers and schools? A common vision of a professional learning community? How could they network their teachers and schools to "multiple mileage" their efforts? What if they designed and assembled a "curriculum" for teacher leadership and change that they all could use, as appropriate? What if they developed strategies for their own professional development, ways to continue learning as well as to "induct" new teacher enhancement projects into their community? Couldn't such an infrastructure have a powerful influence on other providers of professional development? on preservice teacher preparation? on leadership development at state and regional levels? (p. 147)

Clearly, Loucks-Horsley's comments fall within the realm of capacity building and systemic change. What would happen if, indeed, we did pool the work of our best efforts and find some way to share these efforts on a larger scale? As a component of capacity building, what if the results of previous work were summarized and synthesized so that what is known would be available to influence the next steps? NSF mandates could "encourage" the use of such efforts through an expectation that current proposals would demonstrate how they are building substantially on previous work.

Preservice Teacher Preparation

It is essential that we "work backwards," using what we now know are issues in inservice education to inform our directions in preservice education. Teaching involves a process of development; not all the issues of inservice education can be remedied through changes in preservice education. However, how does what we know now inform the practice of teacher preparation? As the *Teaching Standards* (NCTM, 1991) emphasize, teacher preparation and professional development must be viewed as ongoing. The "best" readiness may come from knowing better what we do not know as we begin our teaching careers and accepting the challenge of ongoing, career-long, self-responsibility for professional development.

Preservice teachers' beliefs are based on less extensive knowledge and experience than inservice teachers' beliefs. Teacher educators need to know about and address preservice teachers' beliefs, but the tools that might be used to support or to challenge beliefs may be different or may need to be modified from those used for inservice learning. Lack of experience in the practice of teaching makes it difficult for preservice teachers to "see" what is going on in classrooms and to interpret the importance of instructional events. It may not be wise to assume that materials prepared for work with inservice teachers will work in the same ways for preservice teachers. For example, some of the attendees at the conference (e.g., Bright, Friel, Schifter) currently are exploring the role of reading and/or writing cases in elementary teacher preparation mathematics methods courses. Fundamental to the use of these tools is tapping into preservice teachers' beliefs and skills at reflecting on their own understandings of content, pedagogy, and children's thinking. The ways such cases are used may well support novices as they make a transition to a more reflective mode of inquiry into teaching. A great deal more work needs to be done in understanding the developmental process of what it means to move from novice to practitioner and the kinds of tools and support needed to foster "reform" modes of thinking and behaving.

Both the nature and depth of what preservice teachers choose to reflect about is probably different than that of inservice teachers. Preservice teachers anecdotally seem to be most concerned about classroom "routines" dealing with "how do I get things to work." As was noted earlier, teachers evolve through a series of concerns that are reflected in the kinds of questions they ask (Loucks-Horsley). There are three main stages: self-concerns, management concerns, and impact concerns. The questions that are more self-oriented (e.g., What is teaching all about? How will my being a teacher affect me?) merge into questions that are more task-oriented (e.g., How do I teach students mathematics? What materials do I need and how can I use them efficiently? What is the timing? Do I have enough for students "to do"?). Preservice teachers demonstrate concerns at these stages. The third stage emerges when self and task concerns are largely resolved. An individual now can focus on impact (e.g., Is what I am doing or my students are doing working for my students? What other things do I need to address? Do I want to collaborate with other teachers?). Not only are preservice teachers generally operating at the first and second stages of this model, the very nature of student teaching (i.e., in which a preservice teacher usually assumes responsibility for another teacher's class under that teacher's guidance and the guidance of a university or college supervisor) precludes assuming complete and independent responsibility for one's "own" class. The role of internship or apprenticeship, in a sense, acknowledges that there is a process of developing "into" teaching. Teacher educators need to acknowledge and address the needs for immediacy of preservice teachers, *in addition to* helping them prepare for further growth as reflective teachers who can understand and implement reform in mathematics teaching.

Perhaps the goal of reflection for preservice teachers is different from the goal of reflection for inservice teachers. We want preservice teachers to create an initial personal view of themselves as mathematics teachers, whereas for inservice teachers we want them to build on or change an existing personal view. For preservice teachers, the view is built on perceptions of other teachers (both from many years as a student and from fewer years as a preservice teacher candidate), whereas for inservice teachers the view is built on a perception of themselves in their daily practice. Building a perception of self from observations of others is difficult. As preservice teachers move through internships and student teaching, their views shift to encompass themselves as emerging teachers.

The way that preservice teachers engage in mathematics content may need to go beyond the strategies used in traditional university-level mathematics courses. For example, learning of mathematics might evolve from analysis of children's problem solving. What mathematics do we as adults need to understand in order to interpret what the children are doing? In addition, where preservice teachers are in their program of study may influence what they are willing to learn and interested in learning about mathematics. For example, as juniors, teacher candidates may be very interested in learning the mathematics of the school curriculum, but in the semester immediately preceding their student teaching, they might not be interested in learning new mathematics.

Their focus at this time is mainly on instructional strategies and classroom management issues. For inservice teachers, the timing of inservice on content may not be so critical.

There is a need to integrate knowledge of subject matter, pedagogy, and children's thinking. Perhaps preservice teachers need "inquiry projects" first for themselves to learn about specific content (e.g., the concepts of area and perimeter, the concept of slope). Then second inquiry projects would help them focus on the variety of ways of teaching the content learned. Third projects would investigate what children know about this same content. Finally, only after participating in these experiences, might we expect preservice teachers to develop lessons for helping children learn the selected content.

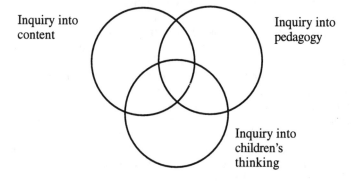

Figure 5: Modes of Inquiry

Perhaps part of the dilemma and confusion about teacher education in mathematics is the failure to distinguish the three components of learning about subject matter, pedagogy, and children's thinking. Doing all three types of projects requires the luxury of time in a teacher education program. It is not reasonable to expect to do all three at once, as often is attempted in methods course assignments. One model is to have a content course in spring of the junior year, followed by methods in fall of the senior year (to address pedagogy and children's thinking). In student teaching, attention is given to the implementation of and experimentation with this knowledge in terms of planning for teaching.

Obviously, preservice teachers' experience with students also is limited, so the way one talks about children's thinking may have to be different than is done with inservice teachers. The aspects of children's thinking that one focuses on may also be different. For example, the notion that students who are doing the same task will think in decidedly different ways is one that is surprising to preservice teachers, particularly prior to their internships in teaching. One first semester senior, as part of an assignment in her mathematics methods course, interviewed three students and returned to class with the results she found (Figure 6). One part of the assignment involved discussing what might be the instructional implications based on the knowledge of students derived from the interviews. This preservice teacher, along with her classmates, realized that the diversity posed instructional challenges that she had not previously considered. However, she was completely "at sea" about what she might choose to do next. One might well expect that that there are many practitioners who would feel equally lost if they were aware of their students' thinking. However, there are many practitioners who do know that this kind of development occurs and have created strategies for addressing individual student needs. Preservice teachers have no such repertoires available; however, their awareness that they can find out what children are thinking is a step toward helping them focus more explicitly on instruction that addresses individual needs.

STUDENT 1

$3 + \square = 7$ Three plus four must equal seven. If three plus three is six then adding one to three makes seven.

$5 + \square = 9$ If five plus five is ten, if you take one away from five you get nine.

$9 + \square = 17$ Ten plus seven is seventeen. So take one away to make nine and add one to the seven to give you eight. The answer is eight.

$6 + \square = 9$ Three plus three is six. If you add one more three you get nine. Two sets of three equal six and one more three gives you nine.

STUDENT TWO

$4 + \square = 12$ She began counting on her fingers at four and counted how many numbers were between four and twelve.

$6 + \square = 9$ If you count the numbers between six to nine you get three. See? (She showed me one finger for each number from six to nine.)

$2 + \square = 11$ She counted on her fingers the numbers from two to eleven. She did this three times before writing down her answer.

STUDENT THREE

$9 + \square = 17$ If ten plus eight equals eighteen, you can take one away from the ten and get seventeen. That would give you nine plus eight equal to seventeen.

$6 + \square = 9$ If six plus three equals nine, then three is the answer.

$2 + \square = 11$ Ten plus two equals twelve. Take one away from ten and you get eleven.

Figure 6: Second/Third Grade Fall, 1995 Interview

Ball, in her paper, addresses the uncertainties of teaching and learning that are created by the new vision of teaching.

> *This new vision of teaching confronts—and embraces—the uncertainties of learning and teaching, and the interaction between the two.... Three sources of uncertainty stand out as endemic to this kind of teaching: the inherently incomplete nature of knowledge in teaching; the multiple commitments with which teachers work; and trying to teach in ways that are responsive to students.* (p. 80)

Ball discusses these uncertainties within a context of a fraction lesson, pointing to the subtleties of knowing mathematics and knowing students. Her rich analysis and personal understanding have developed over a number of years; clearly, first steps for preservice teachers involve building an awareness of the uncertainties that are there.

Role of Technology

The focus on technology at the conference was on professional development provided via technology (vs. professional development about using technology in teaching). There are a number of delivery options that technology provides including videotape and CDs. Indeed, one of the three RFPs addressed the use of such alternative resource. Professional development video materials are becoming increasingly available. How can they be evaluated? How do we know in what to invest limited funds? Video takes a great deal of time to view. Perhaps teachers need to view these at home prior to discussions. Perhaps video tapes ought to be used like cases in the sense that they should be viewed multiple times so that teachers extract the richness of the teaching and learning vignette(s) presented. But is the time it takes to view and interpret such videos reasonable? In addition, video examples are powerful exemplars and may be viewed as "defining" what good teaching is. Who decides whether these are the "right" exemplars?

In addition to the use of video, there is a growing interest in the use of networks (e.g., internet, video conferencing) to support teachers and/or to deliver "short courses" with distance education options. For example, Bank Street College of Education has been experimenting with distance learning through the use of Mathematics Learning Forums. These forums are designed to help teachers introduce new mathematics teaching practices in their classrooms.

Each forum is offered via a telecommunications network making it possible for teachers to communicate with other colleagues throughout the country. During the forum teachers examine their own and other classrooms by viewing videotapes of students and teachers in a range of school settings, and through planning, revising, and implementing activities with their students.

The forums are hosted by a faculty facilitator and focus on the "how" of mathematics instruction, providing ongoing support to teachers as they implement reform in their own classrooms. Throughout the forum the facilitator's role is to raise questions, guide discussion, and provide reflective commentary. Participants actively exchange ideas, share concerns, and construct new understandings as they converse with colleagues and build an on-line community. Each forum focuses on a particular area of instruction including mathematical content, student learning, teaching strategies, and assessment techniques.

> *Each of the Mathematics Learning Forums is eight weeks long and enrollment is limited to twelve.... Forum participants must have internet e-mail accounts, and are expected to spend approximately 2 hours a week actively contributing to and shaping on-line conversation.* (Bank Street College, New York, 1994)

Using internet communication involves several components: getting to know the other participants, study of a problem and reporting back (perhaps repeating this component more than once), and closure. There may be difficulties, for example, in the asynchronization of exchange that can allow for mis-communication to occur or a lessening of face-to-face interaction. On the other hand, the advantage of "anytime response" is that people can formulate their personal views without the "interference" of dialogue. The question of who speaks up when and about what may get dealt with in different ways in electronic communication than in face-to-face communication.

In addition to the more structured electronic forums such as those sponsored by Bank Street College, professional dialogue through listservs and electronic bulletin boards is often touted as a benefit of networking. There seems to be little documentation of what the true effects are of such interactions. Is the dialogue that occurs among participants "better" than that found in face-to-face conversation? Perhaps it is "better" for some teachers, but not for other teachers? Is there a benefit to being able to dialogue with people who are not geographically accessible?

What are the roles for technology in teaching mathematics and how do teachers become educated about these roles? There was some discussion of the "it" (i.e., the mathematics) of inservice. Technology may influence what is important to teach about mathematics, both to teachers and to their students. It is not clear how we decide (or who decides) how technology changes what is important to learn about mathematics content.

Use of technology may change the ways that children understand mathematical structures or connections among mathematics concepts (e.g., interpreting graphs by generating lots of examples with Cricket Graph). Once children have some understanding, technology may change the way that children apply their understanding to problem solving (e.g., finding patterns in large sets of examples as, for example, in seeing relationships between fractions and decimals through generating hundreds of examples in a spreadsheet). Computers and calculators may influence the development of understanding differently because of differences in speed, in types of representations (e.g., there are no non-terminating decimals on calculators or in computers, though it is less obvious in computers), and in record keeping (i.e., memory capacity of the technology).

Summary

Quilts are designed very differently. You have crazy quilts, you have sampler quilts in which every section is different, you have ones that have real designs in them. And you can also have combinations of those. You can have a centerpiece that is a crazy quilt and then build more specialized designs around the outside. But quilting takes a lot of time and it takes attention to detail. That's exactly what we need to be able to do. If you cut a piece slightly wrong, it doesn't fit and then you have to start over again. If you try to put certain colors together even though intuitively they look like they are going to work, you find that they don't so you start over again.

Margaret Cozzens, conference transcript

The quilt for this conference has at its centerpiece the twelve common guiding principles. Around this centerpiece are specialized designs in the form of three RFPs addressing what is needed in order to think more systemically about professional development for K–6 teachers of mathematics. Finally, our quilting points to the presence of false starts and necessary changes that are raised through the discussion of five emerging issues. It seems unlikely that we now need to "start all over again." Clearly, these proceedings will help all of us to "do it better and more wisely" than in the past, designing still other pieces to be added to an already intricately-patterned quilt we have begun here.

References

Bank Street College of Education. (1994). *Distance learning through... mathematics learning forums* [program flyer]. New York: Author.

Belenky, M. F., Clinchy, B. M., Goldberger, N. R., & Tarule, J. M. (1986). *Women's ways of knowing: The development of self, voice, and mind.* New York: Basic Books, Inc.

Hale-Benson, J. E. (1986). *African-American children: Their roots, culture, and learning styles.* Baltimore, MD: Johns Hopkins Press.

Irvine, J. J. (1992). Making teacher education culturally responsive. In M. E. Dilworth (Ed.), *Diversity in teacher education* (pp. 79–92). San Francisco, CA: Jossey-Bass Publishers.

Malloy, C. E. (in press). Including African-American students in the mathematics community. In J. Trentacosta (Ed.), *Multicultural and gender equity in the mathematics classroom: The gift of diversity.* Reston, VA: Author.

National Council of Teachers of Mathematics (1991). *Professional standards for teaching mathematics.* Reston, VA: National Council of Teachers of Mathematics.

Shade, B. (1989). The influence of perceptual development on cognitive style: Cross ethnic comparisons. *Early Child Development and Care. 51*, 137–55.

Solomon, P. (1992). *African-American resistance in high school: Forging a separate culture.* Albany, NY: State University of New York Press.

Stiff, L. V. (1990). African-American students and the promise of the curriculum and evaluation standards. In T. J. Cooney & C. R. Hirsh (Eds.), *Teaching and learning mathematics in the 1990s* (pp. 152–8). Reston, VA: National Council of Teachers of Mathematics.

Willis, M. G. (1992). Learning styles of African-American children: Review of the literature and interventions. In A. K. Burlew, W. C. Banks, H. P. McAdoo, & D. A. Azibo (Eds.), *African-American Psychology* (pp. 260–78). Newbury Park, CA: Sage Publishing.

Appendix A:
Issues Identification Papers

Developing Mathematics Reform: What *Don't* We Know About Teacher Learning— But Would Make Good Working Hypotheses

Deborah Loewenberg Ball
Michigan State University

My task in this paper is to try to frame a set of issues around teacher learning in relation to teaching mathematics. The problem is to take stock of what we know in ways that might help us respond to the Congressional mandate to "reach" many more teachers as they "implement" reform. But the NCTM *Standards* documents are far from a program to be implemented (Ball, 1992). Rather, they are two sets of inspirational, but unfamiliar and incomplete visions for improving mathematics education. Because they are underdetermined, I propose to change the question slightly. Rather than asking, "How might we help more teachers implement the reform?" I want to ask, "How might we engage a wider community in developing and enacting reform?" Although these questions are different, teacher learning is at the heart of both of them. Yet selecting the latter over the former has significant implications for what I discuss below, as well as for moving the reforms forward.

I begin with a few assumptions. First, although reforming mathematics is inescapably dependent on political leverage, economic resources, and public marketing (Mirel, 1994), at its heart is a problem of learning (Cohen & Barnes, 1992). Yet the idea that reform requires learning is often too quickly agreed to, and inadequately examined. And so I begin with a short analysis of why the mathematics reforms require learning, and the nature of that learning. Second, I assume that there are some things we know about teacher learning. And that it might be important to consider our current "knowledge base" in this domain. Finally, I assume that such "knowledge" is a conglomerate of belief, wisdom of practice, folklore, myth, and constraint, and that it would be useful to identify and examine some of what we really may *not* know, for it might well be that the seeds of fruitful work lie in what we *don't* know.

I begin this piece by exploring the question, "What is it that we know about the mathematics reforms and what it takes to help teachers engage with them?" I examine this in three sections:

1. What is the "it" envisioned by the reforms?
2. What do teachers (and others) bring to learning "it?"
3. What do we know and believe about teacher learning?

In the second part of this paper, I pose the question, "What is it that we *don't* know about the reforms and how do we help a larger number of teachers engage productively with them?" With a reexamination of some prematurely-dismissed paths of professional development, I explore some potential working hypotheses about helping people learn to do "it."

What We Know

In Search of "This Kind of Teaching:" What Is the "It" Envisioned by the Reforms?

The multiple foundations of the reform. These are times of ambitious efforts to reform mathematics curriculum and instruction. A host of prominent national reform documents paint a vision of challenging mathematics instruction for all students (NCTM, 1989, 1991; National Research Council, 1989, 1993a, 1993b). The reform's rhetoric takes aim at both patterns of inequity and curricular inadequacy. Students are to learn mathematics with understanding, engage in and be able to solve real-world and meaningful problems, and develop the confidence and power to think mathematically. And these goals are for all students, with particular concern for those who have been traditionally underserved and excluded from mathematics: students of color, poor students, girls.

The foundations for this reform are complex. As part of a tidal wave of education reform, the mathematics education reforms are based on both dissatisfactions with what is, and new aspirations for what could be. On one hand, critics worry about U.S. achievement in mathematics. As a society, we seem to be educating only a tiny fraction of our population to be mathematically literate. For reasons economic, political, and social, the coming decades will demand many more people who can use mathematics competently. Critics also point to the sociological patterns in participation and achievement that show dramatic mathematics dropout rates among female, minority, and poor students.

On the other hand, the reforms also grow from aspirations for what could be. New ideas about learning and knowledge have led to revised Deweyian images in which students interact around important questions as members of learning communities, developing knowledge together. Constructivist theories of learning (Cobb, 1994) have deeply permeated contemporary theoretical work in mathematics education. At the same time, knowledge itself is seen as less definite and more situated in the assumptions and agreed-upon ways of working shared by a community. There is more attention to questions of mathematical argument and discourse—methods of proof, tools of representation. Although there is far from consensus on "the" nature of mathematics, fallibilist and quasi-empirical views of the discipline have gained increased attention (Lakatos, 1974).

Even this brief sketch highlights one central challenge: the scope of the learning that such reforms would demand, not just for teachers but for everyone. The patterns of poor achievement are embedded in the structures of school, inherited ideas about curriculum and about who can learn, and shared images of teaching. These would have to change. And commonsense theories of knowledge as fact, and of learning as remembering information are at odds with these new ideas.[1] These theories too would have to be shaken at their roots. Clearly, reforming mathematics is no short order: It would require profound and extensive societal and individual learning—and unlearning.

But the problem is more complex because of a special quality of the reforms. Despite the laudable rhetoric, what is specifically implied for classroom practice is far from definite. This is our first challenge, namely, that the "it" to which we aim is no clear program for practice.

Inspiring visions, uncertain practices. The NCTM *Standards*, widely touted for their vision, offer perhaps the most detailed images. With vignettes, examples, and illustrations, the *Standards* books—454 pages worth (with a third volume on assessment to follow soon)—are a main resource for reformers. Despite their persuasive, inspiring vignettes, however, these documents are far from programs for practice. They sketch directions and commitments, principles and aspirations. They cannot provide guidance for the specifics of minute-to-minute practice or for the decisions met day to day. For example, one of the teaching standards, in envisioning the teacher's role in classroom discourse, states that teachers have to decide "when to provide information, when to clarify an issue, when to model, when to lead, and when to let a student struggle with a difficulty" (NCTM, 1991, p. 35). True enough. But the challenge is to judge when to do which, and on what basis. When, for instance, is a disagreement among students something worth

---

[1] In his 1989 essay, David Cohen argues persuasively and elegantly that efforts at "ambitious teaching" run repeatedly up against prevailing societal views of knowledge as factual, unchanging, and certain.

continuing? When should the teacher step in and clear up controversy? When is a particular student's statement best left alone? When is it good to probe? (See, for example, Chazan and Ball, 1995.) The *Standards* also speak of "worthwhile mathematical tasks" and specify some elements of such tasks. But, with a particular group of students, what makes a task likely to be productive of learning is much less straightforward—and helping it to be so, even less clear. Sometimes good tasks fizzle to nothing, or run into unanticipated difficulties. How, specifically, can a "good" task be best framed and orchestrated with a particular class?

Some might argue that these questions cannot yet be answered because the reforms are too new and, thus, underspecified. The air is filled with words about which there has been little discussion—problem solving, understanding, meaningfulness, autonomy, authenticity, inquiry. Some assume that, with time, the specifics will be worked out; we will know more and will therefore be able to develop more explicit and helpful guidance for teachers.

Explicating the vision more fully is certainly an important challenge of the reforms. And it will help to have more, and better-specified, articulations of the ideas and their interpretations. Yet no matter how much more specific the vision becomes, it will not be close to a prescription for practice. Shulman (1983) argues that initiatives for change can at best be "a shell within which the kernel of professional judgment and decision making can function comfortably." He argues that such initiatives *cannot* determine directly teachers' actions or decisions, and he concludes that they can, at best, "profess a prevailing view, orienting individuals and institutions toward collectively valued goals, without necessarily mandating specific sets of procedures to which teachers must be accountable" (Shulman, 1983, p. 501).

This relationship between policy and practice is accentuated in the case of the current mathematics reforms. With an eye on new goals of "understanding," teachers ply their trade still closer to the uncertainties of learning and knowledge. This new vision of teaching confronts—and embraces—the uncertainties of learning and teaching, and the interaction between the two (e.g., Cohen, 1989, in preparation; Jackson, 1986; Lampert, 1985). Three sources of uncertainty stand out as endemic to this kind of teaching: the inherently incomplete nature of knowledge in teaching, the multiple commitments with which teachers work, and trying to teach in ways that are responsive to students.

Uncertainty is not a comfortable idea, and certainly not a happy prospect for ambitious reformers. What does it mean? To begin with, knowledge in teaching is most often incomplete. Human understanding is far from a simple, visible phenomenon. To illustrate, I use an example from my own teaching of third grade.[2] One day, in the midst of several weeks of work on fractions, my third graders drew pictures of 4/4 and 5/5 in their notebooks (c.f., Ball & Wilson, in press). Each picture looked like this:

Had I stopped there, I would have concluded that all my students knew that 4/4 was equivalent to 5/5 (even if they would not have used the term "equivalent"). When I asked which was more, 4/4 or 5/5, about half the students thought 5/5 was more and some thought they were the same. One child thought 4/4 was more than 5/5. Why? How could they look at these pictures and think that? As we talked, I discovered that some students thought that since 5/5 has "more pieces," it was actually more. Even though they gave the "correct answer," it was not clear what the students who said the two quantities were "the same" were thinking. At the end of class, I asked everyone to write in their notebooks about 4/4 and 5/5. As I studied what they wrote and drew, I could not tell for sure what they understood. But what they did say and draw made me wonder, make conjectures, and proceed to plan out the next day using my hypotheses. On an ongoing basis, teachers are faced with making such judgments, designing next steps, evaluating students' learning—and with incomplete and indefinitely interpretable evidence.

No matter what kind of research we do in the future—exploring students' knowledge and preconceptions, examining what they know and how—teachers will continue to confront such uncertainty on a daily basis. Can a teacher become more skillful at probing and making sense of students' ideas? Yes. But what teachers know about their students can never be certain or complete.

The practice of teaching itself is uncertain as well. Teachers work in the midst of multiple and oft-competing commitments (Goodlad, 1984; Lampert, 1985). For example, at the core of the reform visions is the

[2]As part of my research, I teach elementary school mathematics on a daily basis. The episode I relate here occurred in my third grade class during the 1989–90 school year. The data on which I am drawing were gathered as part of an NSF project which involved documenting the mathematics teaching and learning across the entire school year in my class and in the fifth grade class of my colleague, Magdalene Lampert. The teacher in whose classroom I was working was Sylvia Rundquist (see Ball & Rundquist, 1992, for a description and examination of our four-year collaboration).

commitment to teach worthwhile content with intellectual integrity. But equally at the core is the commitment to honor students' ideas. When a child presents a novel approach to a problem that is imaginative—and completely nonstandard—what is the right thing for the teacher to do?

This is seldom an easy question to answer. In the episode above, Sheena, one of the African-American girls in my class, argued articulately that 5/5 had to be more than 4/4. She went to the board and presented her original (and persuasive) explanation, rooted cleverly in assumptions about sharing cookies. She drew two circular cookies, dividing them into four and five pieces, and showing that with 5/5 there is enough to pass out one piece to each of your five friends but with 4/4 one friend will not get any cookie.

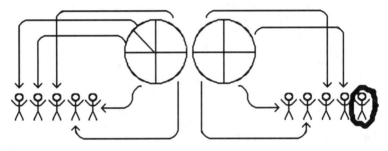

It was important to me that Sheena—a student of color, a quiet girl—displayed enough confidence in herself and her ideas to defend them in the face of classmates' objections. And she is right, given the question she has framed ("Which way of cutting the cookie—into fourths or fifths—will serve more friends?"). Her drawing is another source of uncertainty. Most adults to whom I have shown this picture immediately assume that Sheena does not know that fractions must have equal pieces. But this is actually not clear. Dividing circles into fifths is technically complicated (try it!) and we had not done this in class. I knew that with other pictures, the children had sometimes said, "I know my picture isn't quite right, but just assume that the pieces are the same size." Although Sheena did not say that here, I am not so quick to conclude what she knows—or does not know—about equal parts.

As I listened to Sheena, I knew that next year's teacher might not be charmed by Sheena's way of thinking about this. She might see Sheena as lacking mathematical skills. *Was* she? Sheena *could* complete standard fraction worksheet items correctly (e.g., shade 3/4 of a rectangle) and she got the fraction items right on the end-of-year standardized test. Yet this nonstandard part of Sheena's thinking made me wonder. And I was aware that my twin commitments to teach mathematics with integrity and to honor students' ideas and ways of thinking were in tension in this case: Sheena was being creative. And some aspects of her answer were "right." But her nonstandard approach had actually changed the question. And her response to the original question was "wrong." What should be the "right" answer for me here? To this day, that remains uncertain. The slogans "teaching for understanding" and "mathematics for all" are a lot more complex when viewed up close (Theule-Lubienski, in preparation). Teaching often sits uncomfortably in the cross-talk of several such worthy—and competing—commitments. Wrestling with these in context, on an ongoing basis, is a second source of the uncertainty of teaching.

Third, the kind of teaching envisioned by the reforms aims to be responsive to students, to what they say and do. Teachers often have to adapt and improvise in the face of what happens as lessons unfold. When my students drew the pictures of 4/4 and 5/5 correctly, but then believed that these were still not "the same amount," I had to remap where we were and where we might go. I realized that the phrase "the same amount" was fragile, and searched my mind for new phrasing. I noticed the ambiguity of the idea of "more"—and adaptively began to consider another way to confront the problem that would allow us to explore equivalence without burying the students' alternative interpretations.[3]

Teaching is an interactive practice in a messy terrain of content, politics, and social and individual improvement (compare Cohen, 1989, in preparation). Teachers work with and "on" other human beings, and such work is interdependent in ways that make it quite clearly different from the practice of mathematics or even biology where practitioners (biologists) work with and on materials which they cannot entirely control. This casts a light on the challenge of reform that makes it still more challenging and uncertain.

My sketch here is intended to illustrate one central issue, an issue too often bypassed in our discussions of teacher development in the context of these new reforms: The reforms do not prescribe a specific and identifiable practice. There exists no single "it" to which the reforms aim. Rooted theoretically in the theories and commitments

---

[3]What I mean by this is that I wanted a way of working with the idea of "equivalence" that would facilitate their learning without simply covering up their ways of thinking with a convincing structure that would simply elicit the right answer. I discuss this in more detail in Ball and Wilson (in press).

sketched above, the NCTM documents—as well as other reform documents—are strong on promise, weak on existence proofs.[4] Despite their inspiration in progressive educational ideas, no one has fully developed these ideas on any scale in public schools or even in educational scholarship—at least not to the level of practice. Considerable work lies ahead if the ideas of the reforms are to permeate practices in school in ways that are consistent with their intent. Such work would involve turning these dreams into conjectures, testing them out, revising the revisions.

What does developing "it" require? Although considerable debate exists about what the "stuff" of teaching is (and what counts as knowledge of teaching is perhaps more contested among teachers than mathematical knowledge is among mathematicians), there are nonetheless ideas, principles, insights, theories, and ways of doing things that practitioners know and use. For example, practiced elementary teachers are always on the lookout for opportunities for meaningful counting and can engage young children in enumerating, comparing, sharing equally. Many teachers know that manipulatives can be helpful in helping children to develop mathematical concepts. Most elementary teachers have a repertoire of ways of gaining the attention of the group, and most know particular problems that consistently interest fifth graders. This "stuff" is specialized knowledge of the domain, for it includes a host of things that the ordinary adult, even a parent, does not necessarily know. Note that this body of knowledge is both propositional and procedural—for example, topics that interest students, how to read aloud, ways to gain a class's attention.

In addition to such pedagogical knowledge, there is knowledge of mathematics and knowledge about students. Much has been written in the past decade about the nature of the mathematical understandings that are crucial to teaching mathematics for understanding (e.g., Ball, 1991; Russell, Schifter, Bastable, Yaffee, Lester, & Cohen, 1994; Simon, 1993; Wilson, Shulman, & Richert, 1987). And, equally important, are understandings of the diversity of students with whom teachers work (e.g., Anderson, 1989; Carpenter & Fennema, 1992; Grant & Secada, 1990).

Teaching also involves considerable skill—such as listening to one child while watching thirty others, using one's voice as a tool, "reading" and interpreting the reactions and understandings of others

---

[4]Tyack and Tobin's (1994) notion of a goal as a *hypothesis* appeals to me, for it is neither naively overdetermined—goals as "fixed targets"—nor capriciously unfounded—goals as mere wishes.

who may communicate differently from the teacher, keeping a wide range of details in mind, posing appropriate questions. The kinds of things that play a role in practicing as a teacher of groups of children is more complex than revealed by our usual lists of what teacher need to know. A host of personal qualities matter: patience, curiosity, generosity in listening to and caring about other human beings, confidence, trust, and imagination (Roosevelt, 1994). There is caring about seeing the world from another's perspective, as well as enjoying the humor, sympathizing with the confusion, and caring about the frustration and shame of others. And there are things like tolerance for uncertainty, willingness to take risks, and patience with confusion and mess. The personal resources which teaching demands are not so often discussed, and even less often nurtured. Is the kind of patience that teaching requires something that can be learned? Can empathy grow? If these kinds of resources and qualities are central to teaching, then we need ways of thinking about what might be ways of cultivating and nurturing their development.

But knowledge and skill are not all there is to learning teaching. Another crucial dimension centers on learning to reason and to construct new knowledge in teaching. Three factors underlie this imperative: one rooted in the demands of learning to teach, one in the particularities of practice, and one in the nature of knowledge. As a matter of individual development, learning to teach takes time. It requires taking ideas and images, skills and commitments, and developing a repertoire of professional practice with them. Teaching is also context-specific. Even skilled teachers must adapt their practice in particular situations. Finally, knowledge in teaching is both incomplete and contested; teachers are continually in the position of interpreting conflicting evidence and making choices and judgments. Because knowledge is incomplete, teachers must figure out new things as they teach. They are constantly faced with the data of their own experience. They must develop knowledge of particular children, of the material they are teaching, and of ways to engage students in the content. And, because knowledge is contested, teachers must have ways of working through the alternatives they are offered. They must somehow take stock and assess the relative merits of alternative ideas, interpretations, and strategies. If teachers are to be able to do anything but respond entirely randomly to the flood of claims that are made about what works, what is true, and how things should be done, then they must be able to identify and weigh justifications for various claims.

Confronting Discontinuities and Discomforts of Role, Content, and Practice: What Do Teachers (and Others) Bring to Learning "It?"

There is a gradual recognition that teachers (as well as others such as teacher educators, parents, and school administrators), just like their students, bring experiences and prior understandings that shape their learning (e.g., Ball, 1988; Borko, Eisenhart, Brown, Underhill, Jones, & Agard, 1992; Brown & Borko, 1992; Schifter, 1993; Simon, 1993). These previous experiences often do not help them as they struggle to enact these new reforms. At times, past experiences can act as obstacles. For example, elementary teachers, most of whom experienced school knowledge as given—and who acquired facts and memorized rules—must invent a teaching that engages students in complex reasoning in authentic tasks and contexts. They are faced with trying to find ways to connect students with mathematics and mathematical reasoning, to engage students in genuine experiments. Even though schools have never taught all students equally well, teachers are to find ways to help all of their students.

And so a paradox emerges: elementary teachers are themselves the products of the very system they are now trying to reform. An overwhelming proportion are women, and the majority did not pursue mathematics beyond what was minimally required. Many report their own feelings of inadequacy and incompetence, and can even recall experiences which became turning points when they decided to stop taking mathematics. Rather than becoming critical of the way we "school" mathematics, they often assume that their experiences are due to their own mathematical lacks and to the inherently useless content of mathematics. Those same experiences have equipped them with ideas about the teacher's role, about who can learn mathematics, and about what it takes to learn and know mathematics. Moreover, what teachers bring is not purely cognitive, for some of what they bring includes commitments about how to act with different students, a sense of themselves as helpful and effective, values about a kind of classroom environment. These, too, influence their interpretation of and disposition toward the mathematics reforms.

This mix of things that teachers bring become evident in concrete contexts—such as in viewing videotape or discussing a case. It becomes clear that, given what people's own past experiences are, the reform visions are simultaneously appealing and unsettling, attractive and unfamiliar. When people view and discuss videotapes of alternative approaches to mathematics teaching, they have mixed reactions. On one hand, they are impressed with the children's confidence and civility.

They are attracted by the students' flexible use of drawings and analogies, as well as their articulateness. On the other hand, viewers also find it deeply disturbing to hear the array of students' interpretations. Evidence that students may not understand is not always intriguing, for it can be quite uncomfortable.[5] One major source of teachers' sense of efficacy and satisfaction is the sense that they can help students learn (Lortie, 1975; Smith, 1994). And when we do not ask students to voice their ideas, we run less risk of finding out what they do and do not know. In asking students to talk and otherwise represent publicly their thinking, the gap between their thinking and ours becomes visible. And the ensuing instinct to explain away the apparent misunderstanding is strong: "Did the teacher use manipulatives to show this?" "Had the students been told that the unit has to be the same?" Deeply rooted in teachers is the impulse to help and clarify, to show and tell. It is a good and worthy instinct—and quite right. Teachers are, after all, responsible for helping their students learn. Old complacencies about understanding are called into question when one starts listening more closely to students. My students, who drew rectangles representing 4/4 and 5/5 the same, seemed to understand equivalence until I began asking more questions. Their earlier correct worksheets notwithstanding, I began to see a glimpse of understandings less robust than I had hoped. Moving in the direction of the mathematics reforms means confronting the uncertainties, ambiguities and complexities of what "understanding" and "learning" might really mean and entail.

But things are more complicated still. If student understanding becomes more problematic, one's own understandings are soon more uncertain as well. And this is at least as unsettling. After all, teachers are "supposed to" know what they are teaching. Confronting one's own uncertainties in understanding can make a teacher feel inadequate and ashamed.[6] That the mathematics reforms are aimed at helping students

---

[5]Of course, students can also display exquisite understandings of very complex ideas, glimpses of which are breathtaking. I concentrate deliberately on the less rosy side of listening more closely to students' thinking, for I think it has important implications for what it means to change one's teaching in the direction of the mathematics reforms.

[6]Several poignant and profound examples of this exist in the literature. Heaton (1994) writes about her own struggles to delve into what she had previously considered simple mathematical ideas. Rundquist (Ball & Rundquist, 1992) also describes how vulnerable it made her feel to discover her own confusions, and how personally risky it was to write about it. Other examples can be found in Schifter's (in press a, in press b) books, particularly the chapters by Toney and Yaffee.

understand content in usable and powerful ways is part of the appeal for teachers whose own mathematical histories did not offer them such opportunities. Still, in pursuing such goals, deep anxieties about one's effectiveness and knowledge are likely to surface.

Encounters with the reform visions can be deeply uncomfortable. Despite the obvious fascination of children's nonstandard thinking, if the goal is to help students master content, close views of students' alternative interpretations can threaten established practices. If teachers do the things they have always assumed were helpful and then find that students are thinking differently than what they hoped, this is still more troubling.[7]

The mathematics reforms are attractive and inspiring in many ways. Yet there are also reasonable and powerful disincentives to engage with this agenda, some of which are deeply personal and at the heart of who one is in trying to be a good teacher. Often teachers must defend to parents and administrators things they are trying even before they themselves are convinced or confident. A risky prospect at best, being in this position is understandably unappealing.

Some of what makes learning this kind of practice especially hard includes feeling disconnected from one's past experience with schools and from practice in many contemporary classrooms. With the commitment to attend to what teachers bring, we need to be sensitive to the loss that making a commitment to mathematics reform can engender. What one remembers from third grade is much more useful when trying to learn a more conventional version of practice than it is when one is learning a more novel version of practice. Never having explored the territory this way as a mathematics learner can be disorienting. One's own mathematical understanding and one's ability to listen for and interpret students' thinking plays an important orienting role in navigating the territory in new ways. Being a reformer, an agent for change, can be hard. It takes courage and risk-taking. It takes being adventurous and willing to experiment and try new things in a context that has not typically rewarded or encouraged innovation or rebelliousness. Support, in various forms of communication and community with colleagues engaged in this work, is needed in a very real way.

---

[7]Dick Prawat (personal communication) studied a teacher, who, as she began to decouple learning as a direct outcome of sincere and imaginative teaching, began to doubt that she had ever helped her students "really" understand. As a dedicated twenty-year veteran, she was profoundly distressed.

What Do We Know and Believe about Teacher Learning?

What we know and believe about teacher learning is beginning to be codified in a growing literature. It is also reflected in practice, in the patterns and innovations of teacher change and support.[8] Perhaps, most of all, it is reflected in our talk and the assumptions we reveal about professional development. With a panorama of the literature and programs, I offer below for our collective consideration a tentative list of widely held beliefs about teacher learning. It should be understood that the status of these as "knowledge" is problematic, for the empirical bases for these beliefs vary widely. Some have been investigated in studies of teacher learning and teacher education while some represent current dominant ideology. Even some of those supported by research are the product of studies conducted by teacher educators who design a teacher education experience rooted in one or more of these beliefs. Promising results are then used as evidence for the original assumption. The items on this list, then, possess uneven warrants. They also focus on some aspects of teaching and teacher learning, and not others. But, ubiquitous, they are widely promoted.

1. What teachers bring to learning to teach—prior belief and experience—affects what they learn. Increasingly, teachers' own histories—personal and professional—are thought to play an important role in what they learn from professional development experiences.

2. Learning to create the kinds of teaching envisioned by the mathematics reforms takes a long time and is hard, though what actually makes it hard does not seem to be well-understood nor finely-articulated. Changes do not happen overnight, nor simply by deciding to teach differently. There is as much to unlearn as there is to learn, and what there is to learn is complex and underdeveloped. In ways not well-understood, the odyssey probably entails (at some level) revising deeply-held notions about learning and knowledge, reconsidering one's assumptions about students and images of oneself both as mathematical thinker, a cultural and political being, *and* teacher (Toney, in press; Weissglass, 1994)—all this, and developing new ways of teaching, reflecting and assessing one's work.

3. Often, the most effective staff development model involves follow-up, usually in the form of long-term support (e.g., opportunities to meet with others engaged in the same process) and coaching in teachers' classrooms. Other means that could help teachers continue to develop and learn might also fit this notion of "follow-up."

---

[8]Just as teachers' knowledge can be examined in the contexts of their work—their evolving wisdom of practice—so, too, is knowledge about teacher learning evident in the practice of professional development.

4. Teacher educators and staff developers should model the approaches which they are promoting. This is an oft-heard maxim, quite variously interpreted.

5. Subject matter knowledge matters in learning to teach for understanding. Selecting a generative problem or task for students requires being able to "see" the mathematics latent in its scope. And trying to use tasks and problems—in ways that exploit their potential and support student learning—depends on the teacher's own mathematical understandings. To orchestrate a class discussion of a mathematical conjecture can be treacherous when the teacher feels unsure of the terrain being explored. The teacher's own mathematical knowledge is also an important resource in interpreting students' unexpected statements and solutions.

6. Knowledge of children and their mathematics is crucial to teaching for understanding. Learning more about students, and about listening to them is crucial. How to *hear* what students say is more than a matter of acuity, for it requires seeing the world through another's eyes and perspective, not at all an easy task (especially when those worlds are diverse, sometimes disparate).

7. The contexts in which teachers work affect what they can do. (Included in "context" are students, parents, administrators, tests, district and state objectives and curricular guidelines.) Most often discussed are the ways in which aspects of the context constrain and inhibit teachers' efforts. Students unfamiliar with this kind of teaching resist. Parents protest departures from customary practice. Administrators are intolerant of less-orderly classrooms or fail to provide teachers with materials or time to develop their practice. External curricular guidelines mandate pacing and coverage and impede teachers who want to teach for understanding. There is less understood about promising extant resources although many have claimed that the community can be a significant resource in making reform, that new curriculum and assessments can serve as levers for reform.

8. Reflection is central to learning to teach. For the most part, this perspective focuses on structure and context, emphasizing that teachers need time, space, and encouragement to reflect in ways that facilitate their learning—by talking with others, by keeping a journal, by engaging in action research. Less attention is paid to the specific objects, contexts, and nature of what teachers might reflect *on* and *with*, leaving somewhat out of focus questions about the variety of learnings this might support.

9. Teacher development is especially productive when teachers are in charge of the agenda, determining the focus, nature, and kind of programming or opportunities. In the name of professional autonomy,

many argue that teachers should determine the shape and course of their own development. Little discussion emerges about the dilemma this raises in working toward reform. When teachers set the agenda for their own professional learning, they are likely to be limited by their current vistas. Setting oneself off into a terrain beyond one's current horizons is difficult, if not impossible. Yet, when others set the agenda, they are not necessarily more likely to have vision or sensitivity to teachers' needs and concerns. How to design provocative experiences for teacher learning, that hold real potential for change, for engagement with what is hard about the reforms, and yet that also honor teachers as professionals, is a matter more complex than this maxim suggests.

What We Don't Know

Although these beliefs are widely shared, they are far from a majority view when one considers the enormous "staff development industry." Districts, counties, and private entrepreneurs sponsor workshops, institutes, and after-school dinner meetings to develop, train, refresh, update, and inservice teachers (Sparks & Loucks-Horsley, 1990). Administrators form committees, bring in experts, adopt new textbook series. Teachers read *Teaching Children Mathematics*, *Instructor*, *Learning*, and *American Educator*. They purchase commercial black-line masters for mathematics activities and books. They enroll in master's program courses. These dominant modes of professional development form a substantial infrastructure readily amenable to the current press to reach large numbers of teachers, to "scale up" professional development of teachers. And yet many educators scorn and dismiss them. Do we really know what we need to know about their hidden possibilities? What are their seeds of promise? And what don't we know because it has not been tried and discussed?

The kinds of common activities named in the previous paragraph are disdained for several reasons. Some would argue that they are too brief, too weak, too fragmented. Others would point to their tendency to oversimplify: Providing teachers with activities is unlikely to help them delve into the deeper issues of changing the way they teach mathematics. Still others would note the prevailing tendency toward instrumental goals, and toward technical knowledge imported for teachers' use in their classrooms (Lord, 1994). Yet these criticisms seem to focus on the structure of professional development, rather than on its conceptual orientation, content, or pedagogy.[9] A long-term teacher development' project might develop enthusiasm and yet spur little in the way of serious engagement with reform. A rural Alaska teacher thoughtfully using the new *Investigations* (Russell & Rubin, 1994) mathematics materials with her students miles from any opportunity for professional development might be more stimulated and supported.

Structures offer us a multitude of vehicles and sites for creating possibilities for teacher learning. Some are particularly well-positioned to help meet the challenge of "scaling up" to engage many more teachers in working toward mathematics reform. We should neither write off particular structures without closer consideration, nor uncritically embrace others. For instance, how might electronic mail be a support for professional community?[10] What can people learn from videotape? Are methods courses necessarily of little use? Can mathematics curriculum materials be designed so as to be educative for teachers? How can "follow-up" be provided? That is, what would it take for any particular design to function as an opportunity for sustained learning?[11] Somehow we need to turn our attention toward the aims and orientation of teacher learning opportunities.

---

[9]Feiman-Nemser (1990) argues that structures alone cannot be the determining characteristic of teacher preparation programs, that consideration of conceptual orientations to what teachers need to learn, and in what ways, is crucial in designing alternative approaches.

[10]Although I do not take this up here, there are examples of this worth examining more closely. See, for example, the November 1994 issue of the *Mathematics Teacher*, the special pullout section of *Education Week* (January 11, 1995), and Glazer, 1994.

[11]An image to challenge our assumptions that a deliberative discourse among teachers can only happen when teachers enjoy support, time, and autonomy is that of elementary teachers in China, where external curriculum policies are much stronger and more controlling. Paine and Ma (1993) describe how the common structure provided by a mandated curriculum supports a kind of professional discourse rarely seen in the U.S. except in the context of intensive teacher development programs. Teachers compare notes about particular lessons and problems, discuss how their students respond to specific tasks, and discuss plans.

Exploring "stance" in the orientation of professional development

Traditionally, professional development (such as inservice workshops) and professional forums (such as journals and state meetings) assume a *stance* toward practice that concentrates on answers: conveying information, providing ideas, training in skills (Little, 1993; Lord, 1994; Sparks & Loucks-Horsley, 1990). With enthusiasm and clever quips, leaders distribute ideas, tips, and guidance. Handouts and reproducible worksheets are eagerly collected and filed. In some sessions, participants share ideas—but this is still very much a discourse of answers, a confident stance of certainty. On one hand, this offers participants an enormous assortment of potential resources. However, their potential is restricted by the lack of critical discussion. Seeking to make participants comfortable, staff development leaders rarely challenge teachers' assumptions or provoke disequilibrium or conflict intentionally (Lord, 1994). Because discussions of teaching sometimes resemble "style shows" more than they do professional interaction, teachers' development of their practice is often a highly individual and idiosyncratic matter. The common view that "each teacher has to find his or her own style" is a direct result of working within a discourse of practice that maintains the individualism and isolation of teaching.[12] This individualism not only makes it difficult to develop any sense of common standards, it also makes it difficult to *disagree*. Masking disagreements hides the individual struggles to practice wisely, and so removes an opportunity for learning. Politely refraining from critique and challenge, teachers have no forum for debating and improving their understandings. To the extent that teaching remains a smorgasbord of alternatives with no real sense of community, there is no basis for comparing or choosing from among alternatives, no basis for real and helpful debate.[13] This lack impedes the capacity to grow.

With goals that are uncertain and underdetermined, a stance of certainty and of answers is unlikely to press deeply into the work of

---

[12]I would like to acknowledge Dan Chazan for helping me see this underside of the individualistic culture of teaching. Brian Lord (1994) makes a similar argument related to individual teachers' learning. He argues that because most teachers' conceptions of knowledge, learning, and their role are fundamentally at odds with those that underlie the reform movement, individual and collective challenge and conflict are essential to integrating new ways of thinking about teaching.

[13]Robert Floden, drawing on Campbell (1974/1988), suggests that the lack of debate creates a vacuum around the need for a critical winnowing of the plethora of pedagogical ideas and practices.

reform. We would do well to consider and experiment with fostering a stance of critique and inquiry rather than one of answers—a stance of asking and debating, a discourse of conjecture and deliberation (Fullan, 1982; Little, 1982, 1993; McLaughlin & Marsh, 1978), sometimes called "critical colleagueship" (Lord, 1994). With norms and patterns for discussing alternatives, for arguing about relative merits, for adaptation and evaluation, many more "opportunities" could truly have the possibility of being educative.

What might characterize a stance of critique and inquiry toward practice? One aspect might be the nature of encounters with new ideas—an important part of learning. Such a stance would strive to *make a new idea viable*, getting it on the table for examination, trial, and debate, but not pushing it as "the way." It would involve convincing others that an idea is worth considering, but without "selling" it. A second aspect might center on *considering how other resources and knowledge might be useful* in connection with particular agendas—not as authoritative truth, but as tools for local deliberations. Examining research both inquisitively and skeptically, teachers with such a stance would seek insights from scholarship, but not accord undue truth to its conclusions. This stance would accommodate "the possibility that the available research knowledge is incomplete and there is room for discovery. [It would] neither romanticize teachers' knowledge nor unduly privilege researchers' claims" (Little, 1993, p. 143). A third aspect might entail shifting the emphasis from "implementation" of programs to the *adaptation of innovation* and *generation of new knowledge*. Acknowledging the uncertainties and underdeterminedness of the reform visions, local interpretation and invention is inevitable (McLaughlin, 1976). And desirable. The particularities of local circumstances require tailored innovation. This stance would acknowledge this and embrace it, using the underdeterminedness of the reforms as a resource for developing inspired but locally-tailored innovations (Tyack & Tobin, 1994).

These three aspects all deal in one way or another with relationships with new ideas—how one might engage them, where one might seek them, and how one might develop them—and all with a combined openness to the insights and images of others, and an awareness of the role of critique and adaptation. Missing in these is an explicit concern for community—the final aspect which I will explore.[14] Successful teacher development projects often count among their essential elements the construction of such a community within the project (e.g., Brown,

---

[14]I assume that developing a new stance toward practice will itself entail cycles of invention, experimentation, and re-articulation.

1994; Featherstone, Pfeiffer, & Smith, 1993; Featherstone, Pfeiffer, Smith, Beasley, Corbin, Derksen, Pasek, Shank, & Shears, 1993; Simon & Schifter, 1991). Are there other ways to foster communities of practice, both real (face-to-face) and virtual? A stance of inquiry would also require a sense of membership in some *wider community* of others engaged in reform—in seeking, hearing, envisioning, experimenting, examining, and revising. Connections with others can extend local resources. Such connections are also an antidote for the risks of the self-reflexive tendency inherent in the current enthusiasm for school-based restructuring. Indeed, Lord (1994, p. 197) asks, "In short, how can local efforts to develop critical colleagueship avoid parochialism?" What might be ways to create both local community and connections with a broader community, fostering access to and opportunities to distribute new knowledge and hypotheses for practice?

We need to develop and experiment with such stances within both traditional and nontraditional structures for professional development—in the articles we write, the presentations we give, in the work we do with teachers in schools.[15] What do we know—and *not* know—that can inspire and support experiments with alternative stances within the material, content, and discourse of professional education?[16]

In this last section, below, I propose three sites for the refinement and testing of a set of working hypotheses about ways to engage teachers in working toward the reforms: curriculum materials, videotape, and teacher writing. The first one is conventional—part of the infrastructure I described above—and the second two are novel: vehicles that offer promise and might be worth attention, care, and

---

[15]A special challenge for teacher educators is how unfamiliar all this is for them, too. Many are developing their own practice in the spirit of the reforms, to involve and honor their learners' ideas and ways of thinking, to construct meaningful problems and tasks, and to change the discourse in which they and learners engage. They also vary in their experience with and knowledge of "this kind of teaching" in K–12 classrooms, the albeit incomplete and uncertain "content" of that which they seek to help teachers learn.

[16]The notion that "experiments" could serve to ground and intermingle the development of both theory and practice has its origins in Dewey. Shulman (1994) argues that naturalistic experiments that situate inquiry in the mess of real world contexts are useful to the development of theory. He advocates for "design experiments" [Brown (1992)]: hypotheses formulated as plans, adaptively carried out in a real context, and documented across the course of their evolution. This conjectural stance toward practice fits well with the inherent uncertainties. Based on evolving understandings of learners, content, and context, an approach to developing reform is to design and try out smart hypotheses and to study closely what happens in practice.

experimentation. Each of the three offers a structure potentially amenable to large-scale work. Each offers resources; how each is engaged by teachers could serve to extend the resources of the individual through connections with others around it. Each offers ideas for teaching; each contains the possibility for supporting the generation of new knowledge for teaching. Each holds the possibility for encouraging and supporting a stance of inquiry and experimentation, of critique and deliberation. I propose these as examples of working hypotheses that we will need to develop, refine, test, revise, and try again, if we are to meet the challenges of supporting teachers' learning.

Working Hypotheses: Scaling Up with a Stance of Inquiry

The following three sketches are illustrative. None is yet the design for an experiment (Brown, 1992). Each involves resources of practice—images, understandings, ideas, ways of being or deliberating—and each involves an effort to develop a pedagogical stance that fosters inquiry and critique.

1. *Using redesigned curriculum materials.* Influenced by a big backlash against the teacher-proof curriculum movement, contemporary educators often disparage textbooks, and many reform-oriented teachers—emissaries of the reforms—repudiate them, announcing disdainfully that they do not use textbooks. Yet carefully designed curriculum materials could offer teachers access to mathematical ideas and ways to represent them. Curriculum materials could serve as a rich site for ongoing teacher learning (Remillard, in preparation). They could offer maps of the mathematical territory, helping teachers to reconceive that terrain in ways that reconfigure it around "big ideas" (e.g., Lappan, Fey, Fitzgerald, Friel, & Phillips, in press; Russell, Schifter, Bastable, Yaffee, Lester, & Cohen, 1994). They could provide alternative tasks and discuss their relative advantages and pitfalls. They could offer teachers forecasts of students' likely thinking. With a stance of contributing to an ongoing effort to teach, to a conversation about possibility, text materials would seem to hold untapped potential.

Curriculum could be written with teacher learning as a goal (Russell, 1994). Most curriculum developers have their eye on students rather than on teachers, and attempt to guide teachers without engaging them in pedagogical conversation. Remillard (in preparation) writes about a vision of textbooks that speak *to* rather than *through* teachers, and explores how teachers might come to hold such an expectation for their relationship with a text. To what extent do textbook authors aim to help teachers learn mathematics through the materials they write? And what would it take for teachers to engage in readings—and uses—of such texts that would not convert them to their traditional position of external authoritative guide for the activities of teachers and students?

As teachers build their own understandings and relationships with mathematics, they chart new mathematical courses with their students. And conversely: As they move on new paths together with students, their own mathematical understandings change. Whether and how curriculum materials can be designed to support teachers' exploration of mathematics—their own and their students'—is a question worth fresh investigation. Given the expanse of mathematics to be learned, and the multiple ways in which it can be explored, it would be worthwhile to investigate whether and how materials designed to support both teachers' and students' learning could function as resources for teacher learning rather than as controls for teachers' coverage. Furthermore, there are sites already in place for such exploration. For example, several contemporary professional development projects use curricula as the stimuli for conversations among teachers about teaching (e.g., Acquarelli & Mumme, in press). Using the texts in their own classrooms, reporting on what happened, reflecting on the strengths and weaknesses of different ideas and activities, the teachers in these projects learn about teaching and learning, mathematics and reform.

These projects resurface the crucial pedagogical issue: While curricula could be designed with teacher learning in mind, what teachers learn from such materials will also depend on the ways in which they are engaged with them, what the norms and expectations are surrounding their use. What might be the time frame over which a teacher develops a relationship with the curriculum material, and how might the third year of use be different from the first? Perhaps texts might be deliberately designed to be "outgrown." We have much to learn about the pedagogy of using such materials to support and facilitate teacher learning. In what ways could experiences be shaped around these materials in order to enhance their educative potential?

But these are issues worth working on. Textbooks continue to be a mainstay of the elementary classroom in most schools, and as such, find their way to teachers' elbows and into the daily ticking of their practice. Designing ways to use them more directly in the service of teacher development is strategic.

2. *Watching videotape from classrooms where teachers are seriously engaged in efforts to teach mathematics differently.* The need for "images of reform" is widely-touted. Teachers who have never seen children engaged in a mathematics problem, or discussing mathematics, need to have opportunities to see what this can look like. These serve, in part, as existence proofs that such practice can happen in schools. However, this can also backfire. Teachers can simply dismiss what they

see: "These kids are just very bright—my students would not be able to do this." "This cannot happen every day."

My experience with watching educators (and others) watch, talk about, and refer to videotapes of classroom lessons suggests that, despite the widespread enthusiasm for the medium, we know little about what people attend to and learn while watching tape.[17] Do these tapes infuse new images alongside the deeply-ingrained ones from more conventional classrooms? If so, what aspects of these images are salient—the kind of mathematics, the nature of the discourse, the capabilities of students, the teacher's role? All of these? Perhaps some viewers study teacher moves, voice, stance—and deliberately or unconsciously "try on" unfamiliar ways of being with students. I have seen teachers experiment with asking questions like a teacher on tape, and then note the interesting differences in how their students respond. Such imitation, usually disparaged as not "educative," is something we know little about. Perhaps there are things having to do with ways of being with students, ways of being in oneself, that can be supported through the viewing of tape.[18] Perhaps there are subtle aspects of interaction and manner that are not available for comment or examination in written accounts of teaching, in curriculum materials, or in other kinds of professional development opportunities. What can be learned from videotapes, under what kinds of circumstances, is worth investigating much more closely.

An associated question involves the kinds of tapes and teaching used. What is offered by polished professional quality tapes? What do rough, problematic cases afford? When is watching a novice teacher preferable and why? When are the struggles of experienced teachers crucial to see? Annotations layered onto the video can shape the viewing; we know little about how they affect viewers' opportunities. What features of who the teacher is seem to affect viewers' reactions? Lampert and

---

[17]I draw here on my work with Magdalene Lampert, Kara Suzuka, Ruth Heaton, Angie Eshelman, and Mark Rosenberg, in which we have been investigating the use of primary source materials from Lampert's and my fifth- and third-grade mathematics classes in teacher education contexts (e.g., Lampert & Ball, 1990; Ball, Lampert, & Rosenberg, 1991).

[18]Common interpretations of constructivist theory leaves little room for imitation as a potent form of learning some kinds of things. Yet, in learning to play the piano, listening to a skilled and talented pianist can help develop one's ear, to get a feel for interpretation, to acquire position, motion, and timing (for a marvelous account of what this might be like, see Frank Conroy's novel *Body and Soul*). It is quite likely that there are unexamined aspects of teaching that bear a strong relationship to some of these difficult-to-capture aspects of piano playing.

Eshelman (1995) write about the development of prospective teachers' capacity to view teaching with empathy. Being able to imagine yourself as the teacher on the tape, or being able to understand the teacher's perceptions and decisions whether or not you agree—these seem important for a viewing that connects the viewer with the tape, and thus for the learning that it can make possible: to see through that teacher's eyes, to feel what she feels, to think with her heart and mind.

Necessarily, a videotape is but one slice of classroom life. We know little about the most helpful "slices": Should tapes focus on children and their talk? Should tapes highlight the teacher and her moves? Are some aspects of the curriculum more important to document in such tapes? Maybe any old tape will do, but I doubt it. What is afforded by the availability of additional material, such as copies of children's work, teacher reflections, assessment items? Considering the different aspects or features of tapes that might be significant and exploring the range of their impacts is an important part of learning how these tapes might (or might not) be helpful.

Another, equally important question involves the "pedagogy" of using videotapes. Like any materials, what people learn from the tapes is influenced both by what they bring (e.g., assumptions and values, experiences and beliefs) and how they are engaged (some might say, taught) while viewing the tape. What kinds of discussions are most fruitful? Are there alternative organizational structures in which to use tapes (small groups versus large group settings, pre-viewing, and structured observation during the viewing all come to mind as possibilities)? Are there ways to direct—or widen—participants' attention so as to take the most advantage of the viewed tape? And perhaps, most thorny of all, is the challenge of developing a stance that is less simply evaluative and more analytic of practice.

The small but growing body of literature within teacher education about the use of cases would be a useful source of insight to questions such as these. Scholars and teacher educators have begun to consider the possibilities of using cases to focus and ground discussions (Merseth, 1991; J. Shulman, 1992; L. Shulman, 1992; Sykes & Bird, 1992). While much discussion focuses on the question, "What constitutes a good case?" other discussion focuses on the question, "How does one teach a case?" This is an equally significant question for the viewing of videotapes: How does one structure the experience of viewing in ways that generate learning?

Videotapes have great potential for "reach." Easily distributable to large numbers of people, tapes hold promise as a site for learning. But we need to probe better what shapes fruitful uses, as well as how guidance can be provided for a variety of kinds of use. When, for example, might it make sense to use a tape to *exemplify* a kind of teaching and learning? Under what circumstances might it make sense to use videotape as a springboard for investigation—of the particulars of that tape, as well as of more general issues of teaching, learning, mathematics, purposes?

3. *Reading and writing a literature about efforts to work toward reform in mathematics teaching.* A third possible site is writing (and, hence, reading) about practice. The writing process community has, quite appropriately, spawned a literature produced by writing teachers. These accounts provide glimpses of teachers' work behind their classroom doors (e.g., Elbow, 1986; Graves, 1983; Routman, 1988, 1991). Other teachers find within these stories both inspiration and solace. Practical tips and ideas can be found as well. Many elementary teachers devour these titles (much like a novel by one's favorite author), and await the publication of new ones, or the next installment. They seem to fill a void in the discourse about teaching—in this case, the teaching of writing.

The beginnings of such a literature are emerging in mathematics education (e.g., Burns & Tank, 1988; Featherstone & Beasley, in preparation; Heaton, 1994; Romagnano, 1994; Schifter, 1994, in press a, in press b). Will teachers read such accounts with anything like their appetite for the parallel volumes in writing? It is a genre of professional literature that is underdeveloped and underexplored, but worth investigating. Some teacher development projects have engaged teachers in writing about their efforts as a tool of professional development and found it to be a powerful vehicle for conversation about teaching and learning, both with oneself (the author) and others (Barnett, 1991; Schifter, in press; Shulman & Colbert, 1988). Still, we are only beginning to explore what it might take to help teachers write such books, and differences in the qualities of such texts: What features— content, tone, narrative quality—might affect what teachers gain or learn from reading them? For example, how are upbeat, positive accounts read as compared with ones that reveal struggles, tensions, and uncertainties? How are different authorial stances represented in the pages of these books, and how do they affect readers' experiences of them? Can such books offer teachers paths into other literatures, and would they pursue them, under what conditions? Some of the writing books are accompanied by annotated bibliographies. How are these used, and what impact does further reading have?

We know still less about how teachers who would buy and read books about teaching and learning mathematics might use them. How might such books be promoted and distributed? In what contexts might teachers read them (e.g., alone, as part of a Book Club, as a building staff) and how might these shape the books' role in teachers' practice? The interesting success of this burgeoning literature in the writing movement should encourage those working for mathematics reform to consider and explore the potential.

Still, differences exist between language arts and mathematics that should not be ignored. A key aspect of the writing process work is that it offers a way for teachers to learn in the company of other teachers, and to use one another as resources in learning writing, as well as in teaching writing. The medium *is* the content. Teachers can come to see themselves as writers as they write about their teaching of writing. Teachers' own resources in mathematics tend to be thinner than in reading and writing. Would their writing about mathematics teaching and learning offer similar benefits? Would the products of their writing be as substantial and rich for others teachers' learning?

Associated with this are questions about the writing itself. The aims of the writing projects to which I referred above sit exploratively on a line between a strategy for supporting teacher reflection and inquiry, and the desire to develop a written discourse about teaching that might be shared. On one hand, the potential of private writing—a teaching journal, for example—is an underexplored medium for learning. On the other, the lack of opportunity for connections, for professional exchange, is also well-known. Might writing and sharing writing help to foster new forms of professional communication, community—and learning? And what does it take to do that?

What kinds of learning might be fostered by writing about one's practice? Related to stance are questions of tone and focus, purpose and audience. What is gained from writing "confessional" pieces of one's struggles? Or in the voice of one who has made a Great Change, with a great new world of rosy answers? What about analytic pieces that grapple with some recurring dilemma, a challenge, a student? What about reflections on self?

There is the recurring—and essential—question of pedagogy: What does one need to do to support and facilitate such writing? What risks are associated with the revelations and sharing they may entail? What might be entailed in supporting the sharing of texts about teaching? How can sharing and response develop, and what are some of the pitfalls?

Conclusion: What Might it Mean to "Scale Up" Professional Development to Support More Teachers' Learning?

In the face of the pressure to increase the "reach" of federally-funded professional development, one approach is to identify those things we believe "work" in teacher development, and literally "scale up" their size. Figure 1 provides an image of this approach.

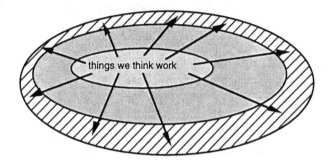

Figure 1. Expanding the "reach" of professional development: Scaling up from "things" we think work

For example, one might take the model of the small teacher study group and extend it by having each participating teacher in such a study group run her own additional teacher group. One might take the long-term focused teacher development project—school-based, and with a weekly mathematics seminar—and institute these in tens of locations. No doubt there is merit in trying to extend the work that has already often successfully supported teachers' growth. But "reaching" hundreds of times as many teachers seems unlikely through this approach alone. This approach tends to underestimate the role of the leader of such groups: what the qualifications and resources for the role are, and what it might take to learn to do it that is different from working on one's own teaching. Moreover, the successful teacher development projects are intensive, personal, resource-dependent, and do not always lend themselves to direct "scaling up."

Therefore, a second important tack is to consider the core conceptual elements of successful professional development projects. For example, many of the successful projects involve long-term follow-up support for participating teachers. Are there other ways to understand both what is fundamentally important about this kind of support, and make conjectures about how else such follow-up could be provided? Conceptual, rather than model-oriented, scaling up holds more promise for dramatically increasing American teachers' opportunities for good professional development. This paper offers a start on such "conceptual" scaling up, with its effort to identify what we think we know about teacher learning. Worth remembering, however, is that our evidence for those beliefs is uneven, and we still have work to do to understand what is important, as well as limited, about various items on that list. We also have more to learn about aspects of teacher learning that the list omits. We know little, for example, about how teachers develop the personal qualities important for more complex forms of teaching—qualities such as courage, confidence, and curiosity. We understand little about how some teachers develop a dissatisfaction with their current practice and the desire and imagination to experiment and study the results of those experiments. We know little about how teachers learn to teach sensitively and well students who are different from themselves.

A third tack is to consider what we *don't* know about professional development and to use this demand for scaling up to experiment with approaches well-suited to larger-scale teacher involvement. Figure 2 offers an image of this approach.

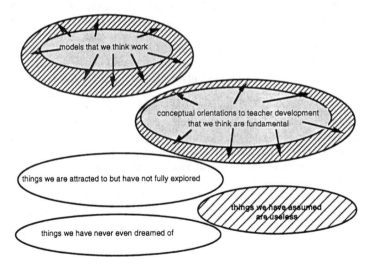

Figure 2. Expanding the "reach" of professional development: A mixed model of scaling up and pursuing new hypotheses

This paper also offers a beginning on this third tack. Although many have been quick to dismiss curriculum materials, I argue that textbooks and other materials are ideally situated to "reach" more teachers, and that we would do well to explore how they could be designed in ways that would especially support teacher development. And while many are enamored of the potential of videotape as a resource for professional development, I argue that we need to experiment with their potential as a tool for teacher learning.

I offer these alternatives to stimulate thought and invite participation in thinking about how to engage teachers in professional development opportunities that will support their learning and push the reforms forward. Others exist. Take the short-term workshop, the bread-and-butter of staff development offices. Are there no things that lend themselves to this format? Are there stances one can take, pedagogical approaches one might try, within such workshops that would alter their assumed limitations? Can series of these be situated in ways that are more generative than the kinds of things we have come to expect of after-school inservice?

My stance is one of inquiry, not certainty, of questions, not answers. The work of professional development is as uncertain as practice itself.[19] The teaching we are trying to help teachers learn is underdetermined, not reducible to programs of practice. Likewise, our understanding of professional development that can support teachers' learning is a mix of myth, belief, and conjecture. Currently, we understand somewhat, but incompletely, what helps teachers learn. We understand, but need to uncover more, about what the resources are that matter in trying to teach all students well. We need to understand better the differences (and similarities) between learning to teach as a beginning teacher and changing or developing one's teaching as an experienced teacher. Adding the challenge of how to engage a much larger number of teachers in the work of these ambitious reforms makes the work all the more uncertain. As teacher educators, teachers, and policy makers, we ourselves will need to make new conjectures based on what we think we know and what we think could be. Our challenge is to experiment, study, reflect on, and reformulate our hypotheses if we are to make progress in engaging a wider community in the work of the mathematics reforms.

---

[19]I am grateful to Suzanne Wilson for pointing out this notable parallel, as well as for much other wisdom about teacher learning—her own, mine, and others'.

Acknowledgments

I am indebted to several of my colleagues for their careful readings and comments on various drafts of this paper: Suzanne Wilson, David Cohen, Magdalene Lampert, Angie Eshelman, Robert Floden, Ruth Heaton, Sue Poppink, Kara Suzuka, Dirck Roosevelt, and Deborah Schifter. I also wish to gratefully acknowledge Angie Eshelman for her assistance with the paper. I also want to acknowledge my co-principal investigators working on the Education Policy and Practice Study at Michigan State University and the University of Michigan: David Cohen, Suzanne Wilson, and Penelope Peterson. The heart of our work is the notion that policymaking and reform are centrally matters of teaching and learning.

References

Acquarelli, K., & Mumme, J. (in press). A renaissance in mathematics education reform. Phi Delta Kappan.

Aichele, D. B. (Ed.). (1994). Professional development for teachers of mathematics. Fifty-Seventh Yearbook of the National Council of Teachers of Mathematics. Reston, VA: National Council of Teachers of Mathematics.

Anderson, L. M. (1989). Learners and learning. In M. C. Reynolds (Ed.), Knowledge base for the beginning teacher (pp. 85–99). New York: Pergamon Press.

Ball, D. L. (1988). Unlearning to teach mathematics. For the Learning of Mathematics, 8(1), 40–8.

Ball, D. L. (1991). Implementing the NCTM Professional Standards for Teaching Mathematics: Improving, not standardizing, teaching. Arithmetic Teacher, 39(1), 18–22.

Ball, D. L. (1992). Magical hopes: Manipulatives and the reform of mathematics education. American Educator, 16(2), 14–18, 46–7.

Ball, D. L., Lampert, M., & Rosenberg, M. L. (1991, April). Using hypermedia to investigate and construct knowledge about mathematics teaching and learning. Paper presented at the annual meeting of the American Educational Research Association, Chicago, IL.

Ball, D. L., & Rundquist, S. (1992). Collaboration as a context for joining teacher learning with learning about teaching. In D. K. Cohen, M. W. McLaughlin, & J. E. Talbert (Eds.), Teaching for understanding: Challenges for practice, research, and policy (pp. 13–42). San Francisco: Jossey Bass.

Ball, D. L., & Wilson, S. M. (in press). Integrity in teaching: How do the knowledge and moral dimensions interact? *American Educational Research Journal.*

Barnett, C. (1991). Building a case-based curriculum to enhance the pedagogical content knowledge of mathematics teachers. *Journal of Teacher Education, 42*(4), 263–72.

Borko, H., Eisenhart, M., Brown, C. A., Underhill, R. G., Jones, D., & Agard, P. C. (1992). Learning to teach hard mathematics: Do novice teachers and their instructors give up too easily? *Journal for Research in Mathematics Education, 23*(3), 194–222.

Brown, A. L. (1992). Design experiments: Theoretical and methodological challenges in creating complex interventions in classroom settings. *The Journal of the Learning Sciences, 2,* 141–78.

Brown, A. L. (1994). The advancement of learning. *Educational Researcher, 23*(8), 4–12.

Brown, C. A., & Borko, H. (1992). Becoming a mathematics teacher. In D. A. Grouws (Ed.), *Handbook of research on mathematics teaching and learning* (pp. 209–39). New York: Macmillan.

Burns, M., & Tank, B. (1988). *A collection of math lessons.* Salinas, CA: Math Solutions.

Campbell, D. T. (1988). Evolutionary epistemology. In E. S. Overman (Ed.), *Methodology and epistemology for social science: Selected papers of Donald T. Campbell* (pp. 393–434). Chicago: University of Chicago Press. (Originally published in 1974.)

Carpenter, T., & Fennema, E. (1992). Cognitively guided instruction: Building on the knowledge of students and teachers. In W. Secada (Ed.), *International Journal of Educational Research: the reform of school mathematics in the United States* (pp. 457–470). Elmsford, NY: Pergamon.

Chazan, D., & Ball, D. L. (1995). Beyond exhortations not to tell: The teacher's role in discussion-intensive mathematics classrooms. Paper submitted for publication.

Cobb, P. (1994). Where is the mind? Constructivist and sociocultural perspectives on mathematical development. *Educational Researcher, 23*(7), 13–20.

Cohen, D. K. (1989). Teaching practice: Plus ça change.... In P. W. Jackson (Ed.), Contributing to educational change: Perspectives on research and practice (pp. 27–84). Berkeley, CA: McCutchan.

Cohen, D. K. (in preparation). Teaching practice and its predicaments. Manuscript in preparation. Ann Arbor, MI: University of Michigan.

Cohen, D. K., & Barnes, C. A. (1992). Pedagogy and policy. In D. K. Cohen, M. W. McLaughlin, & J. E. Talbert (Eds.), Teaching for understanding: Challenges for practice, research, and policy (pp. 207–239). San Francisco: Jossey Bass.

Conroy, F. (1993). *Body and soul.* New York: Dell Publishing.

Elbow, P. (1986). *Embracing contraries: Explorations in learning and teaching.* New York: Oxford University Press.

Featherstone, H., Pfeiffer, L., Smith, S. P., Beasley, K., Corbin, D., Derksen, J., Pasek, L., Shank, C., & Shears, M. (1993, April). *"Could you say more about that?" A conversation about the development of a group's investigation of mathematics teaching.* Paper presented at the annual meeting of the American Educational Research Association, Atlanta, GA.

Featherstone, H., Pfeiffer, L., & Smith, S. P. (1993). *Learning in good company: Report on a pilot study* (Research Report 93–2). East Lansing: Michigan State University, National Center for Research on Teacher Learning.

Featherstone, H., & Beasley, K. (in preparation). *"The big old conversation": Reflections on mathematical tasks and discourse.*

Feiman-Nemser, S. (1990). Teacher preparation: Structural and conceptual alternatives. In W. R. Houston (Ed.), *Handbook of research on teacher education* (pp. 212–33). New York: Macmillan.

Fullan, M. G. (1982). *The meaning of educational change.* New York: Teachers College Press.

Glazer, E. (1994). *An analysis of discourse on an Internet-based listserv for mathematics educators.* Unpublished master's thesis, Champaign-Urbana: University of Illinois.

Goodlad, J. I. (1984). *A place called school: Prospects for the future.* New York: McGraw-Hill.

Grant, C. A., & Secada, W. G. (1990). Preparing teachers for diversity. In W. R. Houston (Ed.), *Handbook of research on teacher education* (pp. 403–22). New York: Macmillan.

Graves, Donald H. (1983). *Writing: Teachers and children at work.* Exeter, N.H.: Heinemann.

Heaton, R. M. (1994). *Creating and studying a practice of teaching elementary mathematics for understanding.* Unpublished doctoral dissertation, East Lansing, MI: Michigan State University.

Jackson, P. W. (1986). *The practice of teaching.* New York: Teachers College Press.

Lakatos, I. (1974). *Proofs and refutations: The logic of mathematical discovery.* Cambridge: Cambridge University Press.

Lampert, M. (1985). How do teachers manage to teach? Perspectives on problems in practice. *Harvard Educational Review, 55,* 178–94.

Lampert, M., & Ball, D. L. (1990). *Using hypermedia technology to support a new pedagogy of teacher education.* (Issue Paper 90-5).

East Lansing: Michigan State University, National Center for Research on Teacher Education.

Lampert, M., & Eshelman, A. S. (1995, April). *Using technology to support effective and responsible teacher education: The case of interactive multimedia in mathematics methods courses.* Paper presented at the annual meeting of the American Educational Research Association, San Francisco.

Lappan, G., Fey, J. T., Fitzgerald, W. M., Friel, S. N., & Phillips, E. D. (in press). *Connected Mathematics Project.* Palo Alto, CA: Dale Seymour Publications.

Little, J. W. (1982). Norms of collegiality and experimentation: Workplace conditions of school success. *American Educational Research Journal, 19*(3), 325–40.

Little, J. W. (1993). Teachers' professional development in a climate of educational reform. *Educational Evaluation and Policy Analysis, 15*(2), 129–51.

Lord, B. (1994). Teachers' professional development: Critical colleagueship and the role of professional communities. In N. Cobb (Ed.), *The future of education: Perspectives on national standards in America* (pp. 175–204). New York: College Entrance Examination Board.

Lortie, D. C. (1975). *Schoolteacher: A sociological study.* Chicago: The University of Chicago Press.

McLaughlin, M. W. (1976). Implementation as mutual adaptation. *Teachers College Record, 77,* 339–51.

McLaughlin, M. W., & Marsh, D. D. (1978). Staff development and school change. *Teachers College Record, 80*(1), 69–94.

Merseth, K. (1991). *The case for cases.* Washington, DC: American Association for Higher Education.

Mirel, J. (1994). School reform unplugged: The Bensenville New American School project, 1991–1993. *American Educational Research Journal, 31*(3), 481–518.

National Council of Teachers of Mathematics. (1989). *Curriculum and evaluation standards for school mathematics.* Reston, VA: Author.

National Council of Teachers of Mathematics. (1991). *Professional standards for teaching mathematics.* Reston, VA: Author.

National Research Council. (1991). *Everybody counts: A report to the nation on the future of mathematics education.* Washington, DC: National Academy Press.

National Research Council. (1993a). *Measuring up: Prototypes for mathematics assessment.* Washington, DC: National Academy Press.

National Research Council. (1993b). *Measuring what counts: A conceptual guide for mathematics assessment.* Washington, DC: National Academy Press.

Paine, L., & Ma, L. (1993). Teachers working together: A dialogue on organizational and cultural perspectives of Chinese teachers. *International Journal of Educational Research, 19,* 675–97.

Prawat, R. S. Personal communication, May, 1988.

Remillard, J. (in preparation). *Changing texts, teachers, and teaching: The role of textbooks in reform in mathematics education.* Unpublished doctoral dissertation, East Lansing, MI: Michigan State University.

Romagnano, L. (1994). *Wrestling with change: The dilemmas of teaching real mathematics.* Portsmouth, NH: Heinemann.

Roosevelt, D. (1994). *Constructing a self: Studying trust, respect, and responsiveness in teaching.* Dissertation in progress.

Routman, R. (1988). *Transitions: From literature to literacy* (1st edition). Portsmouth, NH: Heinemann.

Routman, R. (1991). *Invitations: Changing as teachers and learners K–12.* Portsmouth, NH: Heinemann.

Russell, S. J. (1994). *The role of the teacher in curriculum development (OR, Won't well-prepared teachers make up their own?) (OR, Curriculum: The Right way, a necessary evil, a handy reference, or partner?)* Paper prepared for the conference on teacher enhancement K–6, National Science Foundation, Arlington, VA.

Russell, S. J., & Rubin, A. (1994). *Landmarks in the hundreds.* In *Investigations in Number, Data, and Space.* Palo Alto, CA: Dale Seymour Publications.

Russell, S. J., Schifter, D., Bastable, V., Yaffee, L., Lester, J., & Cohen, S. (1994, November). *Learning mathematics while teaching.* Paper presented at the annual meeting of the North American Chapter of the Psychology of Mathematics Education, Baton Rouge, LA.

Schifter, D. (1993). *Reconstructing mathematics education: Stories of teachers meeting the challenge of reform.* New York: Teachers College Press.

Schifter, D. (1994). *Voicing the new pedagogy: Teachers write about learning and teaching mathematics.* Center for the Development of Teaching Paper Series. Newton, MA: Education Development Center.

Schifter, D. (in press–a). *Constructing new practices/ reconstructing professional identities: Teacher narratives from the mathematics education reform movement.* New York: Teachers College Press.

Schifter, D. (in press–b). *Voicing the new pedagogy: Teachers interpret the rhetoric of mathematics education reform.* New York: Teachers College Press.

Shulman, J. H. (Ed.). (1992). *Case methods in teacher education.* New York: Teachers College Press.

Shulman, L. S. (1983). Autonomy and obligation: The remote control of teaching. In L. Shulman and G. Sykes (Eds.), *Handbook of teaching and policy* (pp. 484–504). New York: Longman.

Shulman, L. S. (1992). Toward a pedagogy of cases. In J. H. Shulman (Ed.), *Case methods in teacher education* (pp. 1–30). New York: Teachers College Press.

Shulman, L. S. (1994, April). *From Brownell to Ball.* Invited address at the American Educational Research Association, New Orleans, LA.

Shulman, J. H., & Colbert, J. A. (1988). *The intern teacher casebook.* San Francisco: Far West Laboratory for Educational Research and Development.

Simon, M. A. (1993). Prospective elementary teachers' knowledge of division. *Journal of Research in Mathematics Education, 24*(3), 233–54.

Simon, M. A., & Schifter, D. (1991). Towards a constructivist perspective: An intervention study of mathematics teacher development. *Educational Studies in Mathematics, 22,* 309–31.

Smith, J. (in press). Efficacy and teaching mathematics by telling: A challenge for reform. *Journal for Research in Mathematics Education.*

Sparks, D., & Loucks-Horsley, S. (1990). Models of staff development. In W. R. Houston (Ed.), *Handbook of research on teacher education* (pp. 234–50). New York: Macmillan.

Sykes, G., & Bird, T. (1992). Teacher education and the case idea. In G. Grant (Ed.), *Review of Research in Education, 18* (pp. 457–521). Washington, DC: American Educational Research Association.

Theule-Lubienski, S. (in preparation). *Mathematics for all? A closer look at teaching and learning mathematics in class.* Unpublished doctoral dissertation, East Lansing, MI: Michigan State University.

Toney, N. (in press). Facing racism in mathematics education. In D. Schifter (Ed.), *Constructing new practices/Reconstructing professional identities: Teacher narratives from the mathematics education reform movement.* New York: Teachers College Press.

Tyack, D., & Tobin, W. (1994). The "grammar" of schooling: Why has it been so hard to change? *American Educational Research Journal, 31*(3), 453–79.

Weissglass, J. (1994). Changing mathematics teaching means changing ourselves: Implications for professional development. In Aichele, D. B. (Ed.), *Professional development for teachers of mathematics. Fifty-seventh yearbook of the National Council of*

Teachers of Mathematics (pp. 67–78). Reston, VA: National Council of Teachers of Mathematics.

Wilson, S. M., Shulman, L. S., & Richert, A. E. (1987). "150 different ways" of knowing: Representations of knowledge in teaching. In J. Calderhead (Ed.), *Exploring teachers' thinking* (pp. 104–24). London: Cassell.

Reform Efforts in Mathematics Education: Reckoning with the Realities

Joan Ferrini-Mundy

University of New Hampshire

The nation's educational communities are engaged in a variety of reform processes, in response to influential reports and the need for improved opportunities for all of our children. In particular, the mathematics education community has been on the forefront of promoting substantial change in mathematics teaching and learning. The National Council of Teachers of Mathematics' documents, *Curriculum and Evaluation Standards for School Mathematics* (NCTM, 1989) and *Professional Standards for Teaching Mathematics* (NCTM, 1991), were designed to provide a shared vision of a new mathematics teaching and learning. The documents have been widely disseminated and discussed, and anecdotal evidence indicates that teachers of mathematics are seeking ways to enact the ideas contained in these documents.

These current reform discussions seem to take more seriously than earlier reforms the centrality and importance of the teacher in enacting new visions of mathematics teaching and learning. Indeed, the *Professional Standards* represents something of a first in its attempt to provide images of pedagogy that are consistent with reformist mathematics teaching and learning. This component of the reform climate, which acknowledges the necessity of professional development of teachers as a means toward reform, is an important dimension. At the same time, the research base about the professional development of mathematics teachers is rapidly expanding, and is addressed in the work of many present at this conference (Ball, 1992; Borko, Eisenhart, Brown, Underhill, Jones, & Agard, 1992; Carpenter & Fennema, 1988; Lampert, 1990; Nelson, 1993; Porter, 1989; Schifter, 1994).

The mathematics education community is involved in providing direction and vision for mathematics reform, in better understanding and conducting the professional development of teachers of mathematics, and in the challenging process of studying and documenting mathematics education reform as it occurs. A number of major projects are concerned with this process of transformative (Silver, 1990) research; that is, studying "what ought to be." This is critical for many reasons, including:

- the need to provide feedback into continuing efforts at change
- the need to build a set of examples from practice to inform continued efforts and discussion
- the need to maintain ever-deeper discussion about reform
- the need to demonstrate to policy-makers the nature and complexity of mathematics reform (Cohen & Ball, 1990)
- the need to explain and justify mathematics reform to a broader community (Ferrini-Mundy, 1992; Schoen, Porter, & Gawronski, 1989)

All of these needs provide a rationale for a range of efforts at documenting and studying mathematics change in schools, and several are underway. In this paper I consider issues arising through NCTM's Recognizing and Recording Reform (R^3M) project (Ferrini-Mundy, Graham, & Johnson, 1993), which is one effort at documenting and understanding change in mathematics education. To some degree I draw also on our beginning experience in Partnerships for Reform in Mathematics Education in New Hampshire (PRIME-NH) (Ferrini-Mundy & Prevost, 1993), a Noyce Foundation-funded effort to support and study reform in three New Hampshire school sites, one of which is a K–4 school.

In particular, I will highlight issues that might bear particular consideration in the design of teacher enhancement programs at the K–6 level. Continuing attempts at juxtaposing the work on school mathematics reform with the challenges of large-scale efforts in teacher enhancement is critical at this time of heightened change and heightened scrutiny. This juxtaposition seems to lead to a call for teacher enhancement activity that is self-reflective and characterized by inquiry (Nelson, 1993; Schön, 1987). It is not at all clear that the most familiar models for teacher enhancement (the summer programs followed by academic year support, the blending of mathematics content and pedagogical emphases, the exposure to many innovative activities) are necessarily the models that will best converge with the realities of mathematics education reform as it exists and develops in schools. Reckoning with the realities of mathematics reform as it proceeds in schools is inevitable for teacher enhancement work at this time.

This paper is not a presentation of findings of the R^3M project, but rather an attempt to highlight issues that are emerging from the data and that remain as puzzles and challenges, but seem worthy of inclusion in thinking about teacher enhancement. In particular, I will describe the R^3M project as necessary to provide the context from which the following observations are drawn. I then will explore recurring themes that are arising within the project, followed by discussion of counterintuitive observations, and end with a section on issues we need to understand better.

Overview of R³M

NCTM is engaged in a multi-year project to assess the influence and depth of knowledge, and interpretation of the NCTM *Standards* in several communities; to develop useful and deep descriptions of "sites of reform," which include schools, clusters of schools, and school districts, where significant change in mathematics teaching and learning is occurring; and to assemble and disseminate what is learned in forms accessible to a variety of publics, particularly practitioners. The project was developed in response to the work of the 1989 NCTM Task Force on monitoring the effects of the *Standards*, whose final report recommended that NCTM "monitor their own and other activities designed to implement the Standards and to monitor (not conduct) a broader program of research and development" (Schoen et al., 1989, p. 27).

It is important to recognize the naiveté of assuming that *Standards* change classroom practice. Bringing about change in practice is a complex process. Sarason (1991) indicates the dangers to reform that may be imposed by those who are not informed about the complexity of the school system, and he cautions that being part of the system is no guarantee that one understands the system in any comprehensive way. The "changer" must know the context in which intervention is to take place. Projects like R³M may be useful to recognizing and recording this context for reform.

The R³M project included a Landscape Cycle, to determine the extent to which teachers understood or were aware of what was contained in the two documents. There is growing evidence that teachers are making changes in the way mathematics is being taught (Weiss, 1992). Teachers are using fewer lectures, increasingly becoming facilitators in cooperative learning situations, and stressing problem solving that is relevant to real life. Manipulatives and technology are finding greater frequency of classroom use.

Seventeen broadly representative sites were selected for the R[3]M study.[1] There were five elementary-level sites, three middle schools, two K–8 sites, five high schools, and two school districts. Of these sites, ten were suburban; six were urban; and two were rural. The selected sites were not considered to be "model" sites; rather, they were schools or districts which typify a variety of attempts to bring about change in their mathematics programs.

Twenty documenters were involved in the site visits. Ten documenters were experienced field researchers, including three ethnographers. This core of researchers was complemented by classroom teachers, mathematics supervisors, and graduate students in mathematics education. Each two-member team visited a site for a two- to six-day period to observe mathematics classes and conduct interviews of teachers, administrators, and other individuals identified by the site as important to the mathematics program. An on-site liaison worked closely with the documentation team to set up schedules and facilitate the visit. Documenters have produced site write-ups and several scenarios for each site. Scenarios are portrayals, built largely out of evidence and material from the site, of what documenters saw as most salient and characteristics of the mathematics reform efforts within the site. These scenarios are being shared with the sites for reaction at this time.

Perspective and Orientation of the R[3]M Project

In developing the mechanisms for studying seventeen sites, with a team of twenty documenters of rather diverse experiences and perspectives, we were faced with challenging discussions about what perspectives might guide our view. The following principles became important as the team of documenters worked to find a common ground from which to proceed.

---

[1] To identify sites in the R[3]M project, we contacted practitioners, researchers, and policy makers in mathematics education throughout the nation. We received 190 recommendations for school sites which saw themselves as engaged in reform efforts toward implementing the NCTM *Standards*. Each nominated site was contacted by letter, and we received 76 completed "Preliminary Information Questionnaires." Five documenters reviewed those questionnaires and narrowed that number to 26. Three of the documenters conducted telephone interviews with the 26 sites. From those interviews and the "Preliminary Information Questionnaires," R[3]M Advisory Board members made the final selection of the 17 project sites.

Interpretation vs. Implementation

The NCTM *Standards* are intended "to direct, but not determine, practice; to guide, but not prescribe, teaching, and diverse interpretations and enactments are inevitable.... If the *Standards* become something mechanical to be implemented, the initiative will probably fail" (Ball, 1992). The *Standards,* according to Apple, provide a "penumbra of vagueness" (Apple, 1992) whose magic lies in their appeal to a broad set of perspectives; almost anyone can find support for their point of view in the document. This creates a challenge in studying *Standards*-based reform, because one documenter's *Standards*-like practice can quite represent another's worst nightmare. We agreed, then, that in project sites (which had been identified and selected on a very subjective hope that something interesting might be going on) we would work to understand the way in which that particular site was choosing to interpret the reforms and directions of the *Standards,* and to do our best to tell the story.

Documentation vs. Evaluation

In keeping with this attempt to develop multiple examples of interpretations of mathematics reform, we also recognized that the project could not be overtly evaluative. Documenters' biases and preferences of course cannot be obliterated and are visible simply through what they chose to observe, report, and discuss. However, we established some ground-rules at least for visits that kept us from making explicit judgments. Thus, when the principal of a secondary school site said to me "So, do we have an avant-garde mathematics program or what?" I was able to refrain from responding. Our slogan became "This is a study, not a contest."

Recognizing the Views from the Site

Consistent with the reality of multiple interpretations, and our commitment to documentation rather than evaluation, we recognized that these stories of reform would need to emerge from what these sites chose to show us, and from the most salient and visible components. We also found that the interpretation of the two *Standards* documents and the view of the change process were rarely consistent among all the key players at a given site. At one site, where there was close collaboration with university mathematicians, the interpretation of who was the catalyst of change—the teachers or the university professors—was very different. Each credited the other for getting the reform effort started. These differences were particularly striking in terms of what teachers at a given site saw as a *Standards*-like pedagogy. These individual differences in interpretation of reform efforts further add to the complexity of developing a particular site's views.

The preparation of this paper provides an occasion to raise a number of issues that have been suggested by the R^3M work. I am drawing heavily on the material provided by documenters through the scenarios that they have created for the project. The issues raised here are particular to K–6 sites and have been selected because they seem appropriate for consideration by those involved in thinking about the directions of teacher enhancement.

Recurring Themes that Seem Important

Certain themes were evident as important in all six sites. There is nothing especially startling or new about these themes. However, it might be helpful to explore, in discussions about teacher enhancement, the possibilities for acknowledging and capitalizing on these themes which emerge from practice.

Specialists of Many Sorts

> *Our mathematics specialists have shown the value and excitement of risk taking. Through their modeling and the realization that the sky doesn't fall in or a bolt of lightening strike when an attempt to instruct isn't as successful as planned, others follow and try, try again.*
>
> (Elementary school principal)

All six of our elementary sites (five school sites and one district site) were characterized by some version of a mathematics specialist, with various levels of official and recognized status within the district. This is not an argument for specialists, but rather, a discussion of the reality that these sites included specialists, and for these sites, this seemed to be an important feature that worked in a positive way. Specialists were "created" in a number of ways; districts decided to fund new positions; outside grant moneys enabled districts to create new positions; or classroom teachers recognized a need and assumed the specialist role in an unofficial capacity. Their roles and the scope of their responsibilities varied considerably. Some were responsible for working in as many as five or as few as one school, some did both mathematics and science, and some were full-time classroom teachers identified as mathematics resource people for the school. In all cases the specialists seemed to be key to the efforts in the school; they were involved in helping to spread ideas, to facilitate communications among teachers, to plan and initiate staff development, and to address political problems with administrators and community members.

The development of leaders has been a long-standing goal of teacher enhancement efforts. Our experience in R^3M suggests that this is reasonable, but we have a thin base of knowledge on which to build the appropriate development experiences for these leaders. The work of specialists or school-based mathematics leaders seems to demand a complex combination of knowledge of mathematics, mathematics pedagogy, skill in communicating with peers, awareness of available materials and resources, strategies for serving as teacher advocates with administrators and community members, and ability to speak supportively of reforms without access to the compelling evidence that would help make the case.

The leadership provided is not necessarily characterized by the active, prescriptive styles sometimes found in leaders. Rather, it is a responsive and contingent leadership. The work that specialists do with their colleagues is professional development, or teacher enhancement, of an individualized and intimate kind—team teaching in classrooms, seeking resources and activities in response to very specific needs and questions, and maintaining the difficult balance of supporting without overstepping bounds. Specialists face challenges in inventing and defining roles that are new and unfamiliar in school cultures and that often are viewed with suspicion by teachers and administrators alike. There are few professional support structures available to mathematics specialists and a paucity of literature. Very little research is available to provide insight into the nature of mathematics specialists' work, the professional development of specialists, and the effects of their efforts in schools. Yet it appears that, increasingly, important professional development of classroom teachers is occurring in their interactions with specialists.

Community Involvement

They were afraid it was the New Math that happened after the sixties; they were afraid it was a fad. (First-grade teacher)

Some of the kids would go home and say that they hadn't done math and it had been four weeks.... Teachers would write on the paper "this was your math today." (Mathematics specialist)

In all six sites it also was important that there was systematic attention to community involvement. This ranged from the usual parent nights and notes of explanation sent home to formal committees, including parents, charged with determining goals for the mathematics program. In one site where parents were kept away from the reform efforts until disaster was imminent, the site developed a very responsive, aggressive, and belated campaign for involving parents. The intricacies of dealing with parents and community members are substantial, and sites are learning a great deal about how critical this area is for sustaining and supporting reform.

In PRIME-NH, in the elementary school site, about 2/3 of the third- and fourth-grade teachers are visibly "committed" to participating in the project. They attend meetings, read and discuss papers, and systematically share classroom episodes. They have decided that they would like to hold a Parents' Night for third- and fourth-grade parents in order to share what they are thinking about relative to mathematics. Should this event be open to all third and fourth-grade parents, even parents of children whose teachers are not actively engaged in the project activities? Does this set up a divisive climate? If all third- and fourth-grade parents are invited, will the teachers who are not involved be made to feel conspicuous? Is there a school-wide, agreed upon "mission" for third- and fourth-grade mathematics? How should that be communicated?

Noting that community involvement and support are very important in reform is hardly an original observation. However, there probably are mathematics-specific issues relative to promoting this involvement that are worth understanding better and perhaps addressing as part of teacher enhancement activity. As teachers struggle to find and learn from images of reform, and make tentative steps into practice that is unfamiliar and short on evidentiary credibility, how can they at the same time reassure parents? In some of our sites, the parents became co-investigators, in a sense, with the teachers. Is it feasible to expect teachers to develop several new styles and modes of collegiality while embarking on their own uncertain journeys? Can teacher enhancement help? A teacher from one site spoke of "finding the courage to be the expert."

Mathematics Reform Centered in the School

> *Once the initial people got excited about it, they began to spread the word among other staff members. It took root and things began to grow beyond that. Somebody else learned about it, saw what was going on, liked it, and began to incorporate it.* (Elementary school principal)

Although every site in the study did have specific connections to outside resources, both in the form of funding and personnel, the school itself, with its teachers, administrators, and community context, was the identified center of the reform activity. These schools provide existence proofs that substantial change in, and attention to, mathematics teaching and learning can occur from a school base. This reality may imply that teacher enhancement models ought to push well beyond even the most forward-looking of the traditional models, parts of which nearly always include bringing groups of teachers together for extended time in the summer. In our sites, the teachers' "laboratories"— the places where they tested their ideas—were their classrooms, and the sustaining forces of continued attention to mathematics teaching and learning issues seemed to reside in the interactions among the teachers, specialists, administrators, and community members. The influence of the outside consultants, the guest workshop leaders, and staff development presentations was less visible. Teachers seemed to learn from what they saw their students doing, from their reflection on attempts at using various curriculum materials, and from their interactions with their colleagues in the school. We heard of the importance of "one-legged conferences," where teachers share ideas and reactions as they lean against the photocopiers (called "tagging up" in the QUASAR project [Brown & Smith, 1994]). These "on-site" instances of professional growth seem important and central. How can teacher enhancement support, catalyze, and document them?

One of the most puzzling quotes in an R^3M scenario is from a university mathematician who occasionally works with elementary school teachers on mathematics in one of our sites. He says "I don't go into their classrooms, not that I wouldn't like to." It seems that he should go ahead in.

Collaborative Communities

We were just getting ready to start our math study group.... I think the primary group just immediately bonded and came together as a group and was very, very supportive.
(Mathematics coordinator)

Perhaps the most striking commonality across the sites was the visibility of close, collegial communities of practitioners engaged in inquiry of various sorts. Sites seemed inclined to invent ways of interacting. We saw teacher-initiated study groups, common planning time used to discuss lessons, specialists orchestrating meetings, regular after school and before school informal discussions, and sharing of articles and ideas "through the mailboxes." It seems that these structures developed relatively naturally and became entrenched, after time, in many of the sites. This phenomenon contributes to a sense of ongoing change, or a constant climate of reform, that has been noted by reform researchers (Fullan, 1991) as critical.

What was more difficult to understand and interpret were the specifics of how these groups functioned. What types of activities, readings, and discussion topics proved fruitful and useful; what was divisive and counterproductive; and what led to deep discussion. These collaborations were, admittedly, at different levels of depth. In some groups, reflective practice was analyzed and discussed in a thorough way; in others, a casual remark of how effective an idea had been in a particular class was all that was needed. Nonetheless, it seems that these interactions may be sites of professional development, and as such they deserve close attention, and warrant a deeper understanding on behalf of those involved in teacher enhancement.

Congruence and Fit: Reform Themes and Context

The children are risk-takers.   (First-grade teacher)

It's hard to change. It's much easier to stay with what you know....Get that area so you feel good about it, next year add another area, then another area, then another area.
                              (Risk-taking teacher, same school)

Of all of the trends that we are noticing in the R^3M data, this concept is the most difficult to articulate and explain. Basically, we are observing that there is often a match, or congruence and fit, between the interpretation of reform that a site chooses and some critical contextual features in the site. There also are philosophical "fits" evident between what is being promoted for children and the ways in which teachers are working to change their practice. We understand these phenomena better in our secondary sites at the moment than in our elementary sites. For example, in a well-to-do suburban-secondary school, the staff determined that technology would be the organizing theme for their reform efforts in mathematics. This appealed strongly to the parent community. To begin, say, with cooperative groups instead would have been a disaster. In a poor, urban, high minority elementary site, the reform theme seems to be manipulatives (a theme which, by the way, can lead to substantial challenges and difficulties relative to coherent mathematical content). By outfitting classrooms in a visible and obvious way with expensive new materials, the innovators made a statement about the value of *providing* for the children. A reform that had started with teacher inquiry and discussion of research papers would have had little chance of community support in that setting. More obvious, and compelling, perhaps, are the philosophical "fits"— teachers working together in groups to devise ways of helping children learn to cooperate and collaborate; teachers engaging with one another in inquiry about teaching, as they promote problem solving and exploration among their students. Sarason (1991) reinforces this notion. "Should not our aim be to judge whatever we do for children in our schools by the criterion of how we are fostering the desire to continue to learn about self, others, and the world, to live in the world of ideas and possibilities, to see the life span as an endless intellectual and personal quest for knowledge and meaning?" (p. 163).

In no case is it clear that these "fits" are anything other than serendipitous. They do not, in general, seem to be strategically engineered. Yet their existence may suggest a new consideration for those involved in teacher enhancement.

Counterintuitive Observations

Our data analysis is currently underway and R^3M is in no position to present findings. However, some preliminary, "counterintuitive observations" seem worth broaching in this context.

Experimenting with Practice Can Change Beliefs

> *She just really shines in the non-standard mathematics. If we were only doing paper/pencil sorts of things, I would never have any idea that she has a wonderful little mind to be able to think through situations. I would never know that if we were only doing calculations in the textbook.* (First-grade teacher)

There are a number of instances in our data, especially when we look at the K–12 spectrum of sites, where it is clear that teachers' beliefs about the value of certain reformist tenets shift as a result of their tentative experimentation with practice. This is connected to the earlier discussion of teachers' classrooms serving as their laboratories, and their motivations for continuing experimentation with mathematics pedagogy being inspired, at least in part, by evidence of student success. The cycle goes something like this: a teacher tries an activity that happens to expose vividly some aspects of children's mathematical thinking or reasoning; the teacher is startled and enchanted with this new opportunity to understand the learner; the teacher becomes more positive about the potential of activities of the sort she tried at the outset. We repeatedly saw skepticism giving way to confidence and belief through experimentation with various types of exploratory and open-ended activities, coupled with perceptive assessment of children's experiences of these situations. If there is anything to this, it might lend additional support to conceptualizations of teacher enhancement that are solidly grounded and based in classrooms, which are the places where teachers can experiment and observe results. The challenge is in orchestrating and encouraging this highly individualized type of professional reflection and growth.

Vision Is a Process, Not a Product

We anticipate all kinds of setbacks.

Fullan (1993) argues that "shared vision, which is essential for success, must evolve through the dynamic interaction of organizational members and leaders" (p. 28). Yet much of the traditional change literature contends that vision and goal-setting is necessary as a first step. Although this seemed to be the means of proceeding in some of our high school sites, it was less prevalent in the K–6 sites. This implies a process which is evolutionary and open ended. Teachers and administrators became more and more articulate and definite about the goals and nature of the mathematics changes as they accumulated experience and evidence from their practice. In particular, we noticed this interaction when we made second visits to several of our sites. Individual teachers who were sitting on the sidelines and watching others make curricular changes in their schools had taken large steps to join their colleagues in reform efforts during the interim (usually six to nine months). The group's efforts toward change were influencing teachers, who, in turn, were influencing and reinforcing the group. It was strikingly apparent with one secondary mathematics teacher who had been sitting on the fence during our first visit. Nine months later he had become an outspoken proponent of his school's reform efforts. We noticed that a greater cohesiveness and sense of direction had also occurred among all members of this mathematics department.

Promising Issues: Worth Trying to Understand

The six elementary sites that have provided a platform for all of this discussion are notable in that they are managing, in different ways and with different effects, the inevitable challenges that accompany change of any kind. Fullan's "problems are our friends" (Fullan, 1993, p. 21) aphorism isn't to be taken tritely; the challenges and difficulties of making *Standards*-like changes in mathematics teaching and learning are enormous. Ball notes in her paper for this conference that many have commented on the difficulty of this change, but beyond that there is little available to help us understand what makes it hard. I agree, and I propose the following areas as areas of difficulty that were thematic in our sites. Although predictable in sites seriously engaged in mathematics reform, we can imagine how any of the following dilemmas can be unsettling at best, and can lead to a derailment of the effort at worst:

1. Caring and the tension of reform
2. Basic skills vs. understanding
3. Being stalled
4. Accommodating everyone
5. Coming to grips with curriculum

Surely others can add to this list of "what makes it hard," and perhaps designers of teacher enhancement experiences can strategize about how these problem areas might be anticipated and addressed. Can teacher enhancement efforts assist here? Perhaps, this can be done by anticipating them, assisting teachers with strategies for addressing them, and monitoring their status throughout the project. This will include recognition that ultimately these dilemmas need to be dealt with locally, to the satisfaction of those involved.

Caring and the Tension of Reform

A major problem in several of the elementary school sites had to do with the disequilibrium and disagreement that seems inevitable in reform, made especially difficult because of the high levels of caring and respect for individuals' feelings and points of view that we witnessed in these elementary schools. Repeatedly we met teachers who were troubled by the differences in viewpoint and opinion exposed in the process of embarking on reform. This was complicated further by new and unfamiliar exposure of individuals' understanding of mathematical concepts, an exposure that becomes inevitable in a climate where children's mathematical thinking is an object of discussion. As collaborative communities of practitioners develop, and as new specialists are imposed into established communities, it seems also that long-standing relationships and patterns of interaction can be upended and rearranged—and this is unsettling. In several sites teachers were startled, and somewhat hurt, by these new challenges in their interactions. Sometimes the efforts at mathematics reform bear the burden of responsibility.

We also found sites who coped well with these situations. What is the implication for teacher enhancement? This seems to come back to the notion of acknowledging the school site as the center for reform, and developing programs that are sensitive to the changed relationships that will emerge.

The Basic Skills vs. Understanding Dilemma

> *I wanted somebody who could actually tell me—if I'm going to use these manipulatives, how do I do it?*
>
> (Third-grade teacher)

This dilemma surfaced repeatedly, and is familiar to everyone working at any level of reform in mathematics, K–14. It appears in different ways: as internal individual confusion; as a bone of contention between K–2 and 3–4 teachers; as an uneasiness between teachers and parents; as a line of demarcation between the "reform" and "traditional" groups of teachers within a school; and even as a philosophical difference between teachers in search of activities and staff developers resisting the dispensing of activities. No matter what its instantiation, the tensions generated by strongly held commitment to development of "basic skills" and developing understanding seem inherent. Sites seem to cope with this by bringing it into the open, spending lots of time discussing it, recognizing that there isn't a simple answer, and staying alert to instances of evidence that can be personally persuasive to teachers. What makes this hard is that teachers seek reassurance and evidence that they will not hurt children by moving in the reform directions, directions that are, as Ball says, underdetermined.

Being Stalled: The Trappings of Reform

> *You can't just take a bunch of gizmos and call it reform—it's a way of thinking.*   (High school teacher)

The dilemma that generated the most concern, interestingly, for the R^3M documenters, was the one they felt when the site simply didn't seem to "measure up" to their expectations of a *Standards*-based example. We had more than one site which on paper, and in telephone interviews, promised to be "the perfect example" (despite our intellectual acceptance of the impossibility of a perfect model). Nonetheless, documenters returned from sites with stories of manipulatives begin used (in their judgments) in meaningless ways, of technology serving as high-speed drill and practice devices, of teacher-developed "worksheets" that had mathematical errors and that led nowhere, of underdeveloped efforts at asking children to collaborate and think together about mathematics, and of uncritical abdication to a textbook or so-called reformist materials.

I do not share this pessimism and have tried to encourage documenters to find different ways of looking at and interpreting these observations. These are, in my mind, natural and expected events in reforming practice, particularly because these "trappings" of reform, because of their tangibility, may be the easiest aspects of the *Standards* to envision and incorporate into practice. When working toward an invisible vision, certainly there is rationale for putting in place at least the physical embodiments. The more interesting part of this process is coming to understand how teachers navigate the tricky path through these superficial embodiments toward deeper innovation. This seems a critical question for inclusion by those studying reform efforts, especially reform efforts that are locally initiated and not part of major research and intervention studies. These pitfalls are also likely in standard teacher enhancement projects and are worthy of systematic attention and effort.

What seems to work in sites who move past these stages, or avoid them altogether? In such sites, we also found evidence of a sustained spirit of inquiry and self examination, particularly in the presence of colleagues. In some cases, teachers have recognized personal needs and interests in better understanding mathematics, as a means toward deeper and more effective use of various pedagogical strategies, and more than one site has found ways of responding to this need. In one of the secondary sites, where a very well-articulated shared perceptive had been developed by the site, they discussed their reform program as "a way of thinking." It seems that commitment to a perspective might also mitigate against the superficiality problem.

Accommodating Everyone

> *I guess I'm a very traditional teacher. I've been teaching a long time and I've seen a lot of different programs come and go, and I just find that in the last few years, while I think it's good to be innovative and offer the children a lot of different aspects and different ways of doing things, but we're finding a lot of basic skills are slipping away.* (Third-grade teacher)

We saw examples of two kinds of challenges. In school sites, individual teachers will inevitably be at different places in terms of their engagement with the ideas of the reforms, and their commitment to examining and exploring their mathematics practice. Understanding and acknowledging these differences, and figuring out how to deal with the dynamics that result, becomes a challenge for everyone, including teachers, specialists, and administrators, especially within the typically close and family-like environment of some elementary school staffs. The presence of teachers not fully engaged in the reform activity was problematic, because colleagues wish to respect their views, but the nay-sayers can undermine the dynamics in a group. On the other hand, determining what to do with teachers who are now "anointed" as leaders is an equally vexing problem. Can teacher enhancement efforts which are school-based, and in some cases school-wide (e.g., Campbell, 1991), provide insights and strategies for anticipating and coping with these challenges?

Coming to Grips With Curriculum

> *I think the minute the workbook becomes the teacher, that's when your math program suffers. You don't have the spontaneity then to take on the theme that the class is involved in at the time.*   (Kindergarten teacher)

We have yet to make sense of the complicated information from our sites regarding the place of curriculum. Our sites had rather clearly visible and developed positions toward curriculum. These ranged widely; in one site, the prevailing mode was to search for activities, something that Schweitzer (in press) also observed. In some sites, we learned how proud they were to have "abandoned textbooks." Indeed, the evidence we saw of problem-driven mathematics instruction was exciting. Yet it is very difficult to learn how, or if, a site such as this envisions the "big picture" or any sort of coherent mathematics experience for children. In another site, the stance toward curriculum was characterized by overwhelming centrality of manipulatives. (I am reminded of methods courses organized by manipulative of the week.) In other sites, innovative commercial or federally-funded curricula were in place, giving teachers particular confidence about their fidelity to the *Standards*, through abdication to the materials.

As sites of reform settle on a position about curriculum, it seems that the teacher enhancement implications might differ quite substantially. Decisions about mathematical content emphasis, pedagogical strategies, etc. might be quite dependent on the nature of the curricular stance. It is not at all clear how teacher enhancement projects might deal with this, but it seems well worth dealing with. Coming to understand and experiment with the varying types of supports and facilitation that teachers might need in these different curricular positions seems important, because diversity is inevitable.

Final Note: Catching and Sharing Images as Teacher Enhancement

It is not enough to suggest active learning and cooperative practices without greater clarity about how teachers might move constructively in these directions.... There is a need for a good description of practice that moves in the direction of the reforms. (Boyer, 1990)

Our work in R^3M highlights constantly the difficulty of catching and sharing images that can assist teachers, policy-makers, and perhaps parents with enriched views of what might be reformed practice in mathematics teaching and learning. The dilemmas are many; who decides which images are worth catching and sharing? If we acknowledge that the *Standards* are to be interpreted, not implemented, then are all interpretations equally good? Because of prevalent expectations for models of good practice, what are the ramifications of sharing and highlighting the challenges, dilemmas, and tensions that occur as teachers and schools undertake reform of mathematics teaching and learning? How do we convey respect for the difficulty and complexity of teachers' work while at the same time inviting critical and deep discussion and debate about specific episodes and instances from school and classroom stories? At this stage, it seems that the best and most available images are those that portray the interactions of individual teachers with small numbers of children—images of mathematics teaching practice in classrooms (Ball, 1990, 1992; Cobb, Wood, Yackel, & Nicholls, 1991; Davis, Maher, & Noddings, 1990; Lampert, 1990). Yet might other images, viewed in a sense at greater distance, also be important? Images of how staffs of teachers interact and engage in inquiry about mathematics teaching and learning? Or images about the practice of specialists? Or images about how administrators and teachers collaborate with community members to secure the political base needed for certain types of change? How do we develop and communicate these images? How important is their inclusion in the teacher enhancement enterprise?

We are not experienced in staging and participating in these exchanges and modes of communication. Yet there are many projects now generating data that can yield very rich collections of images, in video and written form. The potential for teacher enhancement seems quite great, yet our capacity as a community of mathematics educators for using this material effectively is in great need of development.

Acknowledgments

This report was prepared with support from the Exxon Education Foundation, through an award to the National Council of Teachers of Mathematics, and the Noyce Foundation. The ideas presented here do not necessarily represent the views of the Exxon Education Foundation, the National Council of Teachers of Mathematics, or the Noyce Foundation.

I am grateful to Loren Johnson for his assistance in preparing this paper. I also acknowledge the insightful contributions of the R^3M project documenters. Thanks also to Lew Knight and Ferd Prevost for their insights in PRIME-NH discussions.

References

Apple, M. (1992). Do the standards go far enough? Power, policy, and practice in mathematics education. *Journal for Research in Mathematics Education, 23*(5), 412–31.

Ball, D. (1990). Reflections and deflections of policy: The case of Carol Turner. *Educational Evaluation and Policy Analysis, 12*(3), 247–59.

Ball, D. (1992). Magical hopes: Manipulatives and the reform of math education. *American Educator, 16*(2), 14–18, 46–7.

Borko, H., Eisenhart, M., Brown, C. A., Underhill, R. G., Jones, D., & Agard, P. C. (1992). Learning to teach hard mathematics: Do novice teachers and their instructors give up too easily? *Journal for Research in Mathematics Education, 23*(3), 194–222.

Boyer, E. (1990). Reflections on the new reform in mathematics education. *School Science and Mathematics, 90*(6), 561–6.

Brown, C., & Smith, M. (1994, April). *Building capacity for mathematics instructional innovation in urban middle schools: Assisting the development of teachers' capacity*. Paper presented at the annual meeting of the American Educational Research Association, New Orleans, LA.

Campbell, P. (1991). IMPACT: Increasing the mathematical power of all children and teachers. College Park, MD: University of Maryland.

Carpenter, T., & Fennema, E. (1988). Research and cognitively guided instruction. In E. Fennema, T. Carpenter, & S. Lamon (Eds.), Integrating research on teaching and learning mathematics (pp. 1–16). Albany, NY: State University of New York Press.

Cobb, P., Wood, T., Yackel, E., & Nicholls, J. (1991). Assessment of a problem-centered second-grade mathematics project. Journal for Research in Mathematics Education, 22(1), 3–29.

Cohen, D., & Ball, D. (1990). Policy and practice: An overview. Educational Evaluation and Policy Analysis, 12(3), 233–9.

Davis, R., Maher, C., & Noddings, N. (1990). Introduction: Constructivist views on the teaching and learning of mathematics. In R. Davis, C. Maher, & N. Noddings (Eds.), Constructivist views on the teaching and learning of mathematics (pp. 1–3). Reston, VA: National Council of Teachers of Mathematics.

Ferrini-Mundy, J. (1992). Recognizing and recording reform in mathematics education: Surveying and documenting the effects of the National Council of Teachers of Mathematics Curriculum and Evaluation Standards and Professional Standards for Teaching Mathematics. Proposal submitted to Exxon Education Foundation.

Ferrini-Mundy, J., Graham, K., & Johnson, L. (1993, April). Recognizing and recording reform in mathematics education: Focus on the NCTM curriculum and evaluation standards for school mathematics and professional standards for teaching mathematics. Paper presented at the American Educational Research Association, Atlanta, GA.

Ferrini-Mundy, J., & Prevost, F. (1993). *Partnerships for reform in mathematics education in New Hampshire*. Proposal submitted to the Noyce Foundation. Durham, NH: University of New Hampshire.

Fullan, M. (1991). *The new meaning of educational change*. New York: Teachers College Press.

Fullan, M. (1993). *Change forces: Probing the depths of educational reform*. New York: Falmer Press.

Lampert, M. (1990). When the problem is not the question and the solution is not the answer: Mathematical knowing and teaching. *American Educational Research Journal, 27*(1), 29-63.

National Council of Teachers of Mathematics. (1989). *Curriculum and evaluation standards for school mathematics*. Reston, VA: Author.

National Council of Teachers of Mathematics. (1991). *Professional standards for teaching mathematics*. Reston, VA: Author.

Nelson, B. (1993). *Mathematics for tomorrow*. Proposal submitted to National Science Foundation. Newton, MA: Center for Learning, Teaching, and Technology, Education Development Center.

Porter, A. (1989). External standards for good teaching: The pros and cons of telling teachers what to do. *Educational Evaluation and Policy Analysis, 11*, 343–56.

Sarason, S. B. (1991). *The predictable failure of educational reform.* San Francisco, CA: Jossey-Bass.

Schifter, D. (1994). *Voicing the new pedagogy: Teachers write about learning and teaching mathematics.* Newton, MA: Center for the Development of Teaching, Education Development Center.

Schoen, H., Porter, A., & Gawronski, J. (1989). *Final report of the NCTM task force on monitoring the effects of the* Standards. Reston, VA; National Council of Teachers of Mathematics.

Schön, D. (1987). *Educating the reflective practitioner: Toward a new design for teaching and learning in the professions.* San Francisco, CA: Jossey-Bass.

Schweitzer, K. (in press). The search for the perfect resource. In D. Schifter (Ed.), *Constructing a new practice: Issues of teacher development in teacher narratives from the mathematics education reform movement.* New York: Teachers College Press.

Silver, E. (1990). Contributions of research to practice: Applying findings, methods, and perspectives. In T. Cooney (Ed.), *Teaching and learning mathematics in the 1990s* (pp. 1–11). Reston, VA: National Council of Teachers of Mathematics.

Weiss, I. (1992). *The road to reform in mathematics education: How far have we traveled?* (Pilot study). National Council of Teachers of Mathematics.

Teacher Change, Staff Development, and Systemic Change: Reflections from the Eye of a Paradigm Shift

Susan Loucks-Horsley

The National Center for Improving Science Education

Forgive the mixed metaphors in the title, but it is an accurate representation of how this paper has come together for me. I began my teaching and research career at a time when innovation abounded, the late 1960s and early 1970s. Change was the name of the game and schools were rated by the number of innovative programs they could point to. Interest was high in improving the change process, which was typically a traumatic experience and rarely resulted in lasting improvement. In the 1980s things calmed down, as indicated by the limited number of phone calls requesting assistance with change. But as the decade waned, the winds of change blew again, this time reaching gale force as people discussed not only changing what teachers did with students, but the very systems that have for over a hundred years educated our nation's young people.

As the winds of change have built, so too have our understandings of the change process. There is an enormous literature, well synthesized by Michael Fullan (1991). Professional development has been recognized for its critical importance to change, by taking its place as one of only eight National Education Goals. And the "s" word, systemic, is on everyone's lips, although few agree on exactly what it means and what it implies for action.

So, I have found developing an issues paper on teacher change, staff development, and systemic change particularly daunting and challenging at this time. I have sought to find calm for reflection, as if searching for the eye of a hurricane. In what little calm I have found, I have decided to remind us first about what we know. If I had more courage and were not, at least most days, a constructivist, I'd call these "enduring truths." Next, I will suggest where I believe the paradigm for staff development and change is going, through a vision of the future, and raise some issues around that new paradigm for teacher enhancement in mathematics K–6. At all times, I welcome and join in asking questions such as, "Is that really what we know?" "Is that really where we're going?" and "How can we get there?"

Some Principles of Change and Staff Development

When you've worked in this area as long as I have, and as long as many of you have, you sometimes forget how much we know about change and staff development. Often when I work with new project directors, read proposals, talk to groups of teachers, administrators, or state agency staff, and attend conferences and workshops, I realize once again that what we know is not common knowledge, or, if it is, that common knowledge is not common practice. I see or hear about designs for "one-shot," "good-bye, God bless you" workshops; I attend hours of "talk at me" conference sessions; and I see plans to recruit teachers for summer institutes nationally, one at a time. These and many other activities potentially violate principles of effective change and staff development, and I find myself looking carefully in their designs for ways that such activities could actually contribute to the lasting change our education system critically needs. Here are some of those principles.

1. *Fundamental change (learning) occurs over time, through active engagement with new ideas, understandings, and real-life experiences.* This is particularly true for teachers who think about learning and teaching in ways very different from those reflected in the NCTM *Standards*, for example. Change occurs only when beliefs are restructured through new understandings and experimentation with new behaviors. Effective professional development experiences use the same constructivist approaches as do effective learning experiences for students. Yet it's surprising to note how often the principle of constructivism is conveyed to teachers in the context of how they should help their students learn, without its being the basis for how the teachers are helped to learn themselves. (How many lectures on constructivism have you attended?) Modeling constructivist learning is the only way for teachers to understand deeply why it's important for their students. (See Loucks-Horsley, Kapitan, Carlson, Kuerbis, Clark, Melle, Sachse, & Walton, 1990; Little, 1993)

Related to this principle is the issue of what changes first, beliefs and attitudes, or behaviors? The conventional wisdom has long been that, if professional development focuses solely on training in new behaviors, teachers will never adopt them until their beliefs change. Thus, working to change teacher beliefs is the first and primary work of professional development. Naturally, as in most aspects of education, it's not as simple as that. As Fullan (1991) notes, all educational changes of value require new (a) skills, (b) behaviors, and (c) beliefs and understanding. In the best professional development settings, these are developed together. Guskey's (1986) synthesis of research on teacher change indicates that changes in teachers' attitudes often result, not so much when teachers are convinced of its value by an advocate of a new practice, but when they use the new practice and see the benefit to their students. Yet teachers need to have some degree of interest or openness to try something new—at minimum to "suspend disbelief" about its value—if they are to give it a fair try. So change in attitudes and behaviors is iterative; in well designed professional learning experiences, change in one brings and then reinforces change in the other. While this does not argue for the use of mandates in every situation, it does explain why, in some circumstances, teachers required to attend professional development sessions that they would not have selected themselves, find that the practices they learn to use with their students really work—and they come back for more. Success in this situation only occurs, however, when the practice they learn to use is an effective one and they have highly skilled help available as they begin to master its use (Loucks-Horsley, 1989).

2. *As individuals change their practice over time they go through predictable stages in how they feel about the change and how knowledgeable and sophisticated they are in using it.* Some of you know my work on the Concerns-Based Adoption Model, Stages of Concern, and Levels of Use (Hall & Hord, 1987; Hord, Rutherford, Huling-Austin, & Hall, 1987; Loucks-Horsley & Stiegelbauer, 1991). Although our research originated in an earlier era of reform, the basic principles still hold. The model (and other developmental models of its type) holds that people undergoing change evolve in the kinds of questions they ask and in their use of the change. In general, early questions are more self-oriented (What is it? How will it affect me?). When these questions are resolved, questions emerge that are more task-oriented (How do I do it? How can I use these materials efficiently? How can I organize myself? Why is it taking so much time?). Finally, when self and task concerns are largely resolved, the individual can focus on impact (Is this change working for my students? Is there something that will work even better?).

The concerns model identifies and provides ways to assess seven stages of concern and eight levels of use that individuals go through as they implement new programs and practices. These have major implications for professional development. First, they point out the importance of attending to where people are and of addressing the questions they're asking when they're asking them. Often we get to the how-to-do-its before addressing self concerns; we want to focus on student learning before teachers are comfortable with the materials and strategies. The kinds and content of professional development opportunities can be informed by ongoing monitoring of the concerns of teachers. Second, this model suggests the importance of paying attention to implementation for several years because that's how long it takes for early concerns to be resolved and later ones to emerge. We know that teachers need their self concerns addressed before they are ready to attend hands-on workshops. We know that management concerns can last at least a year, especially when teachers are implementing a school year's worth of new curricula and also when new approaches to teaching require practice and each topic brings new surprises. We also know that help over time is necessary to work the kinks out and then to reinforce good teaching once use of the new practice smoothes out. Finally, with all the demands on teachers, it is often the case that once their practice becomes routine, teachers never focus on whether and in what ways students are learning. This often requires some organizational priority setting, as well as some stimulating of interest and concern about specific student learning.

Another implication of the concerns model relates to creating realistic expectations in the system for change. If it takes at least a year for teachers to become comfortable and routine in using a new practice or program, expecting student achievement to change in that short period is unrealistic. Expecting teaching to change is not. Goals for change and designs for formative evaluation can and should be informed by the kinds of information a developmental model such as the CBAM can afford.

3. *Effective professional development programs have many attributes in common with effective teaching.* There are many lists of characteristics of effective professional development programs that have been derived from the literature and research. Here is my favorite (Regional Educational Laboratories, 1995).

    a. *They foster collegiality and collaboration.* Work by Little (1982) and Rosenholtz (1989) illustrate the power, including benefits to student learning, of teachers working together to craft the best learning experiences for their students.

    b. *They promote experimentation and risk taking.* Cognitive research emphasizes the importance of trying out new ideas, challenging others' ideas, and learning from failure. In effective professional development, questions are as important as answers.

    c. *They draw their content from available knowledge bases.* We can no longer afford to try out practices and programs that have no evidence that they work. Effective professional development programs rely on theoretically sound and practical strategies.

d. *They involve participants in decisions about as many aspects as possible.* Although it is sometimes impossible for participants to make all the decisions about what they will learn and how, providing input into design, involvement in decision making about implementation, and recommending ways for programs to be improved increases the ownership of participants in professional development programs and their commitment to using what they have learned.

e. *They provide time to participate, reflect on, and practice what is learned.* As described above, change unfolds slowly and time is critical to make sense of new ideas and craft how to best use them. Practice is needed for complex instructional strategies, especially those that are significantly different from normal. All this takes time, a much sought-after commodity in schools. (See the later discussion about making more time for professional development.)

f. *They provide leadership and sustained support.* Leadership can come from administrators as well as from teacher leadership teams. What is important for professional development is a clear vision and direction that makes teacher learning a priority, backed by behaviors such as allocated resources including time and protection from competing demands. Ongoing support takes many forms, from materials to follow-up problem-solving assistance to released time for collaborative planning and moral support through the rough spots. Reserving half the budget for after initial training signals how important sustained support really is.

g. *They supply appropriate rewards and incentives.* People get rewards in different ways; some value extra compensation; some, recognition; some, an opportunity to train others; some, travel; and some, time to reflect. Effective professional development programs identify the rewards and incentives that are possible and those most appropriate for the participants.

h. *Their designs are based on knowledge of adult learning and change.* Effective professional development is active, constructivist, concerns-based, and unfolds over time.

i. *They integrate individual, school, and district goals.* As noted later in the discussion of a new staff development paradigm, effective programs do not simply meet the needs of individual teacher participants. While doing that, they also attend to organizational goals.

j. *They integrate both organizationally and instructionally with other staff development and change efforts.* Over the years, teachers have been bombarded with professional development opportunities and requirements that address different aspects of teaching and learning with no attempt to integrate or coordinate them, address gaps, and reinforce similarities. Effective professional development recognizes that resources are better spent and teachers benefit when their learning is focused and integrated.

4. *There are other ways to learn than through workshops, courses, and institutes.* Inservice workshops and college course work are overwhelmingly the most common form of professional development in which teachers participate. However, although uncommon and often not legitimized as staff development, many more models are possible. Sparks and Loucks-Horsley (1989) identified four general models in addition to training.

a. *Individually-guided staff development.* This model typically has four phases. First, the teacher identifies a need or interest, which might involve a formal or informal assessment, with or without a supervisor or colleague. Second, he or she develops a plan with a set of learning goals and ways to accomplish them. The learning activities, the third phase, may include course or workshop attendance, reading, visits to other classrooms or schools, or initiation of a seminar or other overtime learning program. Finally, the teacher evaluates the learning and may share it in the form of a written report (especially if this was a formal professional development contract with a supervisor) or interactive session with colleagues. Often the evaluation results in more questions and learning goals to pursue.

b. *Observation and assessment.* This model includes peer coaching and clinical supervision. It typically involves a pre-observation conference, in which the focus for observation is determined, the methods for observation selected, and any special problems noted. During the observation, the focus may be on the students or the teacher, and it can be global or narrow. Patterns found during instruction may be noted. The more structured the observation, the more specific the feedback is apt to be to the teacher. In the post-observation conference, the teacher and observer reflect on the lesson and the observer shares the data collected. Strengths are acknowledged and areas for improvement suggested by either or both participants.

c. *Involvement in a development or improvement process.* In this model, teachers learn through developing or adapting curricula, designing programs, or engaging in systematic school improvement processes whose goal is to improve teaching or curriculum. Typically these projects are initiated to solve a problem and involve learning through reading, analysis, discussion, problem solving, observation, training, and/or trial and error. The result of the process is typically a product; that is, a new curriculum or program or a plan to be implemented.

d. *Inquiry.* This model includes action research and teacher-as-researcher approaches. In the model, the teacher identifies a problem or question of interest, collects and analyzes information to address it, and formulates new understandings and strategies for change.

Other modes that are emerging from both research and practice as powerful vehicles for professional learning are case discussions (Barnett, 1994) and professional networks (Little & McLaughlin, 1993).

5. *Professional development can only succeed with simultaneous attention to changing the system within which educators work.* In the earlier wave of mathematics and science reform, impact studies reported the disturbing finding that many teachers who had experienced exemplary professional development returned to their schools to find no support for the kinds of changes they wanted to make, and therefore no change ultimately occurred. Education and businesses alike have learned a great deal from similar experiences over the past two decades, and what has emerged is new attention to systems. A major premise of systems thinking is that it is not individuals who are to blame for problems, but the systems in which they live and work (Patterson, 1993; Senge, 1990). Educators at all levels are turning their attention to aligning components of the system and strengthening the relationship of the components to one another and to a set of high standards for student learning (Smith & O'Day, 1991). Professional development is viewed as a critical component of reform, one that must be linked to those same clear goals for students, as well as assessment, preservice teacher education, school leadership, and resources and staffing. The context of the school, often blamed for the lack of support teachers feel after they return from professional development experiences, is emerging as nearly as important as the experiences themselves. Professional developers can no longer ignore other parts of the system in which their teacher participants function.

Moving Towards a New Paradigm

These five principles seem to capture much of the learning of those experienced in teacher enhancement programs as well as those who conduct research in the area. They are ones that ring true in my science education community, and I suspect they are also true in mathematics education. However, when I put on my generic professional development hat, I see a new paradigm emerging that is not as much distinct as it is different in its emphasis. Sometimes I think of it as a figure/ground difference. What seems really important in one seems less important in the other, and visa versa.

Dennis Sparks, the executive director of the National Staff Development Council, a professional association to which I have great loyalty, published a commentary in Education Week (16 March 1994) describing a new paradigm for staff development. Because it seemed to embody ideas I've been working with as well, I have used and adapted the characteristics of this paradigm to create a new vision that makes sense to content-focused and generic staff developers alike. The elements of the paradigm are displayed in Figure 1 (Loucks-Horsley, 1995; Sparks, 1994). The following vignette is meant to illustrate the paradigm in action.

From Too Much	To More
Focus on Teacher Needs	Focus on Student Learning Outcomes
Focus on Individual Development	Focus on Individual and System Development
Transmission of Knowledge, Skills, and Strategies	Inquiry into Teaching and Learning
"Pull-Out" Training	Job-Embedded Learning
Generic Teaching Skills	Content and Content-Specific Teaching Skills
Fragmented, Piecemeal, One-Shot Experiences	Driven by Clear, Coherent, Long-Term Strategic Plan
District Direction and Decision Making	School Direction and Decision Making
Professional Developers as Trainers	Professional Developers as Facilitators, Consultants, Planners, Coaches, Trainers
Professional Development as Some People's Jobs	Professional Development as Everyone's Job
Professional Development for Teachers	Professional Development for Everyone
Professional Development as a "Frill"	Professional Development as Essential

Figure 1. A Paradigm for Professional Development in Learning-Centered Schools

Yvonne Montague teaches in Mountainview Elementary School. She is a member of a team that is responsible for the learning of 120 students, ages 9–11. Her team includes three other teachers, one intern spending the fifth year of his teacher preparation program in the school, and two teacher preparation students participating in a semester-long integrated science and mathematics methods experience.

Yvonne arrives at school a bit early. Today the team and students are visiting a nearby reclamation area, where a lake and its feeder streams are being cleaned up after nearly a century of dumping of industrial waste. The trip is part of a month-long inquiry into the water cycle and its interaction with humans. The inquiry is the result of careful planning and research by Yvonne's teaching team, which spent two weeks this past summer with other intermediate grade teams from the district, working with scientists, engineers, and curriculum development specialists. They conducted their own week-long investigation of the reclamation site, and then designed learning experiences for their students to develop knowledge, skills, and attitudes across traditionally separate content areas.

Yvonne's first stop is the cafeteria, where 10 middle-school students await instructions about their role in the trip. Having middle-school students accompany her students on field trips is the result of monthly study group meetings with elementary- and middle-school teachers. Their group is trying to understand what prepares elementary-school students to succeed in middle school and how the middle school scope and sequence can build on students' elementary-school foundations. The middle-school students met with her once before for a briefing on the learning and support needs of elementary-school students, and they are eager to come along.

Yvonne's teammates are also in the cafeteria. They quickly check on last-minute logistics, but spend most of the time reviewing the particular concepts they are trying to develop during the trip. They also remind themselves how to be good learning coaches and ask good questions of the students. They smile as they share that they're all still learning how to do this well.

As the trip progresses, Yvonne spends time taking notes on the experiences and reactions of two relatively older students who have peaked her interest this past month. During one of their team meetings focused on mathematics, Yvonne had mentioned that these two students were puzzling to her. They were champions in their neighborhood chess club, yet they could not seem to do the basic mathematics required to understand the impact of various concentrations of pollutants on plants and animals. She was determined to understand their conceptions of the relevant mathematics principles and see what was blocking their thinking. She had promised to share what she learned with her team so they could devise some strategies to help these and other students learn.

Back at school by mid-afternoon, Yvonne oversees the debriefing with the students. They are working in their learning teams to synthesize their data, check to see if the questions they had generated before the trip had been addressed, and identify what new questions they now have. As they end the day by writing in their journals, Yvonne notes the different paths the learning teams have taken as they explore different questions and choose to demonstrate their new understandings in different ways.

At the end of the school day, the meeting of their teaching team is at once lively and exhausting. As teachers have committed to new ways of helping their students learn, they've made so many changes that it's often hard to keep track. While the middle school students are present, they discuss what happened, what they did that seemed to make a difference, and what indications they had of learning by the students. What aspects of the inquiry did they think would help the students succeed in middle school?

They spend a few minutes hearing the observations of the two preservice teachers taking the science and mathematics methods course. They had chosen to work with a group of girls who had shown little motivation for the field trip. Their description of the girls' science and mathematics anxiety and the conviction that they'd "never learn this stuff," prompt them to suggest asking the girls if they would be interested in a special mini-study, maybe one that would examine federal regulations for fast food ingredients and testing. They leave to further develop their ideas. They'll begin by searching the Internet on the team's computer for relevant material from federal agencies.

The team's discussion returns to the big picture. How does this trip fit into their thematic program? How does it fit with the school wide focus on the environment and individual responsibility? How well are they applying the alternative assessment strategies that have been a special priority for the school over the past two years? How will the rest of the week play out as students do library research and talk with various scientists they have invited in to further their knowledge and address their additional questions? How can the final group projects be structured to best reflect the students' developing knowledge and skills?

After the team meeting, Yvonne lingers in the team's office to check her e-mail on their computer. They're hooked up through their state's education department. Yvonne is particularly interested in checking the bulletin board for the regional elementary mathematics and science network. Last week, she wrote a question in the "Perplexing Problems Conference." How do you help parents of traditionally high achieving students understand and appreciate the participation of their children in heterogeneous teams? Their team has been troubled by several parents who voice opposition on the grounds that their children spend all their time helping others learn, and not learning themselves. This opportunity to poll other teachers in the network has been helpful in the past.

On the bulletin board she also notes the formation of an action research group, where members will work with a university qualitative researcher to refine their skills in asking and pursuing answers to the questions they have about their students' learning. She wonders if her focus on the two students and their mathematics concepts would be helped by participating in the group.

As she leaves for the day, Yvonne passes the "new arrivals" shelf of the professional development library and notices a book called *Leadership and the New Science* (Wheatley, 1992). This book, it seems, might combine her interest in working better with her team and her hunger to learn as much as she can about new science concepts like quantum physics and chaos theory. She checks out the book on the library's computer as she muses about how different from the past it is to work in a school that encourages her to learn.

If teachers are going to create new (more active, real-world, integrated) learning opportunities and environments for their students, then they need to experience those same kinds of learning opportunities and experiences for themselves. This vignette is intended to illustrate what such an environment might look like—one where teachers have the support, time, and expert resources to pursue their own learning needs as well as those of their students. Although learning can certainly occur outside of the teaching-learning setting, if it doesn't continue there it is unlikely to "take." If we in teacher enhancement can shift the emphasis of our concerns from our "pull out" programs to the place where the teacher does his or her job, we may be able to make a quantum leap of difference in our impact.

Questions and Issues for Teacher Change, Staff Development, and Systemic Change

Shifting into this new paradigm also raises new questions and issues for us to ponder. A few are discussed below.

1. *What is the source of new knowledge?* One of the main features of the new paradigm is that professional development decisions are made largely at the school level. In the current paradigm, individual teachers select which workshops, institutes, or courses to take. Decisions about areas in which to sponsor opportunities (e.g., inservice sessions) are frequently made at the district level, often on the basis of a needs

assessment, and then selections are made by individual teachers. The new paradigm emphasizes that the school is the unit that builds the learning community for its students, so it needs a unifying set of learning goals and a strategic plan to meet those goals. Consequently, professional development choices are made in areas congruent with the plan.

Decentralized decision making can empower teachers and ensure that curriculum and instruction meet the needs of the school's population (Darling-Hammond, 1993). But, writers such as Schlecty (1990) and Fullan (1993) have argued that it can also have the effect of "the blind leading the blind." While wise in many important ways, veteran teachers who have not had broad exposure to new research and teaching approaches, and who distrust universities, state, and district staff who have traditionally not been much help, are often limited in their openness and awareness of new resources. Nor have they had a great deal of practice analyzing and critiquing research and literature, and selecting among new programs and practices. In the past, this issue has been difficult enough at the district level, where textbook adoption has typically occurred; decentralizing the strategic planning and decision making to the school compounds the challenge. Where will the teachers—now the planners and decision makers—get the new knowledge they need to make well informed decisions?

This knowledge issue extends beyond organizational decision making to teaching, and is especially keen in elementary schools. School-wide improvement efforts often focus on issues that either ignore or threaten content, because they respond to school wide needs. For example, workshops in cooperative learning or alternative assessment emphasize generic processes and skill development, and only secondarily, content. Curriculum integration or interdisciplinary instruction can threaten the integrity of disciplines if not done well (e.g., students may end up reading and writing about science rather than doing it). Where and how can deepening teachers' understanding of mathematics (science, history, etc.) fit into school strategic plans? How can the important emphasis on teachers' developing pedagogical content knowledge (Shulman, 1987) become a priority for the school's professional development resources? My own experience is that these questions are far from the minds of school-based decision makers. How can the development of knowledge and skills in content and content-specific pedagogy take their place in schools' priorities and get the attention of those making these important decisions?

2. *At what level should teacher enhancement occur?* The easy answer to this is, of course, at all levels, but what should happen at each? Typically, teacher enhancement has been "y'all come." That is,

individual teachers who were interested signed up and attended. The new paradigm calls for more school-focus than individual-focus, so working with teams of teachers or whole schools makes more sense. As the level changes, the nature of the work also changes, from individual understanding and lesson development (although that needs to be there, too) to development of curricula and strategies that articulate across a team or school (or even a district). Participants in teacher enhancement suddenly include more than the individual teacher (or, the teacher who specializes in mathematics); often all teachers, and building administrators, support staff, and even parents are involved. Schools who have strong partnerships with businesses and/or other community agencies may find it appropriate to have them represented as well.

If the goals of teacher enhancement enlarge to include developing the school community's ability and strategies to facilitate student learning of mathematics, then the nature of many of the activities will clearly be different. Programs will need to provide, but then move beyond, the original content focus to include strategies for engaging other professionals, leadership and change agent skills and strategies, and understanding and practice in systems thinking. Teacher enhancement will need to take on an organizational development component as well.

3. *Where do we find the time?* This issue can no longer be ignored. The kind of teacher enhancement that is portrayed in the new paradigm cannot be accomplished in four inservice days spread throughout the year. Shanker (1991) indicated that 20% of a teacher's time should be focused on professional growth. Fullan (1993) and Sparks (1994) have stressed that unless a school rethinks its time schedule (school year, week, day), then neither students nor their teachers will have optimal conditions for learning.

The movement towards school-based decision making is based on decisions being made "closer to the customer," and decisions about reorganizing time are no exception. Within certain general parameters set by the district and state (some states, like Indiana and Connecticut are actively exploring alternatives to traditional time allocations), schools can think creatively about time allocations. The current literature has many examples of creative use of time (e.g., Castle & Watts, 1992; Joyce & Showers, 1987; Price, 1993; Raywid, 1993). Teacher enhancement projects that are committed to helping teachers learn "on the job" can offer many ideas for consideration by the teachers in their school planning and decision making.

4. *How can this new paradigm become a reality?* Time allocation is clearly not the only thing that would have to change for teachers like Yvonne Montague to work in a rich learning environment. Like effective mathematics teaching and learning, the new paradigm for

professional development is an innovation that calls for a change in attitudes, beliefs, knowledge, skills, strategies, and context. As an innovation, it requires opportunities for people to become aware of its nature and importance, engage in developing their own understandings of its implications for them and their work, develop commitment to experimenting with it, learn and practice skills and new behaviors, and maintain a continuous feedback loop for adjustments and refinements. My experiences in using a similar process to build collaborative, comprehensive systems for staff development in schools and districts (Arbuckle & Murray, 1989) indicate that such change is possible, although time-consuming and complex. It involves changing the culture as well as the schedule and the structure of the school as a place for learning.

5. *What is the role of teacher enhancement?* It is obvious from discussion of these issues that, to move towards the new paradigm for professional development, much about current teacher enhancement projects will need to change. Many are already moving towards a school-based design with resources allocated for follow-up. Many have built in components to develop teacher leadership and change agent skills. Others have begun to work with the systems as well as the teachers. All of these changes are critical, as are working with the same teachers for extended periods of time, increasing the critical mass in schools, and building special expertise either in the school or district to maintain the changes that have occurred over time.

Yet there are still many questions to address. First, working with smaller numbers of teachers over time increases the cost per participant. Are there less intense strategies that have pay-off in change in practice? What are the best strategies for the critical mass in a school to bring others into the fold? A second, related, question is the role of professional networks. Especially at the secondary level, teachers often have important reasons to network with others outside their school rather than inside. Creating and supporting professional networks can be a powerful strategy for systemic change (Little & McLaughlin, 1993), but what influence can it have on building strong in-school learning communities? How can teachers be members of professional networks both inside and outside of their schools to take advantage of both kinds of support?

A final question I will raise, although far from the only one that remains, is the value of a teacher enhancement infrastructure to support the new paradigm. In the past, teacher development projects have been fairly independent, linking with each other periodically, but rarely working together. Many of the state systemic initiatives have sought to coordinate teacher enhancement efforts, but few have succeeded in more than enhancing communication between them and with potential participants.

If schools are indeed to become professional learning settings for teachers, they will need a strong infrastructure to help them "reculture" and to maintain that new culture. Given where they are starting, they will need a lot of help in doing so. How could teacher enhancement projects become that infrastructure or part of it? What could they do beyond carrying out their own projects? What would it be like if they had a common set of beliefs and ways of working with teachers and schools or a common vision of a professional learning community? How could they network their teachers and schools to "multiple mileage" their efforts? What if they designed and assembled a "curriculum" for teacher leadership and change agentry that they all could use, as appropriate? What if they developed strategies for their own professional development, ways to continue learning as well as "induct" new teacher enhancement projects into their community? Couldn't such an infrastructure have a powerful influence on other providers of professional development, on preservice teacher preparation, and on leadership development at the state and regional level?

As in most areas of education, pushing the edge in professional development raises more questions and issues than it answers. However, having a common vision for professional development, one that is grounded in evaluation, research, and best practice, is one good way for a community to weather the winds on the other side of the hurricane's eye. It's simultaneously a challenge and an honor to be part of that teacher enhancement/professional development community.

References

Arbuckle, M. A., & Murray, L. B. (1989). *Building systems for professional growth: An action guide.* Andover, MA: The Regional Laboratory for Educational Improvement of the Northeast and Islands.

Barnett, C. (1994). *Dilemmas of teaching: Math cases to promote inquiry, discussion and reflection.* Portsmouth, NH: Heinemann.

Castle, S., & Watts, G. D. (1992). The tyranny of time. *Doubts and Certainties, 7*(2), 1–4.

Darling-Hammond, L. (1993). Reframing the school reform agenda: Developing capacity for school transformation. *Phi Delta Kappan, 74*(10), 753–61.

148   *Reflecting on Our Work*

Fullan, M. G., & Stiegelbauer, S. (1991). *The new meaning of educational change.* New York: Teachers College Press.

Fullan, M. G. (1993). *Change forces: Probing the depths of educational reform.* London: Falmer Press.

Guskey, T. (1986). Staff development and the process of teacher change. *Educational Researcher, 15*(5), 5–12.

Hall, G. E., & Hord, S. M. (1987). *Change in schools: Facilitating the process.* Albany, NY: SUNY Press.

Hord, S. M., Rutherford, W. L., Huling-Austin, L., & Hall, G. E. (1987). *Taking charge of change.* Alexandria, VA: Association for Supervision and Curriculum Development.

Joyce, B., & Showers, B. (1987). Low-cost arrangements for peer-coaching. *Journal of Staff Development, 8*(1), 22–4.

Little, J. W. (1993). Teachers' professional development in a climate of educational reform. *Educational Evaluation and Policy Analysis, 15,* 129–51.

Little, J. W., & McLaughlin, M. W. (1993). *Teachers' work: Individuals, colleagues, and contexts.* New York: Teachers College Press.

Loucks-Horsley, S. (1989). Managing change: An integral part of staff development. In S. Caldwell (Ed.), *Staff development: A handbook of effective practices* (pp. 114–25). Oxford, OH: National Staff Development Council.

Loucks-Horsley, S. (1995). Professional development and the learner-centered school. *Theory into Practice, 34*(4), 265–71.

Loucks-Horsley, S., Kapitan, R., Carlson, M. D., Kuerbis, P. J., Clark, R. C., Melle, G. M., Sachse, T. P., & Walton, E. (1990). *Elementary school science for the '90s.* Andover, MA: The NETWORK, Inc.; and Alexandria, VA: Association for Supervision and Curriculum Development.

Loucks-Horsley, S., & Stiegelbauer, S. (1991). Using knowledge of change to guide staff development. In A. Lieberman & L. Miller (Eds.), *Staff development for education in the '90s: New demands, new realities, new perspectives* (pp. 15–36). New York: Teachers College Press.

Patterson, J. L. (1993). *Leadership for tomorrow's schools.* Alexandria, VA: Association for Supervision and Curriculum Development.

Price, H. (1993, May 12). Teacher professional development: It's about time. *Education Week.*

Raywid, M. A. (1993). Finding time for collaboration. *Education Leadership, 51*(1), 30–4.

Regional Educational Laboratories. (1995). *Facilitating systemic change in science and mathematics education: A toolkit for professional developers.* Andover, MA: The Regional Laboratory for Educational Improvement of the Northeast and Islands.

Rosenholtz, S. (1989). *Teachers' workplace: The social organization of schools.* New York: Longman.

Senge, P. M. (1990). *The fifth discipline: The art and practice of the learning organization.* New York: Doubleday.

Smith, M. S., & O'Day, J. (1991). *Systemic school reform.* New Brunswick, NJ: Center for Policy Reform in Education.

Sparks, D. (1994, March 16). A paradigm shift in staff development. *Education Week.*

Shanker, A. (1990). Staff development and the restructured school. In B. Joyce (Ed.), *Changing school culture through staff development, 1990 yearbook of the Association for Supervision and Curriculum Development* (pp. 91–103). Alexandria, VA: Association for Supervision and Curriculum Development.

Shulman, L. S. (1987). Knowledge and teaching: Foundations of the new reform. *Harvard Educational Review, 57,* 1–22.

Sparks, D., & Loucks-Horsley, S. (1989). Five models of staff development for teachers, *Journal of Staff Development, 10*(4), 40–57.

Wheatley, M. (1992). *Leadership and the new science.* San Francisco, CA: Berrett-Koehler.

The Logic of Program Evaluation: What Should We Evaluate in Teacher Enhancement Projects?

George E. Hein
Lesley College

Tip O'Neill, former speaker of the House of Representatives, said, "All politics is local." So is education. No matter how grand our educational schemes for systemic change, they need to be assessed for their local impact; for their effect on children. The purpose of public schools is to educate children. Any change—any scheme to reform schools—must be judged by the extent to which it helps children become fully functioning, competent, educated adults.

The truism above does not immediately translate into the conclusion that evaluation of educational programs must necessarily involve an assessment of the extent to which a program has resulted in increased learning by children. (In this paper I shall only explore *whether* student assessment is appropriate as part of the program evaluation task, not *how* student performance should be assessed.) In fact, I will argue in this paper that the proper subject for the evaluation of teacher enhancement efforts is the impact of these efforts on *teachers*. The argument will be based on the analysis of a simple, visual model of the structure of schooling.

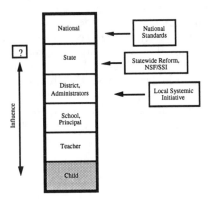

Figure 1. A Simple View of the U.S. Educational System

A Structural Model for Schooling

The U.S. education system can be conceived as a hierarchical structure ranging from the national level to the level of children as indicated in Figure 1. This figure represents the *logical structure* of the national education system, not necessarily the relative importance of the various levels. It emphasizes the systemic, bureaucratic elements of the system, not all the aspects of society that contribute to children's learning.

The model is particularly appropriate for this discussion of the logic of evaluation of teacher enhancement programs because much of the initiative and most of the funding for reform, no matter what level targeted, comes from national and state sources. As far as program evaluation is concerned, the national and state funding levels play a disproportionately significant role. Most of the local school funds—the property taxes that supply the basic, day-to-day operating expenses of schools—are usually not subject to external program evaluation. As indicated in the introduction, however, all interventions, no matter what their intended level, must ultimately be justified by their effect on children's learning. Thus, the level of the child is emphasized by the shaded section.

The schematic diagram also indicates the traditional view of the education system as a hierarchical structure in which policies developed at any level are likely to influence those levels below it. (The terms "below" and "above" or "higher" and "lower" applied to this model refer to the level of aggregation of the system; they have no value implications. A state system of education is a higher; i.e., larger; organizational level than a single school, although it is farther removed from the children.) There is an expectation that national educational policy will somehow trickle down to the level of the child through the various layers of the structure. An open question, and one that is currently much discussed by writers about organizational change (e.g., Fullan, 1991), is the extent to which reform at any lower organizational level can and needs to influence higher organizational levels in order to bring about systemic change. These expectations of influence are indicated by the arrow along side the model, with the question mark emphasizing that the degree of influence from lower to higher levels is open to debate.

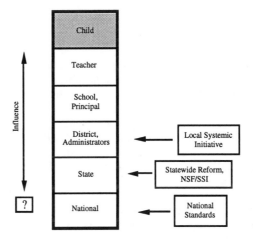

Figure 2. School Structure (Child Centered)

The schematic in Figure 1 can also be inverted to emphasize the importance of the child in education; the lowest organizational unit is, in fact, the most important one, as illustrated in Figure 2. In addition, the many components that influence education, such as family and community, business and industry, and especially, various agencies dedicated to improving education, can be added to provide a more complete picture of the structure of the U. S. education system. This is illustrated in Figure 3. (A much earlier, but similar, model is provided by Dewey, 1900.)

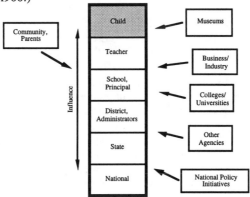

Figure 3. A More Complete View of the U.S. Educational System

Examples of national interventions to bring about school change abound. When the Secretary of Education publishes a document such as *A Nation at Risk* the intention is to influence education across the country. Examples of other initiatives intended to influence education nationally would be the National Standards effort, movements to require (or ban) prayer in schools across the United States, or Supreme Court decisions that influence racial distribution of children nationally.

Another set of efforts is directed primarily at the state-wide organizational level. Such initiatives may arise within a state, such as the various state frameworks and state assessment programs instituted in the past decade, or they may result from a distribution of federal funds to the states, such as the NSF sponsored Statewide Systemic Initiative (SSI). In the latter program, the NSF has targeted individual state school systems as the level of intervention. How the state actually uses the funds to implement school reform—by carrying out state-wide activities or initiatives at the level of individual districts or schools—is determined by the proposals submitted to NSF by individual states.

Evaluation of any Proposed School Reform

Applying the model outlined above to the evaluation of school reform basic questions concerning any school intervention can be formulated:

1. At what level(s) is the intervention targeted?
2. What is the strategy for influencing this level?
3. To what extent does the program influence the targeted level?
4. What is the logical argument that an intervention at the targeted level will influence the education of children?
5. Is there a strategy for influencing all levels?

All of these questions are significant for any intervention, and each requires careful attention. Program implementers must be clear about what level (or levels) they propose to influence by their actions; they must have an action plan, specific mechanisms and tactics for accomplishing what they propose to do; and they need to be clear about why they believe this particular set of activities has the potential to make a difference for the education of children.

But an evaluator's perspective is different. Not every step in the logic of the argument that is intended to result in improved education for children is a component of the evaluation of a specific program targeted at a particular audience. Program evaluators have two major concerns. One is a need to understand the logic of the program being evaluated. What is intended, how is it supposed to work? Although there have been suggestions that evaluation should be goal free and that evaluators might even intentionally be ignorant of program goals (Scriven, 1972), most of us believe that unless we understand a program's basic assumptions, we cannot adequately evaluate it. The rationale for a program is embodied in the answers to questions 1, 2, 4, and 5 above.

The second concern of the evaluator is to document and evaluate the actual program activities and consequences. In order to carry out the evaluation, the evaluator needs to understand the logic behind the program, but the evaluation work itself focuses on the activities of the program and the outcomes associated with those activities. In carrying out the evaluation, the evaluator will address primarily question 3 above.

An example will illustrate the situation. *Goals 2000*, first an activity sponsored by the National Governors' Association and now a federal school reform package passed by Congress and signed into law by President Clinton in 1994, is a *national* initiative intended to change the education of children. The intervention itself, however, is targeted at the level of the *states*; the Goals 2000 Program requires each state to submit statewide plans that include standards and assessments to improve schools. Its strategy for change is twofold, it distributes money to states so they can carry out their plans, and it lends moral force to the efforts around the national goals, most of which refer to student outcomes such as student readiness for school and student achievement in various subjects. The argument that the funding strategy will effect the education of children will, presumably, be contained in the individual state plans. If history is any guide, this logic may be somewhat tenuous, relying heavily on assumptions about education.

But from an evaluator's standpoint, the evaluation of the program is straightforward. The first task would be to determine whether the actual program—the plan to distribute funds to the states in response to their plans—has in fact occurred. In this brief discussion we are not distinguishing between *formative evaluation*, which would be used to improve the funding mechanism in response to state plans, and *summative evaluation*, which would report on the results of the funding program. The second level would be to examine the state plans and see if the funds had accomplished what the plans had proposed. Most likely, the funds will be used for activities such as teacher education, development of assessment systems, school building and program improvements, rather than direct services to children. It remains to be seen whether the plans call for direct state support of activities at the level of districts, of individual schools, or of new entities that are, in turn, supposed to carry out activities within the state. An example of such an organizational structure would be regional centers (as utilized by some SSI Programs) to facilitate implementation of their programs in different regions of a state.

The logic of the Goals 2000 Program as I have just described it is contained in Figure 4. One task would be to evaluate process X, the mechanism for distributing funds to the states. This corresponds to questions 1 and 2 discussed above. Another task would be to examine the various state proposals and then evaluate the processes they propose to achieve the Goals 2000. One state (illustrated by arrow A) may propose to provide funds directly to individual schools. Another (arrow B) may chose to intervene at the district level, while a third (arrow C) might set up an intermediate entity with the intention of influencing districts, schools or teachers. Again, the evaluator's responsibility would be to assess the proposed programs, A, B, or C, and to determine the extent to which they were able to carry out the activities described by each. In addition, an evaluation of the Goals 2000 Program will provide information on the relative effectiveness of the different strategies, A, B, or C, in accomplishing project goals.

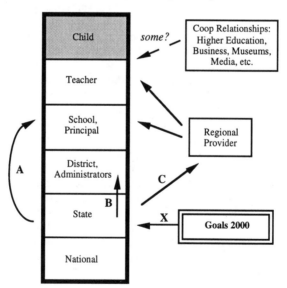

Figure 4. Hypothetical Goals 2000 Structure to Guide an Evaluation Plan

It should be incumbent on program staff to articulate why they believe that the activities they carry out, whether teacher enhancement, local school restructuring, or new state mandates that apply to all school systems, can be expected to lead to changes in students' performance. That is, they need to address questions 1, 4, and 5. But it is not logical to expect that program evaluations of the state programs will directly answer this question.

The reason there is a logical leap between program evaluation and assessment of children's progress in school is that there are a host of local, environmental factors that may intervene between a program's activities and student outcomes. *Although a valid rationale for any program's impact on children is a* necessary *component to justify an intervention at any level, it is not a* sufficient *one to assure an observable outcome at the level of the child.* In any particular instance, a program that could, in principle, benefit children may be overwhelmed in a state that has cut overall support for schools; another program may be badly implemented because of local teacher-administration labor disputes; and the positive effects of a third program may be overshadowed by a larger school reform effort that occurs simultaneously. Program evaluation that focuses at education levels other than those targeted for intervention may miss the significant features of that particular reform effort. It must examine implementation where it happens, not indirectly through its (possible) effect on children, who may be several levels removed from the "action."

An analogous situation would be provided by an evaluation of a particular intervention to treat tuberculosis victims with an anti-TB medication at a hospital outpatient clinic. In this instance, the clinic can be compared to a school setting, and the program to distribute the drug to a school-based intervention. The actual efficacy of a particular chemical for the treatment of a disease, will be determined by the following:

1. The evidence (logic of the argument) that connects that particular chemical structure with an effect on the course of the disease.

2. The environmental factors that determine its value in any specific situation. A drug that is effective in principle may still not be effective in practice because of expense, difficulty in administration, public antipathy towards the treatment or a host of local confounding conditions. The appropriate level of analysis for this program would be the treatment program at the clinic. Evaluation questions could focus on such issues as, was the correct patient group targeted for treatment?

Did the staff follow up on treatment? Were patients satisfied with their care? Did the patients stay with the regimen?

If the evaluation focused primarily on an analysis of the changes in the incidence of TB in the community, then it would be impossible to ascertain whether any changes (or lack of them) were caused by the outpatient treatment program, the efficacy of that particular chemical, the incidence of a new drug resistant form of TB, the fact that patients were or were not taking their medication, or any one of a number of other environmental and economic factors influencing the course of the disease. In order to carry out a study to cover all these factors, it would be necessary to follow the lives of individual patients and be able to isolate the various factors that influence their health.

The analogy here is of limited applicability because in clinical drug evaluation no substance can be tested in community settings (analogous to a school intervention) before both the safety and efficacy of the drug have been demonstrated in controlled, laboratory settings. In education we sometimes initiate new processes at various levels without compelling evidence for their value at *any* level.

The Model Applied to Local Systemic Reform

The NSF Local Systemic Initiative Program (LSI) is intended to bring about reform through intervention at the school district level. The intention is similar to the goals of the Urban Systemic Initiative (USI), and indeed, the LSI Program solicitation cross-references the parallel USI Program. The solicitation goes farther. It not only specifies the unit within which reform should be implemented, but also points out that systemic change involves an entire organizational unit and then identifies school districts as the target for the solicitation, emphasizing that they should focus on teacher enhancement for teachers from an entire district.

The LSI Program has an added specification, as is evident from its placement within the category of teacher enhancement projects. It specifies that the school reform should take place through "a focus on teacher enhancement with the attention to the implementation of exemplary instructional materials" (NSF, 1994, p. 1). The solicitation does not say anything, for example, either about how school districts are organized within a state or how they relate to state initiatives (a "higher" level of school structure than is included in this program), nor about how the districts need to connect their teacher enhancement activities to activities undertaken by children (a "lower" organizational level than the one addressed by this solicitation). All the discussion in the solicitation refers to the school district as the target for the intervention.

Using our model, the LSI Program can be illustrated as indicated in Figure 5. The program will fund a series of projects that will operate either by mechanism X or Y to carry out activities in districts. All the projects will have some impact on teachers, either directly (path A), through schools (path B), or some combination of these two mechanisms with the expected outcome to be some form of teacher enhancement.

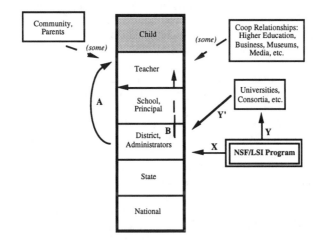

Figure 5. Schematic View of LSI Projects

Evaluation of any LSI project can reasonably be expected to determine the extent to which these activities have been effective in bringing about the proposed teacher enhancements. It is reasonable to expect evaluations to document changes in teacher beliefs and behaviors as a result of participation in the LSI projects. If both paths A and B are used, information may be generated on the relative efficacy of the two paths in fostering these changes. In the course of their evaluation activities, evaluators are likely to obtain evidence concerning environmental factors that influence the extent to which the teacher enhancement activities are likely to have an impact at any level. A dysfunctional school, in which teachers and the principal are feuding, may not be able to show the results of the enhancement activities on the teachers, and certainly not on the students one level further removed.

Impact on Students (but Are the Kids Learning Anything?)

Despite the argument given above, that program evaluation must be focused at the level of the intervention, all of us concerned about education still need to worry about the most important members of the school structure, the children. Activities proposed under the LSI initiative are only worth carrying out if there is reason to believe that they have the possibility of improving the education of children. An answer to question 4 above, is necessary both to justify the project and to permit the evaluator to carry out an appropriate evaluation.

The RFP for the LSI Program makes a series of statements that assume a relationship between teacher behavior and student outcomes. It argues that the following attributes of school systems are of value:

1. Creation of professional communities where teachers are empowered to bring about change and encouraged to reflect on their own teaching and learning.

2. New beliefs, new skills and new behaviors must be learned and explored (by teachers) within a supportive school culture which itself is engaged in renewal.

3. Just as students should learn mathematics, science and technology through the process of inquiry, so too should their teachers.

These teacher behaviors are linked to "making significant progress towards reaching national goals for the teaching of mathematics, science and technology education" (NSF, 1994, p. 1). The rationale for the connection between these teacher behaviors and student outcomes comes from a whole series of research studies and policy papers that delineate the appropriate teacher behaviors that lead to desired student outcomes (e.g., Gabel, 1994). These studies fall into two general categories:

1. *Research* findings based on some form of controlled setting. Whether the research involved a treatment and control group or whether it was more naturalistic, the essence of any research study that tries to make a connection between teacher behaviors and children's learning necessarily requires a rather narrow focus. The researcher specifies a set of conditions and then notes what happens.

2. *Descriptions* of classroom life. Over the past twenty years we have been provided with a wide range of descriptions of "real" school life (e.g., Cohen & Ball, 1990; Stake & Easley, 1978). Some of these have been horrendous examples of the worst of our classrooms; others have been glowing accounts of stellar efforts to educate children.

For this discussion, what we can generalize from both kinds of studies is that any proposal to develop evidence concerning the connection between teacher behavior and student learning is major activity by itself. To attempt it within the framework of the LSI projects would be well beyond the scope of most program evaluations associated with NSF funded teacher enhancement projects. If the LSI projects attempt to carry out such research, they will have neither time nor funds left to carry out what they are intended to do: bring about systemic changes in teacher beliefs and behavior. Within the NSF there are other programs specifically committed to funding research on student learning and how it relates to teacher behavior. Our knowledge base in this area may be inadequate, but it will not be enhanced if program evaluators for LSI projects are asked to carry out studies beyond the means available to them, and studies which are primarily late extensions and additions to projects that were conceptually developed for another purpose.

Conclusion

The evaluation of Teacher Enhancement efforts must focus on observable outcomes for teachers. Projects must explain how they expect these changes to impact students. The research base that links teacher behavior and student learning is still inadequate. Additional research studies are necessary to provide more evidence for this connection and to describe more fully the ecological circumstances that influence it. But it is important to make the distinction between the capacity of project evaluators to provide information about implementation efforts—and to assist in improving these through formative evaluation—and studies that attempt to link teacher behavior with student outcomes. If evaluators are asked to assess teacher enhancement programs by the student outcomes that may or may not be associated with them, they will produce primarily uninterpretable data without being able to develop a better understanding of the factors that encourage or hinder teacher enhancement.

Acknowledgments

I wish to acknowledge with gratitude critical comments from Susan Baker Cohen, Mary Ellen Harmon, Sabra Price, Susan Snyder, Iris Weiss, Max West, and Karen Worth, as well as members of the PERG discussion group. They all helped me to strengthen the argument and clarify the writing.

References

Cohen, D. K., & Ball, D. L. (Issue Organizers) (1990, Fall). *Educational evaluation and policy analysis, 12.*

Dewey, J. (1900). *The school and society.* Chicago, IL: University of Chicago Press.

ERIC Review, Systemic Education Reform, 3(2) Fall, 1994, p. 10, U. S. Department of Education.

Fullan, M. (1991). *The new meaning of educational change* (2nd. edition). New York: Teacher's College Press.

Gabel, D. L. (Ed.). (1994). *Handbook of research on science teaching and learning.* New York: Macmillan.

National Science Foundation. (1994). *Local systemic change through teacher enhancement: Grades K–8: Program solicitation and guidelines* (draft). Washington, DC: Author.

Scriven, M. (1972). Pros and cons about goal-free evaluation. *Evaluation Comment, 3*(4), 1–7.

Stake, R. E., & Easley, J. (1978). *Case studies in science education.* Champaign, IL: University of Illinois.

Appendix B:
Project Descriptions

FIRST Project: School-Based Elementary School Mathematics Professional Development

George W. Bright and Anne-Courtney Miller
The University of North Carolina at Greensboro

Catherine R. Nesbit and Josephine D. Wallace
The University of North Carolina at Charlotte

This three-year project, funded by the National Programs component of the Eisenhower Mathematics and Science Education Program, was designed to help elementary teachers at the building level to develop and implement School Improvement Plans (SIPs) for enhancing instruction in mathematics and science, especially in elementary schools with high percentages of traditionally under-served groups. Only the mathematics portion of this project is discussed here. In total, 357 teachers and 181 principals from 181 schools in North Carolina participated, 46% for three years (called "year-one teachers") and 54% for the last two years only (called "year-two teachers"). These teachers from each building worked in cooperation with the principal from that building to form a team whose mission was to improve the teaching of mathematics and science. The teachers can be viewed as "lead teachers," but it must be remembered that principals were also involved (in varying intensity) in leading reform efforts.

The goals of the project were to (a) develop and implement in each school a science or mathematics SIP formulated with input from the teachers and administrators, that would focus on standards of the National Science Teachers Association or the National Council of Teachers of Mathematics, (b) improve the science or mathematics teaching competency of all teachers in these buildings, (c) increase teachers' positive attitudes toward science and mathematics teaching, (d) build local peer training teams that would continue the work of the project, and (e) develop a model for school-wide improvement that included a school-based planning strategy and a leadership development component for peer teachers. The project was conducted at seven university sites during year one and eight sites during year two; each site had a coordinator who was responsible for selecting the schools to participate (12 schools per site per year). Priority was given to schools with high minority student populations, schools with large numbers of students in free or reduced lunch programs, and schools located in small towns or rural areas.

During the first month of the project, the site coordinators met with additional mathematics and science educators from the state to develop needs assessment surveys (one in mathematics and one in science) for teachers and principals to complete. The heart of each survey was 30 statements concerning content, instructional practices, assessment, and classroom climate. A sample statement is "Mathematics is taught in a way that makes it applicable and relevant to students' lives." Teachers and principals rated each statement according to (a) how important they felt the practice was to their school's program (importance) and (b) what degree they were implementing the practice in their current program (achievement).

Shortly after selection for participation in the project, teams of lead teachers and principals participated in visioning and assessment sessions. The visioning sessions were designed to help the teams see that there were many ways to think about teaching, assessment, and curriculum in ways that were consistent with national standards. The assessment sessions involved providing each school with sufficient copies of appropriate needs assessment instrument(s) so that all teachers and the principal/assistant principal(s) in each building could complete the survey. Seven of the sites only dealt with one content area (mathematics or science), so teachers in buildings at those sites completed only one of the needs assessment forms. The eighth site dealt with the integration of mathematics and science, so teachers and principals in buildings at this site completed both sets of needs assessment forms. Data from each building were first tallied by the lead teachers and principal from that building. As the perceived discrepancies between the importance and achievement in practices were identified, the strengths and weaknesses of each school's programs emerged. The lead teachers were then expected to work with the principal and "other teachers" in each building to develop a SIP based on the needs identified in the survey. The SIPs were collected by each site coordinator and used to develop plans for a three-week summer workshop (75 hours) to respond to the common needs of the schools at that site. As expected, the teachers generally responded very favorably to the workshops; teachers saw them as relevant to their needs and useful in implementing SIPs.

The site coordinator met with lead teachers several times during the following academic year. These follow-up sessions included opportunities for lead teachers to share their experiences as well as to receive additional professional development. Lead teachers were expected to work with their peers during this academic year to implement their SIPs. This could include conducting building-level workshops, demonstrating teaching strategies, organizing materials and resources, and so forth. Collectively, lead teachers and the site coordinator planned a one-week follow-up workshop during the second summer. Whenever possible, teachers were helped to visit each others' classrooms. In most cases this was accomplished by scheduling follow-up meetings at different school buildings; teachers were released from their own teaching to go to that school early in the day to observe. Teachers at several sites asked for the development of a reporting mechanism that would help them track changes in their own buildings. Forms were developed by site coordinators and given to teachers to use.

A second, one-week workshop (25 hours) was scheduled during the next summer as a capstone experience for these teachers. Lead teachers had direct input to planning the content and organization of this workshop.

What Have We Learned from the FIRST Project?

Involving all teachers and the principal in a building in the needs assessment process seemed to be a powerful technique for opening up dialogue about needed changes in mathematics instruction. Each person brought a slightly different perspective, and the resulting consensus was richer because of the differing contributions. Overall, the data on importance and achievement in mathematics show that there are important differences among the three subgroups. Analysis of the responses revealed, overall, that achievement rankings were somewhat lower than importance rankings. Analysis of responses of the lead teachers, the other teachers, and the principals revealed that for the importance responses the principals generally ranked items highest, followed by lead teachers, followed by the other teachers. For the achievement responses, however, the pattern was reversed; generally, the other teachers ranked the items highest, followed by lead teachers, followed by principals. The discrepancy between importance and achievement was greatest for the principals and least for the other teachers. In other words, the principals saw more need for improvement than the lead teacher, who in turn saw more need for improvement than the other teachers.

It is possible that the principals ranked items as more important than the lead teachers and the other teachers because they generally must view a school's program in a more global context; not only the context of the district but also the context of statewide reporting of the performance of individual school buildings. It is possible that the teachers ranked achievement of practices higher than principals because teachers work closely with children on a day-by-day basis and know more intimately what is gong on in classrooms. Principals may see the discrepancy between the average test performance for the building and the performance of other schools in the state and may seek to close whatever gaps there are, reasoning "Our children are as smart as other children, so we should be scoring as high as other schools." The lead teachers, because they are possibly more interested in improving the mathematics instructional program, may interpret the performance of children as indicating a need for improvement on a school-wide basis, while the other teachers, who perhaps do not see the same urgency for change, may be more-or-less satisfied with the achievement of their students, in the sense that teachers are "doing the best they can for the children in this school."

The initial "visioning" sessions seemed to make the development of SIPs easier. Teachers and principals, especially those in isolated settings, may need some help in knowing what is possible. It is important for them to have a sense of options. At some schools, there was a separate "visioning" session prior to the first summer workshop for all the faculty in the building. One purpose of this session was to prepare the other teachers for the fact that the lead teachers would be returning in the fall with new and better ways to teach mathematics and science. The tone was set that all teachers would need to incorporate these techniques into their instruction during the following school year. This seemed to be important in heading off attempts by teachers to plan their instruction without at least considering whether the new techniques might be more effective.

The receptivity of the lead teachers to the content of the summer workshops seemed to be related to the fact that the teachers felt that they influenced specification of the workshop content through their SIPs. In addition, having the lead teachers tally the data from all teachers and principals in their building may have given them a better sense of the strengths, weaknesses, and needs of their colleagues.

It was also clear that the buildings where the most change was noted tended to be those in which the principal's support was the greatest. This was not a surprise. When principals and teachers value the same goals, it is easier for them to work together as a team. In addition, it seemed important to have two teachers working together in a building, since they could support each other. In retrospect, it might have been more effective to have two teachers from the primary grades and two from the intermediate grades.

The visits of teachers to other buildings were very popular, and teachers reported that they learned a lot from watching their peers teach. Having teachers visit each others' classrooms diminishes some of the sense of isolation common to elementary teachers.

In follow-up study (Nesbit, Wallace, & Miller, 1995) of the implementation of leadership roles by the lead teachers, most lead teachers identified a variety of experiences that helped prepare them for those roles: the hands-on approach presented in the professional development sequence, the presentation of up-to-date content and curriculum materials, and the opportunity to talk to other teachers about common problems. In addition, some teachers identified other factors: observations in schools, visits by project staff, and modeling of effective pedagogy as well as leadership techniques by project staff.

When asked about factors that helped or hindered in carrying out leadership roles, the following factors were often listed as helpful: principals that cooperated in implementing the SIP, close networking among lead teachers, and explicit attention in the inservice for lead teachers given to understanding factors that inhibit change. Factors that were often listed as inhibiting included the following: poor working relationship with the principal, limited networking among lead teachers, little attention in the inservice for lead teachers on topics associated with leadership development.

What Advice Can We Give for Large-Scale Teacher Change Programs?

Teachers need to have options for ways to change. They need a vision of what is possible and what is desired by current reform efforts. Many teachers spend a great deal of time in one environment (e.g., school district), thus making it difficult for them to have a clear sense of options that might be available.

Lead teachers have the potential to serve as mediators between the teaching staff and school administrators. That is, their views about reform and about the strengths and weaknesses in the school seem to tend to be somewhere between the views of the other teachers and the administrators. Lead teachers need to be helped, however, to learn how to play this mediation role, and other parties (especially administrators) need to be helped to come to accept this mediation role of the lead teachers.

Needs assessment should be carried out within a clear framework for change. The national mathematics or science standards provide one such framework, but there are others that may need to be considered (e.g., state curriculum frameworks). It seems key, however, to have a context within which teachers can interpret change.

Teachers and administrators need to learn how to talk together about needed changes and to plan for implementation of those changes that seem most important locally. Discussion needs to be built on knowledge of what is going on locally and on knowledge of what local teachers and administrators want to have happen.

Although the site coordinators had somewhat different visions of leadership, data from this project suggest that lead teachers at a site were able to understand and begin to implement the particular vision that was advocated at that site. However, site coordinators need to think carefully about which vision of leadership they want to advocate through leadership training activities. Activities should be explicitly organized to help teachers attain this vision.

The data also seem to support the notion that it takes at least two years for change to occur at the building level. Analogous results have occurred across a wide variety of projects, but often the change has been measured at the individual teacher level rather than at the building level. Too, this project included on-going support for teachers from site coordinators and other university personnel. That support is a confounding factor in the design of the project.

The lead teachers identified a variety of factors that should be included in professional development: leadership development, curriculum knowledge, peer teaching, active modeling of pedagogy as well as leadership by project staff, and close collaboration with principals. The items in this list are consistent with elements cited by other researchers (e.g., Devaney, 1987; Gehrke, 1991; Graebill & Phillips, 1990; Lieberman, Saxl, & Miles, 1988; Loucks-Horsley, 1992; Price, 1990; Sparks, 1983; Taylor, 1986).

How Might Such Programs Be Monitored?

In addition to monitoring student performance and teachers' instructional practices, there needs to be monitoring of changes in teachers' and principals' visions about reform (Nesbit & Wallace, 1994). It is important to understand how teachers and principals conceptualize a framework for change.

Changes in teaching need to be observed in the context of the teachers' own classrooms. Teachers seem to be most comfortable and most able to make changes in their own classrooms. But observation of the building-level and district-level environment for change is equally important. Individual change cannot be interpreted without knowing how those changes relate to larger contexts. In our project, having a larger vision seemed important for interpreting the level of success of individual teachers. Similarly, understanding changes in students' performance is more easily interpreted when some sense of the larger context is available.

The development and use of the form as a means for documenting changes within buildings allowed all teachers within those buildings to be able to point to changes that they contributed to the improvement of instruction. This seemed like a fairly non-threatening way for all teachers to participate in change.

References

Devaney, K. (1987). *The lead teacher: Ways to begin*. New York: Carnegie Forum on Education and the Economy.

Gehrke, N. (1991). *Developing teachers' leadership skills (ERIC digest)*. Washington, DC: Office of Educational Research and Improvement.

Graebill, L., & Phillips, E. (1990). A summer math institute for elementary teachers: Development, implementation, and follow-up. *School Science and Mathematics, 90*, 134–41.

Lieberman, A., Saxl, E., & Miles, M. (1988). Teacher leadership: Ideology and practice. In A. Lieberman (Ed.), *Building a professional culture in schools* (pp. 148–66). New York: Teachers College Press.

Loucks-Horsley, S. (1992). *Effective teacher development programs*. Paper presented at annual National Eisenhower Program Conference, Washington, DC.

Nesbitt, C. R., & Wallace, J. D. (1994, March). *The impact of leadership development on perceptions of the elementary lead science teacher role*. Paper presented at the annual meeting of the National Association for Research in Science Teaching, Anaheim, CA.

Nesbitt, C. R., Wallace, J. D., & Miller, A. C. (1995, April). *A comparison of program coordinators' leadership models in science and mathematics and lead teachers' implementation of those leadership roles in the schools: Is there a match?* Paper presented at the annual meeting of the National Association for Research in Science Teaching, San Francisco, CA.

Price, E. C. (1990, August). *Enhancing the professionalization of teachers through effective leadership training*. Paper presented at the summer workshop of the Association of Teacher Educators, Baltimore, MD.

Sparks, G. M. (1983). Synthesis of research on staff development for effective teaching. *Educational Leadership, 52,* 65–72.

Taylor, R. (1986). *Professional development for teachers of mathematics: A handbook.* Reston, VA: National Council of Teachers of Mathematics.

The Kentucky K–4 Mathematics Specialist Program

William S. Bush
University of Kentucky

Over the past four years, the Kentucky K–4 Mathematics Specialist Program established a network of 435 K–4 mathematics specialists in 143 districts and 25 private schools across Kentucky. In addition to establishing a network, the program's primary goals were to implement the recommendations of the NCTM *Standards* in elementary classrooms across the state and to provide opportunities for collaboration among university faculty, classroom teachers, and school administrators.

In 1990 and 1991, eight regional teams of university mathematics educators, university mathematicians, classroom teachers, and school administrators collectively developed a 45-hour seminar to prepare K–4 teachers as mathematics specialists. In 1991 and 1992, 435 teachers (K–4) attended the seminar at 16 different sites across Kentucky. The seminar immersed teachers in a variety of activities focusing on topics in number, geometry, measurement, and statistics. The seminar helped teachers incorporate problem solving, manipulatives, cooperative groups, technology, and alternative forms of assessment in their mathematics teaching. It also provided the teachers assistance in increasing parental involvement and in conducting workshops for other teachers.

After the seminars, each regional team member was assigned to work with 6-10 mathematics specialists in their geographic areas. The team members and mathematics specialists met monthly during the year following the seminars. At these meetings, team members and mathematics specialists shared successes and concerns in implementing the ideas presented in the seminars. The regional team members also assisted the mathematics specialists in planning and delivering workshops to other teachers in their schools or districts. During the past two years, the network of mathematics specialists has been maintained through regional workshops funded by three state Eisenhower grants.

What We Have Learned

Although the Kentucky K–4 Mathematics Specialist Program had several limitations, it confirmed many ideas its developers had about large-scale teacher enhancement programs. First, the program confirmed the importance of changing teacher attitudes and beliefs about learning, teaching, and mathematics. The program was successful in getting teachers to establish classroom environments in which students learned mathematics by solving problems in cooperative groups. Most participating teachers began to enjoy doing mathematics and became confident in their ability to teach mathematics. As a result of the seminars, teachers broadened their views of mathematics to include geometry, statistics, number sense, and estimation.

Second, the program's use of regional teams comprised of mathematics educators, mathematicians, classroom teachers, and school administrators was highly effective. Bringing these groups together into regional teams to develop and deliver the seminars had two major benefits. The regional team members gained a mutual respect for each other. Mathematicians learned to appreciate the complex task of teaching elementary school. Teachers learned to appreciate the mathematical and pedagogical expertise of the university faculty. The teachers also began to appreciate the depth of mathematics and theoretical perspectives held by the university faculty. In addition, the seminars were strengthened by the input and collaboration of persons with different backgrounds. The activities and information provided in seminars were mathematically sound, pedagogically sound, and classroom tested. The classroom teachers on the regional teams often brought samples of their students' work on seminar activities. This enabled participating teachers to get a better sense of what was possible for their students.

Third, the program, through the network it established, created a voice for elementary mathematics in the state. Elementary teachers began attending and participating in the Kentucky Council of Teachers of Mathematics. They also were asked to join state curriculum and assessment committees focusing on mathematics.

Through some of its shortcomings, the Kentucky K–4 Mathematics Specialist Program also provided its developers much insight into large-scale teacher enhancement. First, the program was not particularly effective in helping elementary teachers develop a sufficient mathematics background to enable students to understand mathematical concepts and to build mathematical connections. Most of the mathematics specialists entered the program with a limited background in mathematics—at most one or two courses in their undergraduate program. They learned some mathematics in the program through their participation in seminar activities and through weekly problem-solving assignments. However, these activities and assignments were not sufficient to provide them the background to understand many mathematical concepts or procedures. In our observations, we noted that teachers performed very well with cooperative groups and technology. Most used a variety of problem solving and exploratory activities in their mathematics lessons. Yet, the lessons were often filled with mathematical misconceptions and errors, and they often lacked mathematical depth. In observed lessons, teachers missed opportunities to challenge students mathematically. On some occasions, students completed activities and were still confused about mathematical concepts and procedures.

Second, not all mathematics specialists' were successful in carrying the program goals and ideas back to their schools or districts. Their success seemed to be based on the following factors:

1. The specialists' willingness to work with other teachers in their district or school
2. The specialists' ability to work with other teachers in their district or school
3. Support from building and central administrators
4. The specialists' approach to professional development

The first two factors listed above should be obvious. Several of our mathematics specialists returned to their classroom and worked on their own teaching. Some were reluctant, and even refused, to work with other teachers. Others, because of personality or political dynamics in the school, had little credibility with other teachers in the school. Often, this lack of credibility was the result of a difference between the mathematics specialists' goals and the other teachers' needs.

Administrators offered substantial support in schools and districts where the mathematics specialists had the greatest impact. It was only on rare occasions when the teachers would meet informally on their own without the knowledge and support of administrators. By and large, workshops and meetings were arranged and supported by building principals or district supervisors.

The K–4 Program could not dictate to schools and districts how the mathematics specialists should be used. However, mathematics specialists invited school administrators to one of the sessions near the end of the seminars. At this session, regional team members provided an overview of the project, including sample activities, and had administrators and mathematics specialists develop action plans for how the mathematics specialists would be used in their school or district.

The nature of the professional development activities also had an impact on the success of the mathematics specialists. Regional team members encouraged the mathematics specialists to establish support groups and conduct workshops. The support groups were much more effective than the workshops. Conducting one or two workshops, as might be expected, helped other teachers become more aware of the NCTM *Standards*. However, they did not have much impact on the classroom practices of the other teachers. Support groups which met regularly to share ideas and concerns seemed to be effective. Only on rare occasions did mathematics specialists visit other classrooms or team teach with other teachers.

Advice for Others

Based on our experiences in the Kentucky K–4 Mathematics Specialist Program, we recommend developers of large-scale teacher enhancement for elementary teachers consider the following guidelines.

1. A program should enable teachers to develop a sufficient pedagogical knowledge in mathematics to establish an environment of inquiry and reflection. This pedagogical knowledge is not easily acquired. Most university mathematics or methods courses do not focus on the mathematics elementary teachers need to understand in order to challenge their students. Possible strategies might be to encourage teachers to establish "communities of learners," whereby teachers study mathematics together. Another strategy would be to have university faculty work as mathematical mentors with groups of teachers.

2. A program should use professional development models which include mentoring, peer coaching, team teaching, and reflection. Professional development activities for teachers must be more sustaining than a series of workshops. Teachers should work with other teachers in classrooms and with students, rather than in isolated inservice workshops.

3. A program should take advantage of the multiple perspectives of mathematics educators, mathematicians, classroom teachers, and school administrators. These multiple perspectives ensure that all participants learn new ideas and approaches. The quality of the professional development is enhanced significantly through the involvement of educators with different backgrounds and perspectives.

4. For sustained change and impact, a program should actively involve school administrators and obtain their commitment to the goals and philosophy of the program. District-wide or school-wide change is more likely when administrators understand and adopt the vision of teachers participating in the program. Administrators need not be involved in all aspects of the program, but their understanding and support is absolutely essential for systemic change.

Suggestions for Evaluation

The evaluation of large-scale teacher enhancement programs is difficult. While it is relatively easy to determine a program's impact on teachers, we found it virtually impossible to determine its direct effect on students. In our program, we assessed changes in teachers beliefs, attitudes, knowledge, and professional growth through writing prompts and surveys. We obtained more specific information about individual teachers by interviewing and observing randomly selected participants. We believe the use of "stories" to be particularly useful in describing the impact of a program. An accumulation of stories from and about participants can provide a means to describe a program's impact.

Project IMPACT:
Increasing the Mathematical Power of All
Children and Teachers

Patricia F. Campbell
University of Maryland at College Park

Josepha Robles
Rolling Terrace Elementary School

Project IMPACT is a collaborative project between the University of Maryland at College Park and Montgomery County Public Schools, Maryland (MCPS). The objective of the project is to design, implement, and evaluate a model for elementary mathematics instruction that will enhance student understanding and support teacher change in predominantly minority schools. The emphasis in Project IMPACT is on mathematical understanding, emphasizing problem solving and concept development. Project IMPACT addresses a constructivist perspective of mathematics learning and focuses on how to promote student and teacher understanding through interaction and collaboration. The intent is for teachers to organize their instruction to build on children's existing knowledge, relating mathematical procedures and curriculum objectives to problem solving. In IMPACT schools, children are to do more than solve mathematics problems, they are to explain how they solved a problem and why they solved a problem in that way. Project IMPACT is not limited to one strand of the MCPS mathematics curriculum; it seeks to support teachers as they attempt change across the entire spectrum of mathematical topics for which they are accountable. Further, Project IMPACT examines equity issues, particularly in terms of access and learning outcomes, as teachers grapple with differentiation, grouping, questioning, expectations, classroom organization and management, and instructional responses.

Where Is Project IMPACT?

Phase One of implementation (1990–93) was limited to the K–3 grades at three schools. Project IMPACT is a school-based model that requires the participating sites to commit the cooperation of all of their mathematics teachers. Three other schools representing similar demographic and academic populations served as the comparable sites for Phase One evaluation purposes. The six schools were selected based on the following criteria: percentage of minority students in the school population; percentage of low socioeconomic families; percentage of low scores on the third-grade statewide mathematics assessment mandated in the state of Maryland; and percentage of students categorized as being "below grade level" on the school district's mathematics assessment as of entry to fourth grade. In the summer of 1993, MCPS and Project IMPACT offered a summer inservice program for those K–3 teachers at the comparable-site schools who wished to participate. Phase Two of Project IMPACT (1993–95) involves fourth- and fifth-grade implementation in the five elementary schools that are associated with the six primary schools involved in Phase One.

What Happens in Project IMPACT?

The IMPACT teacher enhancement model involves (a) a summer inservice program, (b) an on-site mathematics specialist, (c) manipulative materials, and (d) a common grade-level mathematics planning period each week. The summer program addresses the pedagogical content knowledge, the mathematics content knowledge, and the beliefs of the teachers. Topics include (a) adult-level mathematics content, (b) teaching mathematics for understanding, including questioning, use of manipulative materials, and integration of mathematical topics, (c) research on children's learning of mathematics, and (d) teaching mathematics in culturally diverse classrooms. Teachers consider a variety of instructional approaches that support a constructivist perspective of mathematics learning, emphasizing interaction and collaboration rather than limiting instruction to a direct model. The summer program provides time for the teachers to practice instructional strategies with a small group of children and to plan for the coming year. A mathematics specialist is assigned to each participating school to observe and assist teachers as they implement their new approaches with a classroom of children, serving to resolve teachers' concern and to support change throughout the school year.

How Is Project IMPACT Being Evaluated?

Monitoring of Project IMPACT includes classroom observation to determine the degree and character of the implementation and project-developed small-group and individual student mathematics assessments.

What We Have Learned: A School-Based Model

Project IMPACT seeks to implement a school-based teacher enhancement model encompassing all of the mathematics teachers in a building. The assumption behind this model is that the critical unit for change in mathematics instruction and learning is the school. Although students' mathematics instruction occurs in classrooms with individual teachers, our hypothesis is that it will be beneficial to students, teachers, and parents if there is one mathematics program in the school with a common perspective regarding mathematics teaching and learning. Thus Project IMPACT seeks to address school-wide mathematics reform. There is variance in how the teachers within a building approach a "strongly encouraged" inservice effort and even greater variance in the strengths and beliefs that teachers bring to the effort. Nevertheless, IMPACT demonstrates that not only can school-based mathematics reform be implemented, it can yield some results in every classroom and outstanding results in many classrooms. Once teachers are involved in the summer inservice, they generally acknowledge the benefit of having all of the teachers of a given grade working together.

It is our belief that individual teacher change in the IMPACT schools has been facilitated by the involvement of all of the mathematics teachers in the building. Change is not easy; it is demanding, threatening, and risky. Individual teachers in urban schools work in settings that abound with constraining conditions. It may be unreasonable to expect sustained and reflective reform in isolated classrooms across urban settings. It is not unreasonable to address reform in urban schools where teachers and administrators are working together to develop a shared purpose and perspective.

At the conclusion of our five summer programs, we surveyed the teachers to determine if they would have volunteered for Project IMPACT if they had been given an option. Of the 99 respondents, 62 said they would have volunteered, 30 said they would not have volunteered, and 7 teachers did not comment. During the last four summer programs, the teachers were also asked: "How do you think the goals of Project IMPACT would be affected if all teachers of a grade level in a school were not required to participate?" Of the 74 teachers who were surveyed, 62 teachers said the goals of the Project would be negatively influenced, 5 teachers said it would not influence the goals of the Project, and 7 teachers did not respond. Comments included the following:

> *I think that to start, it really provides more support to have everyone doing it. I think it would be hard to stick to it if a teacher felt pressure from other teachers or parents to abandon IMPACT ways. I really think that it has to be strongly school supported by the whole school!*

> *I think it would lose a lot of 'IMPACT!' Let's face it. The hidden agenda of team teaching with style/age differences merging for edification and cooperation has many benefits for each teacher and for the team rapport.*

> *I really think it would make implementation difficult. If all students are not included it could be a nightmare in terms of parents' attitudes. Some may feel their child is being excluded because of intellectual ability or included because of some lack of ability.*

> *I believe the goals of IMPACT would be less effectively met if teachers self-selected into the program.... While rewarding on some levels, preaching to the converted does not affect broad change.*

> *I don't think it would be as successful because it might allow people to work at cross purposes rather than toward a collective goal in math instruction.*

Mathematics Teacher Specialists

A critical component of Project IMPACT's teacher enhancement model is the assignment of a mathematics specialist to each school. Specialists assist teachers in their efforts to implement new approaches in the classroom. When asked to delineate their role, IMPACT specialists noted that they assisted teachers in making connections between mathematical topics and between mathematics and other disciplines, creating "non-contrived" problems that were meaningful to the culture of the classroom and addressed critical mathematical objectives, developing questioning and wait time, responding to incorrect answers and fostering involvement and growth among all children, supporting reflection regarding instruction and student needs, learning how to share with colleagues and how to support colleagues, and communicating with parents and the principal.

The teachers are adamant in their belief that the specialist is crucial. In reality, what is critical is some mechanism to support change, to foster implementation, to promote reflection, to applaud efforts, and to challenge further growth. In Project IMPACT, that mechanism happens to be the specialist. The common weekly planning period also encourages reflection and supports professional interaction, but without a "leader," these planning periods can easily become stressful and potentially divisive.

To illustrate the importance of a continuing support mechanism, consider the following. In 1991, three teachers from Atlanta, Georgia, participated in IMPACT's summer program, but there was no accompanying mathematics specialist. Thus, this site was viewed as a pilot of how well the IMPACT summer enhancement would succeed without follow-up support. Unfortunately, analysis of this pilot revealed that implementation simply did not occur. The most stunning indication of inertia at this site, as opposed to change, occurred in February, 1992. Project IMPACT sent one of its staff to Atlanta to visit the school, to observe instruction, and to interact with the three teachers. Teacher directed, procedurally focused, "model and practice" instruction was observed as opposed to any activity-based or problem-solving student investigation. When the IMPACT staff member inquired as to the location of the manipulatives, because none were evident in the classrooms, she was taken to a closet where the entire shipment of manipulative materials was stored, still sealed in its original packaging!

Content and Research versus Distributed Activities

Project IMPACT's summer program addresses the mathematical and pedagogical knowledge of the teachers. Teachers are taught adult-level mathematics with instructors modeling the approaches that are being suggested for use in their classrooms. This not only serves to address the mathematical knowledge of the teachers, it also serves to convince them that one can indeed learn mathematics in this fashion. Project IMPACT also interprets research addressing children's learning of mathematical topics that are critical to a given grade level. This serves to foster and support teachers' instructional decision making. Both of these components are critical.

Project IMPACT does not provide teachers with "ready-to-use" activities for the classroom. During our first summer program, the Project provided only a minimal number of sample activities. During our second year, the Project provided many activities. The differences in implementation during these two academic years were stunning. None of the teachers who participated in the first summer program expected IMPACT to provide them with daily activities. They expected to reflect on the needs of their children and to work with their team and their specialist to determine what activities, problems, or resources they should access. During the second year, many of the teachers returned to their specialists, noted that they had used some activity from the summer, and asked, "What should I do now?" It was as if these teachers viewed their responsibility as being limited to delivering a prepackaged lesson. As a result, Project IMPACT no longer provides a collection of "approved tasks" to teachers.

Instead, three approaches are utilized in the summer teacher enhancement program. One scheme is to make time available to examine and discuss examples of commercial materials that address mathematical topics appropriate for children. The second venue is to offer examples of activities or tasks, but always with another purpose in mind. For example, a problem may be offered as an illustration of how one could facilitate a child's re-examination of a mathematical construct. In another setting, a task may be presented, and the teachers may be asked to write questions that they could ask to determine what mathematical ideas the children were constructing as they completed that task. A third approach is to follow an adult-level mathematics session with the challenge to the teachers to define a task that would address that same mathematical topic at a level appropriate for their students. Thus, the teachers leave the summer program with a collection of appropriate problems and activities as well as with knowledge of commercial materials, but they leave with the perspective that, with their team and with their specialist, they can make decisions and determine needed tasks.

Lastly, Project IMPACT has learned that no one outside of the classroom can demand that a teacher change. What can be done is to communicate an expectation of change, to consistently encourage change, and to provide teachers with support and interaction to foster the construction of the knowledge that they will need in order to change. It is also crucial to expect each teacher to define how he or she will attempt change and then to create a setting that supports that change.

Fostering Large-Scale Teacher Change Across Diverse Settings

If the profession is serious about the need to address instructional reform across the nation, it is critical that we stop relying on volunteer teacher enhancement. Further, it is necessary to recognize that for teachers to change the way they teach is a risk, and ultimately it is a risk taken by each individual teacher. There is much that we do not know about how instructional change will play out in the classroom; the truth is we will never know every aspect of what a teacher will face because it is a product of the culture of each classroom. We must admit this to teachers. But we must also admit that current practice is not sufficient, that children are being limited, that more can be accomplished, and that individual teachers will not be left alone to accomplish it. It is easier to attempt change in an atmosphere of support; it is easier to succeed when people work together for a common goal relevant to their needs.

To involve each teacher requires advance planning. It is very difficult for teachers to understand and attempt change through after-school and Saturday sessions, unless those teachers are self-motivated. In a non-volunteer program, all teachers are not self-motivated. Therefore, Project IMPACT uses a summer inservice program to introduce the mechanisms of change. Further, IMPACT's experience is that teachers should attend grade-specific summer sessions. In this way the summer program is viewed as being more relevant to the needs of the teachers. If teachers know of the summer program by the preceding February and know that this will be the mathematics program of their grade, then teachers will agree to come. Our experience has been that very few teachers leave a building to avoid the inservice. Quite the contrary, teachers will view the summer inservice with either acceptance or eagerness.

A teacher enhancement program must have a vehicle for on-site support during initial implementation. The journal entries of the IMPACT specialists indicate that teacher change is a very slow process, quite susceptible to outside personal pressures, individual fears, and school climate. Teachers vary in their pedagogical experience and in their mathematical expertise. Some teachers are self-actualizing and goal oriented, while other teachers are passive or complacent. School-based implementation must address the challenge of these variables as they are manifested in individual teachers, coupled with the personal feelings of doubt, anxiety, insecurity, and loss that individual change triggers. In addition, it must be recognized that as individual teachers struggle with these personal challenges, each teacher is also struggling to inform and define that school's grade-level mathematics program, as that teacher reflects on personal classroom practice. At the same time, teachers are expected to defend their "as-yet-emerging" perspective to parents and administrators. Instructional change is demanding and threatening during initial implementation. Continued classroom support is critical.

Despite the intensity of the challenge present in urban schools, the potential for substantial teacher change is quite real, and the implications for student learning are quite remarkable. At the conclusion of the summer inservice program, each Project IMPACT teacher is asked to clarify exactly what aspect of teaching he or she intends to initially address. That is, our approach is to ask each teacher what aspect of instructional change that teacher will initially attempt to modify. In consultation with a school specialist, each teacher then begins to consider how to approach that goal. Once a teacher is able to effect some level of modification towards that self-determined goal, with an accompanying positive response from the students, the promise for continued teacher change is activated. As teachers see children in their classrooms truly engaged in figuring out how to address a mathematical problem and as teachers recognize that their students are indeed learning, the teachers become more willing to try again and to gradually address additional goals. Instructional change can happen in urban classrooms.

Monitoring and Evaluating Teacher and Student Change

It is critical that both teacher change and student change be monitored. Classroom observation to support individual needs and to foster individual change is not abhorrent to teachers. If supervisory classroom observation standards do not create dissonance with the proposed vision of instructional change and if supervisors are cognizant of an individual teacher's growth, then supervisory observation can actually support change. In those Project IMPACT schools where the atmosphere can be characterized as "the teachers and the principal are in this together," the phenomenon of change is in fact catalyzed. Student assessments provide a mechanism to address and to inform instruction. However, the assessment used to monitor student change must correspond to the vision of instruction being promoted. Neither teachers nor students can tolerate being in a position where the standards for instruction and the standards for characterizing students' mathematical success in the classroom do not mirror the accountability device.

Talking Mathematics: Supporting Discourse in Elementary School Classrooms

Rebecca B. Corwin
TERC

Talking Mathematics is a teacher enhancement project developed to look at ways of supporting mathematical discourse in elementary school classrooms by developing resources designed to support school-based staff developers in conducting inservice seminars. Our inquiry has focused on understanding some of the ways teachers have changed their pedagogy as they deepen their own mathematical knowledge.

Most discourse in elementary school mathematics focuses on individual students supplying the right answer, but there are alternatives—learners comparing strategies, generating conjectures, and challenging each others' mathematical ideas. Because few elementary school teachers have experienced good mathematical talk themselves, our project developed a context that encourages such discourse. We began with the assumption that doing mathematics together in a responsive group creates a safe professional community in which to explore issues and raise questions about both mathematics and pedagogy.

The first group of twelve participating teachers were selected in 1990, half from Boston Public Schools and half from other local systems. They participated in seminars through June, 1993. The second group, with the same school representations as the first, worked with the project for one calendar year.

The first group participated in a three-week seminar conducted by TERC staff with a consulting mathematician. They did mathematics for themselves and discussed related pedagogical issues as they were raised. In the following three years these teachers participated in bi-weekly seminars, doing and discussing mathematics, viewing videotapes of their mathematics classes, and discussing classroom practice. Videotapes of their classrooms were used to focus seminar discussions on pedagogy and to support the exploration of project research questions.

To pilot the materials being considered for staff developers (the Resource Package), 24 teachers were selected to participate in a two-week seminar in the summer of 1992. These teachers also did mathematics, discussed selected reading, observed classroom videos, and reflected on their own practice.

The Staff Developers' Resource Package

Building knowledge gained from working with the Talking Mathematics teachers we are now developing a unique package of resources for staff developers, that empower teachers as *doers* and *teachers* of mathematics. This collection includes 8 videotapes, a staff developers' manual, and a classroom teacher's book, all designed to help group leaders extend and enhance teachers' classroom practice. Key players in school-based staff development work (including mathematics coordinators, inservice educators, university faculty, and teacher/leaders) need resources—"the stuff" of teacher development experiences for site-based teacher programs that support a new culture of classroom mathematics and a model or framework to help staff developers think about long-term teacher enhancement in elementary mathematics. To meet this need, the Talking Mathematics staff has developed a resource package for staff developers that will be commercially published; it contains the following:

1. videotapes of real-life mathematics teaching designed to illustrate a wide range of the classroom talk including discussion questions
2. a manual that helps discussion leaders plan their seminars
3. readings and related discussion topics for seminar leaders
4. selection of mathematics problems that have engaged teachers' interest

What We Have Learned

We are now confident that doing mathematics and reflecting on it make a major contribution to a paradigm shift for many teachers in a long-term staff development program. Shifting the focus from their teaching helps some teachers pursue their own mathematical identities. Subsequently they develop more mathematical confidence.

Some of the principles we have learned in conducting these seminars may be useful to large-scale teacher projects. Others may be less relevant. Some consideration of the following ideas is essential to planning an effective long-term staff development program:

1. *An effective staff development program takes place over a long time.* Meeting biweekly during the follow-up years was essential to sustaining individual teachers as they investigated discourse in their classrooms. The meetings sustained mathematical community and gave participants an opportunity to reflect on their practice Even the group that participated for one year was strongly impacted, and many members sought mechanisms for continuing their work (Schifter and Russell's project, Teaching to the Big Ideas, was one of those mechanisms).

2. *Effective staff development encourages an atmosphere of inquiry.* Just as we need literate teachers—teachers who love to read, who enjoy the quirks of language, who write to communicate a variety of ideas, we need numerate teachers who enjoy finding patterns and exploring relationships—teachers who are open to the rhythms and balances of spatial and numerical relationships, interested in questions of "what if" in mathematics. Keeping an exploratory frame of mind alive in staff development experiences is essential if we want teachers to replicate that mindset in their classrooms. A challenge for large programs, it is still necessary to find ways of retaining tentativeness, serendipity, and spontaneity.

3. *Doing mathematics is engaging for many teachers.* Many teacher enhancement programs have a skills-oriented emphasis. Teachers learn to teach using manipulative materials; they learn to teach a specific curriculum; they develop particular skills in assessing children's mathematical knowledge. What they do not do is explore adult mathematics, strengthen their appreciation of mathematical processes, and develop their abilities to understand and pose mathematical questions. In short, they have not done enough mathematics to develop their mathematical identities.

Richly textured mathematics problems lend themselves to complex, multi-layered investigations, and we recommend that long-term teacher seminars engage teachers in doing mathematical investigations. Too often in inservice meetings teachers' own mathematics is not being enhanced because the mathematics in teacher enhancement seminars is done *for the children.* When teachers know that their seminar will continue for a long time, it is easier for them to let go and do their own mathematics; with a long time-frame they assume that there will ultimately be classroom relevance so they can relax and engage in mathematical work on a personal as well as professional level. Ultimately, they can even begin to pose their own mathematical questions. Large-scale programs will have to work hard to put in place ongoing school-based seminars that maintain a focus on inquiry into practice alongside inquiry into mathematics.

4. *Focusing on pedagogy can be done through a variety of frameworks.* A new idea (e.g., children's thinking, data analysis, implementing a new curriculum) is engaging for many teachers, perhaps because fewer preconceptions allow freer thinking about strategies to engage children. We chose to emphasize ways of supporting discourse in pedagogical discussions—a new focus for many teachers.

To move participants beyond the level of bromides ("they need concrete experiences;" "all children need to feel accepted;" "it's important to individualize"), there must be shared images of instruction. The necessity of grounding talk in shared ideas and images was clear to us. We found four strategies:

a. participants' mathematical experiences in the seminar
b. videotaped classroom episodes
c. cases teachers wrote about dilemmas in their own teaching
d. selected readings about practice

Videotapes of participants' classrooms seemed to us especially salient. The role of videotapes as objects to thing *with* is very similar to the role of mathematics problems as objects to think *about*. Just as materials or diagrams model a problem in mathematics, set constraints, and provide grounding for discourse, videotapes model moments in teaching, set constraints, and provide grounds for discussion.

5. *Community supports risk-taking and reflection.* Through interviews before, during, and after the project it is clear that teachers valued their teaching community. The creation of community is an essential part of any long-term teacher enhancement plan and should be the centerpiece of the program at the start. The creation of community translates to participants' classrooms in a variety of ways and is a palpable dividend of doing mathematics together. Creating mathematical community is a challenge for large-scale programs, but we believe that with care, school-based communities can be formed.

6. *Teacher development is complex, often uneven, and seldom unidimensional.* As we analyzed data, we saw that change happened differently for different individuals. Slow, incremental change was typical of some participants; spurts of growth and change more common for others. Some teachers' behaviors changed first in their classrooms; for some the changes emerged in the seminars. Beliefs changed slowly for many and surprisingly quickly for some; connections between beliefs and practice seemed different for each teacher, and characterizing those connections is complicated. To date we have not seen evidence of teachers following one developmental route,

although all are growing. We are confident that at this point in their careers these experienced teachers are adapting mathematical and pedagogical ideas to their own teaching.

There are many contributors to the pace and direction of teachers' pedagogical growth. Their views of mathematics and teaching are likely affected by their personal and career development, past experiences with mathematics, and other events and priorities in their lives. Teachers appropriate mathematical and pedagogical ideas along many personal, mathematical, and pedagogical dimensions. This may make large-scale program monitoring very difficult.

7. *There are plateaus in teachers' pedagogical growth.* Once teachers find that they can successfully do mathematics and thus feel empowered, many look for a place to start to shift practice. Some of our participants began by looking for questions to ask their students. A few selected one question and stayed with it for a very long time. ("Why do you think so?" or "Why does it make that pattern?" were favorites of some participants.) Others accepted every method or solution strategy as equally worthy. They did not find ways to help students compare and evaluate strategies, seeming so excited to have their students do and talk about real mathematics that they did not hone, refine, or compare students' ideas and methods. (We called this the "I'm OK, you're OK" technique.)

Although each of these approaches is irritating and problematic, they nevertheless reflect the awareness that mathematics is a human endeavor in which everyone can participate. Large-scale staff development programs need to address these issues in mathematically-sound ways; we anticipate that the sensitivity to deal with developmental challenges is not likely to be a feature of staff development programs that are geared toward prescribed measurable change.

Concerns about Planning for Large-Scale Change

1. *Staff developers need support materials, community, and time for reflection in the same way that teacher-participants do.* As a profession we need to provide a variety of entry points for reinventing practice—no particular way will work for every teacher and every staff developer. We have to allow significant time for staff developers to engage in their own mathematical activity and reflect on their work if we expect them to help teachers reinvent their practice. As professionals we need to resist the "quick fix" solution, whether it is a few months or a few workshops in length. We need to cultivate habits of inquiry and

reflection at all levels of the profession. When considering large-scale programs we must think about how we train staff developers so that we get a multiplier effect rather than the distortions we encounter in the children's game of "telephone."

2. *The process of change is difficult and may not fit a timetable.* In order to make any difference in schools, our approach must be to provide strong support for school-based teacher enhancement efforts that are flexible enough to be truly owned by the leaders and teachers involved. We cannot expect all teachers in a district or a school to "change" because of outside pressures; rather we should look for ways to attract the growing edge of many different teachers.

We advocate a delicate mix of *doing* mathematics and *reflecting* on practice; few resources exist to help in this task. Expecting teacher educators to create the experiences and resources they need as they work with teachers is unrealistic.

3. *There are problems as we think about large-scale programs.* Teachers are grateful for the respect, interest, and challenge of a program that supports their development as mathematicians and as teachers. It is not clear that these elements can be mass-produced. Staff developers vary along many of the same dimensions as the teachers they work with: It may or may not be a good year to change; it may be a year for this individual to hunker down and tend to business rather than stretch to meet new challenges.

From our work with teachers we find a growing need to know more about what compels teachers to change their pedagogy. What images are catalysts for teachers' professional growth? What is the right impetus for the second-grade teachers with twenty-five years' classroom experience? What experiences convince the fifth-year sixth-grade teacher that he is not teaching mathematics as he would like? We need to know more about teachers' growing edges.

4. *Assessment and rich description of teacher change would provide some guidelines for future program development.* If we could identify the images of practice a teacher is drawn to and the source of that image, we might understand the complexity of teacher change and development. Conducting longitudinal studies of teachers who are just introduced to enhancement programs might help us identify the images of practice associated with their professional growth. A constructivist view of professional growth and pedagogical content knowledge needs to be developed, with all its complexity and contradiction.

Cognitively Guided Instruction (CGI)

Elizabeth Fennema and Thomas P. Carpenter
University of Wisconsin–Madison

Megan L. Franke
University of California–Los Angeles

How Cognitively Guided Instruction (CGI) Works

For the last 10 years, we have been investigating the impact of a staff development program focused on helping primary teachers to understand their children's mathematical thinking. Our modus operandi has been to help teachers gain an understanding of children's thinking by having them construct relationships between an explicit research-based model of children's thinking and their own children's thinking. We have encouraged and supported teachers as they have used the research-based model to develop their own understanding of their children's thinking and decided how to use this understanding during instruction. We have studied how the program affected teachers' knowledge and beliefs, their instruction, and their children's learning.

Our research-based model starts with precise definitions of content domains and relates these definitions to solution strategies that young children typically use to solve problems within the domains. The model is robust in that most young children use the solution strategies and they are readily observed by teachers. Thus, teachers establish the validity of the model and modify it as they assess their own children's thinking. In other words, this knowledge enables teachers to find out what their own children know and understand about mathematics. (See Carpenter, Fennema, & Franke, 1996, for a complete discussion of our research-based model.)

Consistent with our model of children's thinking, we recognize that teachers construct their own understandings of children's thinking, and we do not presume that teachers simply assimilate the research-based model. We believe, and our research has confirmed, that teachers approach CGI workshops with a great deal of informal, although somewhat unfocused, knowledge about children's mathematical thinking that is similar to our analysis. The goal of our work with teachers is to help them to focus and build on this initial knowledge.

The emphasis throughout all workshops is on helping teachers develop principled understanding of children's thinking and to explore how to use this knowledge in instruction. We structure the workshops so that participants do activities which enable them to consider the research-based model in relationship to children. Together with us, they view video tapes of children solving problems and identify relationships between the solution strategies and the problem types. We examine how the solution strategies they see can be used to predict how other problems can be solved. We suggest ways they could interact with their own students so that the students' thinking became visible.

The workshops' environment is arranged so that teachers engage in discussions about children's thinking and how their own children's thinking can inform their instructional decisions. We provide written materials which explicate the research-based model, and provide workshop time for reflection and discussion of how the readings relate to their own children's thinking.

We do not suggest explicitly how classes should be organized for instruction, but we do share some examples which the teachers are able to adapt for their own use. Experienced teachers assist in some of the workshops by responding to teachers' questions and concerns about how their classrooms are organized and how they use children's thinking. We do not provide the teachers with materials that they can use to instruct children, although they sometimes collaborate among themselves to create problems which children can be asked to solve. We do not tell them that they should or should not use a textbook or any other instructional materials.

What Have We Learned?

From 1985 to 1989, we investigated how learning about children's thinking in addition and subtraction influenced first grade teachers' instruction, beliefs, and the learning of their children. We reported (Carpenter & Fennema, 1992) that experimental teachers who had been in CGI workshops spent more time having children solve problems, expected multiple solution strategies from their children, and listened to their children more than did control teachers. We also reported positive relationships between students' learning, their teachers' beliefs, and their teachers' knowledge about their own students' thinking. We described an expert teacher using this knowledge to make instructional decisions and reported how another teacher learned to use it to fundamentally change her classroom instruction to include many of the components of classrooms envisioned in the reform movement.

From 1989 to 1993, we investigated how learning about children's thinking in whole number arithmetic influenced teachers in grades 1–3 to change their beliefs and instruction and what impact this change had on their children's learning. During the study, 18 of the 21 teachers' instruction changed so that their children spent more time solving problems and discussing their thinking. The beliefs of 18 teachers also changed so that they believed more strongly that children can and should solve problems without direct instruction. For every teacher for whom four years of data were available, class achievement in concepts and problem solving was higher at the end of the study than it was before the workshops. For most teachers, a shift in emphasis from drill on procedures to problem solving did not lead to a deterioration in traditional computational skill (Fennema, Carpenter, Franke, Levi, Jacobs, & Empson, 1996). We also investigated and confirmed the value of CGI with African-American children and their teachers (Carey, Fennema, Carpenter, & Franke, 1995), and the use of CGI in pre-service education of elementary teachers (Vacc & Bright, 1994).

Advice to Those Planning Large-Scale Teacher Change

CGI has proved to be very successful with teachers and their children and some of our findings which are applicable to large-scale teacher change are as follows:

1. Knowledge of their own children's thinking enables teachers to make instructional decisions so that children's learning of mathematics improves. Learning the explicit research-based model of children's thinking that we used will make a significant contribution to teachers' being able to understand their own children's thinking in mathematics so that they become increasingly able to build instruction on children's knowledge and to structure their teaching around authentic problem solving.

2. Learning to find out what children know about mathematics and to use that knowledge to make instructional decisions is not simple. It takes time for teachers to come to believe that they should consider children's thinking and to learn how to do it. Follow-up workshops and support for teachers which includes time for discussion and reflection are critical.

3. There is wide variation among teachers in believing in the importance of children's thinking and learning to use children's thinking in ongoing classroom activities.

4. Teachers more readily change their instruction when they can see that an innovation is beneficial for themselves and their children.

5. Teachers themselves become change agents when they see that innovations result in better learning for their children.

References

Carey, D. A., Fennema, E., Carpenter, T. P., & Franke, M. L. (1995). Equity and mathematics education. In W. S. Secada, E. Fennema, & L. B. Adajian, (Eds.), *New directions in equity for mathematics education* (pp. 93–125). New York: Teachers College Press.

Carpenter, T. P., & Fennema, E. (1992). Cognitively guided instruction: Building on the knowledge of students and teachers. *International Journal of Educational Research, 17*(5), 457–70.

Carpenter, T. P., Fennema, E., & Franke, M. L. (1996). Cognitively guided instruction: A knowledge base for reform in primary mathematics instruction. Submitted for publication to *Elementary School Journal.*

Fennema, E., Carpenter, T. P., Franke, M. L., Levi, L., Jacobs, V., & Empson, S. (1996). Mathematics instruction and teachers' beliefs: A longitudinal study of using children's thinking. *Journal of Research in Mathematics Education, 27,* 403–34.

Vacc, N. N., & Bright, G. W. (1994). Changing preservice teacher-education programs. In D. B. Aichele & A. F. Coxford (Eds.), *Professional development of teachers* (pp. 116–27). Reston, VA: National Council of Teachers of Mathematics.

Teach-Stat: A Key to Better Mathematics

Susan N. Friel
University of North Carolina at Chapel Hill

Mary Lee Danielson, Statistics Educator
Chapel Hill Public Schools

This project combined a large-scale implementation plan with a plan for research and evaluation in statistics education to address teacher education needs in statistics for elementary teachers. The overall goal was to develop and implement a comprehensive program to teach and to research the teaching and learning of statistics in the elementary grades (1–6) throughout the state of North Carolina. Three major aspects of this goal are as follows:

1. Developing a statistics professional development curriculum designed for inservice education of elementary teachers
2. Assisting elementary teachers in using the teaching of statistics as an organizing framework for the elementary mathematics curriculum and as a tool for integrating mathematics with other disciplines, particularly science and social studies
3. Preparing over 80 *Teach-Stat* participants as Statistics Educators to provide professional development in statistics for elementary teachers across the state

This project involved nine sites that are part of the UNC Mathematics and Science Education Network (MSEN). Each of the nine MSEN Center Directors oversaw the project in terms of coordination and logistics. In addition, there were eleven faculty involved: one from each of seven sites and two from each of two sites. These faculty were responsible for the planning and implementation of the program. Two Research/Evaluation Coordinators met on a regular basis to plan the research and evaluation program.

We developed and implemented a program of professional development for elementary teachers. We also developed and implemented a staff development program to prepare approximately 80 Statistics Educators to serve as resource persons who can offer the original *Teach-Stat* professional development program to other elementary teachers across the state. Our products (outside the human element—approximately 480 teachers over three years) are a fairly complete set of materials that will permit others to replicate our program of professional development and implementation.

1. *Teach-Stat for Teachers: Professional Development Manual* (Friel & Joyner, 1997). Provides a "how to" discussion for planning and implementing a three-week teacher education institute. It is written in a way that addresses *teachers'* needs for in-service education, and its audience is mainly those who provide professional development programs for elementary-grades teachers.

2. *Teach-Stat for Statistics Educators: Staff Developers' Manual.* (Gleason, Vesilind, Friel, & Joyner, 1996) Provides a "how to" discussion for planning and implementing a one-week Statistics Educators Institute. This institute is designed for teachers who will serve as staff development resource people (statistics educators), who have participated in a three-week program in statistics education and have previously taught statistics to students.

3. *Teach-Stat for Students: Investigations for the Classroom 1–3* and *Teach-Stat for Students: Investigations for the Classroom 3–6* (Joyner, Pfieffer, Friel, & Vesilind, 1997a, 1997b) Provides "how to" discussions of the planning and implementation of activities for elementary-grades students that promote the learning of statistics using the process of statistical investigation. The activities are designed to provide a variety of "investigation starters;" many were developed by and used in the classrooms of teachers in the *Teach-Stat* project.

What Have We Learned?

Exploring statistics as a content area and using the process of statistical investigation appear to work as a catalyst for helping teachers think about new ways for teaching and learning. The process of statistical investigation is centered in inquiry. Student explorations more often than not do not have "right answers;" opinions supported by evidence are valued. Critical thinking and discussion are seen as essential, and a teacher's focus is on the use of "questioning strategies" that provoke students' involvement. Teachers quickly find many ways in which connections among content areas can be made through the use of the *process* of statistical investigation. Indeed, one way to think about interdisciplinary teaching is by identifying interdisciplinary processes as organizing themes. The content of statistics is not perceived as an "add on" to an already crowded curriculum because of its potential for integration. In addition, statistics is a topic that is engaging and accessible to all students. Teachers don't have preconceived notions of what students can/can't do and, often, are surprised by what occurs. Very possibly, teaching teachers to implement a statistics education program with their students provides a first manageable step in promoting inquiry (constructivist) teaching.

What Advice Can We Give?

The project was designed so that, during the first year, each of the nine faculty who were providing the professional development program selected 6–7 teachers from their site as a pilot team; the three-week institute was offered as a residential program at a central site. The faculty worked in teams of three and were responsible for various parts of the program. All faculty and teachers (57 teachers) participated together in this institute. Each faculty member met with and visited his/her regional teacher team throughout the following school year, jointly exploring with the teachers what it meant for them to teach statistics and integrate statistics with other subject areas.

In the second year, each of the nine sites offered a revised version (non-residential) of the three-week professional development program to 24 teachers in each of their regions. The faculty member and the pilot team of six or seven teachers worked together to plan and deliver the workshop. This was somewhat serendipitous! Originally, the teachers were going to be available to help *but not to teach.* However, by the second summer, faculty and teachers had developed such a good working relationship that the model of a "professional development team" naturally emerged and was very successful. The second-year participants were able to hear from teachers who had spent the year implementing the program and had lots of actual examples to show them. The first-year teachers received a great deal of support, informal "how-to-be-a-staff-developer training," and coaching/ mentoring from their respective faculty leaders.

Project staff noted that the experiences of the first-year teachers with their respective site faculty leaders appeared to be quite powerful for all involved. These experiences included participating in the first *Teach-Stat* institute, teaching with their students during the 1992-93 school year, and participating as part of a professional development team (summer 1993) in conducting the second-year regional institutes. In order to try to capture summary impressions and reflections of these experiences, hour-long phone interviews were conducted in fall 1993 with 20 of the first-year teachers. A number of topics were addressed in these interviews, one being a discussion of their involvement in providing professional development for their peers during the second summer; at all sites "professional development teams" emerged as a model used. Stone (1995) characterizes some of the teachers' views about these experiences in her summary of major themes from the interviews:

> Mrs. Robinson [a teacher] relays an insightful anecdote about the team's workings and teacher relationships with the university professor. She is, Robinson reveals, a kind of advisor that the teachers look to for leadership. But, this advisor also learned during the institute.
> *She told us that she was so nervous about turning us loose to let us do this workshop because she wanted it to go well. But she said, after the first days, 'I am not nervous anymore—you guys are doing great.'*
> This experience was a first for Ms. Baker. And "it was a wonderful workshop." Part of the reason was the leadership of her team's professor who helped allay initial fears of teaching adults. The team met a couple of times in the spring for pre-planning and then met specifically to assign and plan lessons. What was interesting for Baker was that adults did have a different knowledge base than children, of course, but that one uses "the same strategies, just at a different level."
> This support was particularly evident during the second summer workshop when the team taught peers *Teach-Stat* for the first time. Some members like Mrs. Bates had conduced workshops in the past; other had not. This is how Bates puts this:
> *We were very supportive of each other. We stayed right in the room ... but not in an obvious way. Because we didn't want any one of us to look less professional than anyone else.... We were very careful of each other's feelings yet at the same time, very, very professional.*
> Part of this professionalism also was careful preparation of the workshop lessons: being prepared to do one's own lessons and knowing that others were doing as well. Finally Bates emphasizes two team elements. One is the idea that teachers never "talk down" when teaching—a model they appropriated from the Meredith College experience [the first-year institute in which they participated]. A second, significantly, is the relationship of the team's teachers to their "leader." She had

become, it is explained, a kind of equal partner in *Teach-Stat* activities.

Ms. Peterson says that the team members were personally selected by the professor who "did an excellent job getting a group of people who are the same and very different." Some are organizers, some are creative, some are perfectionists, some are not. Her job, as she sees it, is to add "creative spunk;" others present very well or demonstrate materials beautifully. And, they work so well together.

Project staff characterized this model simplistically as "take the course, apprentice teach the course with a "master" experienced instructor, teach the course." Collins, Brown, and Newman (1989) note that before schools appeared, apprenticeship was the most common means of learning and was used to transmit the knowledge required for expert practice (p. 453). Apprentices learn expert practice through participation in a process of observations/modeling, coaching, and fading.

In looking at the earlier teacher comments we can see the apprenticeship model in operation. The observation/modeling component of this process is noted as a reference to the "Meredith College experience." Indeed, as the faculty participated together in the first-year professional development program (held at Meredith College), the notion of "modeling a process of teaching" was consciously addressed. When the teachers joined with the faculty leaders at each site in the second-year professional development program, they were given numerous opportunities to teach their peers. Several of the teacher comments point to the coaching role provided by the site faculty leaders. In addition, they highlight the important coaching role of their teammates during the workshops; further comments about the roles of teammates suggest that these teachers also functioned as models (sometimes successful and sometimes not so successful) for each other. Finally, faculty assumed the "fading" role, allowing the teachers to take on differing levels of responsibility and control during the workshops based on their readiness (which the teachers identified for themselves) to do so.

The benefit of a structure like MSEN is that it provides access to the state's school systems and assists in maintaining a consistent level of quality in the professional development programs it provides. However, North Carolina still lacks the capacity to provide high quality opportunities for the majority of elementary teachers to deepen their subject matter knowledge and to continuously examine and modify their teaching practice. The *Teach-Stat* project sought to address the "capacity question" not only by providing professional development for a large number of teachers on a regional basis but, more importantly, by developing teachers (statistics educators) who can work with other elementary teachers in support of their learning statistics and about how to teach statistics and teach using statistics.

The final teams of statistics educators varied in composition; some teams included only first-year teachers, some included a balance of first- and second-year teachers, and some included a few or no first-year teachers with the preponderance of second-year teachers. They were selected based on their interest *and* on their potential ability to provide professional development to their peers. In cases where first- and second-year teachers were balanced, we found that teaming of a first-year teacher with a second-year teacher created a mentor/coach arrangement that seemed to support the second-year teachers in their initial experiences teaching other teachers. It was assumed that, in most cases, these teachers would work in teams of two statistics educators to provide such experiences for other teachers once they "graduated" as statistics educators.

Teachers selected for this opportunity participated in an additional week's professional development program that helped them explore staff development issues and ways to conduct a workshop. The Statistics Educators Institutes included content on adult learning, the change process, and statistics pedagogical content knowledge. Statistics educators completed 3–4 days of work prior to the *Teach-Stat* workshop they taught for third-year teachers; the remainder of the work was done as part of a "looking back" effort to reflect on what happened during the workshop.

As part of their participation, approximately half the statistics educators participated in a study (Frost, 1995) to investigate the effects of classroom teachers becoming *Teach-Stat* workshop leaders. They responded to three different instruments, and some also participated in interviews. These were completed at three points in time: at the beginning and again at the end of the Statistics Educators Institute and after teaching the third-year *Teach-Stat* summer workshops.

This study is rich with information. For purposes here, the results suggest that staff development designs built upon teachers becoming workshop leaders should provide special assistance to help teachers develop in this role over time.

1. Opportunities to develop and/or demonstrate strong content knowledge in mathematics before becoming a workshop leader should be an important consideration in staff development.

2. Teachers' classroom experiences are valuable assets to their work as workshop leaders. Classroom experiences using teaching activities like those presented in workshops provide the workshop leader with "personal memory tapes" of the practical, as well as the pedagogical, issues related to the activities.

3. Teachers who become workshop leaders may need specialized assistance in conceptualizing effective staff development. The study suggests that workshop leaders progress through stages of growth in their conceptions about effective staff development; such stages can be used as "benchmarks" to assess readiness or potential of the teacher to serve as a workshop leader.

4. Teachers who become workshop leaders need opportunities to develop their own understanding of the nature of adult learners and of creating a climate conducive for adult learning. Further, there is a need to help workshop leaders explore pedagogical content knowledge related to teaching adults.

What Can We Say about Evaluation?

We used a variety of assessment and evaluation strategies. First, we developed and administered (several times) a statistics content test to first-year and second-year teachers. The test was developed prior to the professional development curriculum and was not modified. The greatest change in performance occurred from before to after the workshop. We believe that teachers' knowledge about statistics continued to change in subtle ways, but our content instrument failed to provide us with needed insights. A later phone interview survey of a selected number of first-year teachers revealed information about their use of statistics with students, but it failed to clarify their developing statistical knowledge. A few select and quick visits to Statistics Educators classrooms have raised our awareness that we can tell much about a teacher's understandings of content when we watch her/him teach; however, this was not a strategy implemented in this project's evaluation plan.

Second, we developed and administered (several times) a pedagogy survey to first-year and second-year teachers. The survey was developed prior to the professional development curriculum and was not modified. We saw teachers change from a somewhat fragmented and narrow view of what teaching statistics is all about to a view of teaching statistics as involving a process of statistical investigation and linking topics like measures of center and representations of data. The instrument we used did not provide insights into actual classroom behaviors. Through self-report and faculty visits we have a sense that teachers feel they have made major changes in how they teach, believing that they now do much better at questioning and encouraging inquiry. Again, classroom observations are really needed; it is not clear that teachers have actually "moved" to the level we may think when we hear them describe changes. However, it is clear that teachers believe that being involved with and implementing what they learned through *Teach-Stat* has had a strong positive impact on how they view teaching and on how their students respond to their teaching.

Third, we have had reports from *Teach-Stat* teachers and their administrators in selected cases that students are doing "better in mathematics" as a result of *Teach-Stat*. We don't know what this means. We have tried (not very successfully) to track *Teach-Stat* students' performance on the statistics items on the North Carolina end-of-grade tests (newly revised) to see if we can make some comments on impact of the program.

Our project officially ended on August 31, 1994. Now the Statistics Educators are working with other teachers and/or schools to provide professional development programs. We are trying to implement a follow-up program in which we will ask selected Statistics Educators to keep portfolios of their year, documenting any professional development experiences they conduct as well as their own teaching. For remaining first-year and second-year teachers, we are mailing out an impact survey that looks at self-report about students behaviors, mathematics teaching, attitudes towards mathematics, sharing information with others, and effects of the project. Finally, three of the *Teach-Stat* faculty and eight of the Statistics Educators are working together on a project to look at grade 5–8 students' understanding of graphing before and after instruction. We do not have good strategies for exploring the long-term impact on both participants and on the second tier teachers who are served in some capacity by the participants, particularly because, as the project ends, there is still much of the work of the project to be completed!

What Is the Impact on Preservice Education?

There are obvious and not-so-obvious impacts with respect to the professional development of a large group (11) of college faculty: 7 mathematics educators, 3 statisticians, and 1 science educator. The first year of the project was a planning year; the faculty worked together to learn about what was available and about research related to teaching and learning of students K–6 in statistics. They also participated in the creation (and implementation) of the professional development curriculum. All the faculty report that they valued the sharing and the collegiality that grew over the life of the project. Several faculty also reported changes in the way they teach their university content and/or methods courses. Some feel that they lecture less, have increased their "wait time," and promote discourse more. Some now include data analysis as a topic in Modern Algebra, Mathematics for Liberal Arts, and Calculus courses as well as in their methods courses. Statisticians have chosen to use some of the *Teach-Stat* activities (e.g., raisins!) to help students visualize concepts; these strategies have been carried to other colleagues outside the project as well.

References

Berenson, S. B., Friel, S. N., & Bright, G. W. (1993). The development of elementary teachers' statistical concepts in relation to graphical representations. In J. R. Becker & B. J. Pence, (Eds.), *Proceedings of the fifteenth annual meeting, North American Chapter of the International Group for the Psychology Mathematics Education* (vol. 1, pp. 285–91). San Jose, CA: San Jose State University.

Berenson, S. B., Friel, S. N., & Bright, G. W. (1993, February). *Elementary teachers' conceptions of graphical representations of statistical data.* Paper presented at the annual meeting of the Research Council for Diagnostic and Prescriptive Mathematics, Melbourne, FL.

Berenson, S. B., Friel, S. N., & Bright, G. W. (1993, April). *Elementary teachers' fixation on graphical features to interpret statistical data.* Paper presented at the annual meeting of the American Education Research Association, Atlanta, GA.

Bright, G. W., Berenson, S. B., & Friel, S. N. (1993, February). *Teachers' knowledge of statistics pedagogy.* Paper presented at the annual meeting of the Research Council for Diagnostic and Prescriptive Mathematics, Melbourne, FL.

Bright, G. W., & Friel, S. N. (1993, April). *Elementary teachers' representations of relationships among statistics concepts.* Paper presented at the annual meeting of the American Education Research Association, Atlanta, GA.

Bright, G. W., Friel, S. N., & Berenson, S. B. (1993). Statistics knowledge of elementary teachers. In J. R. Becker & B. J. Pence (Eds.), *Proceedings of the fifteenth annual meeting, North American Chapter of the International Group for the Psychology Mathematics Education* (vol. 1, pp. 292–98). San Jose, CA: San Jose State University.

Bright, G. W. (1995). *Final report of Teach-Stat pedagogy survey.* Greensboro, NC: University of North Carolina at Greensboro.

Brown, J. S., Collins, A., & Duguid, P. Situated cognition and the culture of learning. *Educational Researcher, 18*(1), 332–42.

Collins, A., Brown, J. S., & Newman, S. E. (1989). Cognitive apprenticeship: Teaching the crafts of reading, writing, and mathematics. In L. B. Resnick (Ed.), *Knowing, learning, and instruction: Essays in honor of Robert Glaser* (pp. 453–94). Hillsdale, NJ: Lawrence Erlbaum.

Friel, S. N., & Bright, G. W. (in press). Teach-Stat: A model for professional development in data analysis and statistics for teachers K–6. In S. Lajoie (Ed.), *Reflections on statistics: Agendas for learning, teaching, and assessment in K–12*. Hillsdale, NJ: Lawrence Erlbaum.

Friel, S. N., McMillen, B., & Botsford, S. J. (1996). *Teach-Stat follow-up evaluation.* Chapel Hill, NC: University of North Carolina Mathematics and Science Education Network.

Friel, S., & Joyner, J. (Eds.) (1997). *Teach-Stat for teachers: Professional development manual.* Palo Alto, CA: Dale Seymour Publications.

Frost, D. L. (1995). *Elementary teachers' conceptions of mathematics staff development and their roles as workshop leaders.* Unpublished doctoral dissertation. Greensboro, NC: UNC–Greensboro.

Gleason, J., Vesilind, E., Friel, S., & Joyner, J. (Eds.) (1996). *Teach-Stat for statistics educators: Staff development manual.* Palo Alto, CA: Dale Seymour.

Gregorio, L. M., Vidakovic, D., & Berenson, S. B. (1995). *Teach-Stat evaluation report.* Raleigh, NC: Center for Research in Mathematics and Science Education.

Joyner, J., Pfieffer, S., Friel, S., & Vesilind, E. (Eds.) (1997a) *Teach-Stat for students: Activities for grades 1–3.* Palo Alto, CA: Dale Seymour.

Joyner, J., Pfieffer, S., Friel, S., & Vesilind, E. (Eds.) (1997b) *Teach-Stat for students: Activities for grades 4–6.* Palo Alto, CA: Dale Seymour.

McMillen, B. J., Botsford, S. J., & Friel, S. N. (1995). *Workshop evaluation.* Chapel Hill, NC: University of North Carolina Mathematics and Science Education Network.

Stone, L. (1995). *Teachers on Teach-Stat: A first report.* Chapel Hill, NC: University of North Carolina Mathematics and Science Education Network.

Elementary and Middle School Math and Technology Project

Ann Grady
Boston Public Schools

Since June 1988, Boston Public Schools has been engaged in an intensive Elementary and Middle School Math and Technology (EM-MAT) Project to improve mathematics education through teacher enhancement and implementation of the NCTM *Standards* in elementary and middle school mathematics instruction. The major goal of the EM-MAT project has been to develop Math Leader Teachers in Boston's elementary and middle schools.

The project involved 220 teachers (grades K–8) from 100 Boston elementary and middle schools over six years. Each year approximately 35 teachers were selected for the project through a competitive selective process. Each participant participated in intensive mathematics courses during a two-week Summer Institute and one release day per month in the academic year following the Institute. The courses included mathematics content presentations as well as integration of manipulatives, computers, calculators, and problem solving approaches in classroom teaching. The mathematics content sessions were conducted by Dr. Robert Willcutt of Boston University. Classroom applications sessions were conducted by experienced EM-MAT teachers. Each participating teacher received a budget to purchase manipulatives and software; two computers for each class were provided by Boston Public Schools. In addition, each participating school received a modem and phone line for telecommunications, as well as training in and accounts on Boston Public School telecommunications board, BoSNET.

During the academic year, EM-MAT Project staff members visited each teacher in her classroom at least four times. These visits included conducting model lessons, team teaching with the teacher, observing a teacher developed lesson, and trouble shooting computer problems. In each successive year following a teacher's active involvement as an EM-MAT teacher, she was invited to attend a minimum of two "Alumni meetings" which followed the same format as the first year release days, but covered more advanced mathematics content and new technology applications. These Alumni meetings provided an important opportunity for experienced EM-MAT teachers to stay connected to the Project and share their concerns and successes with one another and the Project staff.

In addition, the EM-MAT Project developed a number of resource opportunities to support teachers back in the classroom.

* Production of videotapes showing Boston Math Leader Teachers using manipulatives and technology in their teaching and showing Boston parents engaged in family mathematics activities with their children. These videotapes are being widely used in both teacher and parent workshops conducted by the Math Leader Teachers.

* Production of a bimonthly newsletter, *EM-MAT Times*, featuring articles about elementary- and middle-school mathematics projects and events, show casing teachers' and students' work.

* Organization of a Math Manipulative and Software Resource Library. The library contains more than one hundred of the most highly regarded pieces of mathematics software and many commonly used mathematics manipulatives and is in constant use by the EM-MAT teachers.

* Organization of EM-MAT Demonstration Grants providing an opportunity for teachers who have developed excellent mathematics project based curriculum units to mentor groups of 10–12 additional teachers, as they change their classroom teaching practice.

* Organization of a Kids Fair attended by more than 200 day campers. This event provides an opportunity for EM-MAT teachers to develop and implement hands-on mathematics activities for students during the Summer Institute, while they are receiving the daily support of project staff.

* Organization of a School-Wide Implementation Project, where schools could apply for a mini-grant to release their Leader Teacher for one week to work in classrooms with five additional teachers committed to changing their mathematics practice. EM-MAT paid for a permanent substitute, a trained mathematics teacher who covered Leader Teachers' classes. Participating schools agreed to provide funding for after-school workshops for participating teachers.

The EM-MAT Project has developed a groups of teachers, strongly committed to improving their own mathematics teaching and interested in continuing to upgrade their own mathematics background. This group of teachers has become an excellent resource for a number of mathematics reform initiatives in Massachusetts. EM-MAT has developed an excellent reputation, and EM-MAT teachers are approached when projects are looking for strong urban educators. This collaboration with groups ranging from NSF-funded projects such as the Massachusetts State Systemic Initiative, Northwestern University's Comprehensive Regional Center for Minorities, to TERC's Used Numbers, Talking Math, and Teaching to the Big Ideas, EDC's Logo Action Research Center, and the Algebra Project, have enriched the EM-MAT Project as well as the projects in which EM-MAT teachers were involved. In addition, EM-MAT teachers are now regularly listed as presenters at local and national conferences (more that 20 were accepted to present at NCTM/Boston in April).

Supporting Elementary Teachers' Improvement of Mathematics Instruction

In independent evaluations of the EM-MAT Project, teachers have spoken to the need they have for support so they are comfortable in changing their teaching practice. The factors they observed included the following:

- Strong mathematics content sessions given by a mathematician who has a practicing experience of the elementary classroom. Bob Willcutt, our principal mathematics consultant spent two days a week in classrooms, modeling the teaching that he demonstrated in teacher workshops. These classroom visits also provided an opportunity to document to the EM-MAT teacher, principal, and other visitors who gathered to observe the lesson, that hands-on mathematics can open worlds to students previously unsuccessful in mathematics.
- Follow-up activities led by their peers. Each monthly release day included a two hour session led by an experienced EM-MAT teacher, teaching at the same grade level, who provided classroom tested lesson ideas and technology suggestions for implementing the day's mathematics topic. These Team Leaders received the highest reviews in evaluations of the Project, and the Team Leaders themselves said that the experience gave them the confidence to go back and conduct similar workshops in their schools.
- Mentoring visits four times a year by EM-MAT staff. These visits provided an opportunity for participants to try a new activity, knowing that they would have an "extra pair of hands."

The visits also provided a level of accountability. Teachers took the visits very seriously and were anxious to have their students show off the new mathematics worlds which they had explored.

- Additional opportunities to continue their own mathematics professional development and to develop collegial relationships with others who shared the same goals. EM-MAT teachers who have continued to be involved in Alumni Days, Demonstrator Grants, and other mathematics projects, report that their momentum for mathematics reform has continued.

- Additional opportunities to continue their own mathematics professional development and to develop collegial relationships with others who shared the same goals. EM-MAT teachers who have continued to be involved in Alumni Days, Demonstrator Grants, and other mathematics projects, report that their momentum for mathematics reform has continued.

EM-MAT has consciously worked to develop successful models for teaching mathematics to all students. The selection process for EM-MAT teachers insured that the group reflected teachers of all Boston students. EM-MAT teachers include bilingual teachers (6 different languages), teachers of students with special needs, and teachers of gifted and talented students, as well as regular education students. These teachers were a strong resource in the development and successful implementation of reformed mathematics instruction for all students in urban classrooms. (Boston's population is 80% minority, 90% low income, 33% students with special needs, and 25% bilingual.) Many of our schools are working hard to o develop models for successfully teaching a wide range of students in the same classroom and EM-MAT teachers have used their training to make a significant contribution to that effort. They report that the hands-on, project based, technology infused developed through EM-MAT are very successful in meeting the needs of a diverse group of students.

Planning for Large-Scale Change

EM-MAT has clearly achieved some significant successes, but it has also shown the enormity of the problem of effecting substantive, system-wide change for a large group of teachers. EM-MAT underestimated what was required to achieve school-wide change in the teaching of mathematics. An EM-MAT teacher stated the problem well.

EM-MAT trained me to rethink the way I taught math, but that seemed like the easy part! I've found it difficult to implement change outside my classroom. I've given workshops at my school, but the effort seems to have stalled at this point. I need better strategies for convincing other teachers—and my principal that this is the way we should be teaching math.   (Sixth-grade teacher)

It was unrealistic to assume that Leader Teachers who have successfully modified their own teaching practices, and have conducted workshops for their colleagues, can automatically bring about change in the mathematics teaching of an entire faculty. When the independent evaluator for the EM-MAT Project and Project Staff surveyed EM-MAT teachers, they also critiqued and analyzed two schools that have been most successful in beginning the process of school-wide reform. They determined from their analysis that there are additional elements needed to provide excellent mathematics instruction to all students in a school:

- A concrete and concise school-based plan for change and professional development from which to work.
- Strong, well-informed principal leadership. The principal (or the Director of Instruction in a large school) must understand and embrace the NCTM *Standards* herself and be comfortable in her role as curriculum leader. The one-day workshop provided by EM-MAT was not sufficient for most principals.
- Leadership training that supports Leader Teachers' efforts to move beyond their own classrooms to support their colleagues' efforts to reform their own mathematics teaching.
- More than two mathematics leaders in a school. The schools that were most successful recruited additional teachers to share in the responsibility of bringing "math-rich worlds" to *all* students in their schools.
- Leader Teachers who extend their own mathematics backgrounds through participation in additional mathematics professional development programs. These Leader Teachers clearly articulated that one year of professional development is not enough, and that if they are to be effective in their roles as leaders, that they need on-going professional development and a sustained support system.
- Change in methods used to assess mathematics learning. EM-MAT teachers who participated in the pilot assessments conducted by the Center for the Study of Testing, Evaluation and Educational Policy at Boston College found that their assessments

more accurately reflected and supported the changes they were undertaking in mathematics teaching than did the Metropolitan Achievement Test administered by the Boston School Department.

- Families who understand and support the changes in mathematics teaching and learning that have occurred since they were in school. Teachers report that children are most successful when their parents share in the belief of the importance and excitement involved in good mathematics education, and understand how important it is that all students are involved in a challenging mathematics program that will guarantee their access to further study in mathematics and science.

- Strong support for technology by the principal, teachers and parents who understand the richness that technology can bring to the learning of mathematics, and are willing to make the human and monetary investment in integrating that technology with student learning.

Supporting this change in individual schools doesn't happen quickly or simply. Much has been written recently about systemic reform and clearly, that is a piece of the answer. Teacher change on a large scale cannot come about without parallel reforms in curriculum and assessment, and without the leadership necessary to build administrative and family support. That for us has been the difficult part; Boston is not different from many urban school systems, in that budget cuts have virtually eliminated funds for revising curriculum and assessment, for updating classroom materials and instructional technology, and for large scale professional development. Without the political and administrative support needed to change this situation, very little can be accomplished of a systemic nature. Boston Public Schools has begun to address these issues with its application for an Urban Systemic Initiative Grant.

In another instance, Boston's political situation has worked to our advantage in reaching a diverse teacher population. Boston has for many years, been under a court order to diversify its teaching staff; this has resulted in a richly diverse pool of applicants for EM-MAT. The diversity of EM-MAT was also enhanced by its very first reputation; the initial Teacher Advisory Board was consciously chosen to reflect a strong multi-ethnic group of teacher leaders. This Teacher Advisory Board was very active in our initial recruitment for EM-MAT and quickly established EM-MAT as a program which both welcomed and nurtured diversity.

A model which is enabling us to reach an ever widening circle of teachers is the distance learning model. Boston has participated for the past five years in the TEAMS interactive distance learning project developed by the Los Angeles County Public Schools. TEAMS has developed an excellent reputation for quality, hands-on mathematics and science instruction for students in grades 4–6. Teachers and schools are eager to participate, and teachers learn along with their students as they participate in projects ranging from dissecting owl pellets to scale drawing. TEAMS works best in schools where there are strong Leader Teachers (often EM-MAT teachers) who support the rest of the faculty as they deal with the technical and logistical issues of distance learning. TEAMS requires an investment in technology and infrastructure (cable and phone lines), and the support of the principal for required schedule and room changes, etc., but the model appears successful in beginning to change school-wide mathematics and science cultures.

Project Evaluation

Large scale projects still need individual contact between teachers and Project Staff. Alternative models can include distance learning, but some face to face contact is essential. Leader Teachers and supportive principals can serve an important role as liaison between Project Staff and the larger group of faculty, but time and again, we have found that teachers change their practice most successfully when they feel a personal connection to those asking them to change.

Successful evaluation models for the EM-MAT Project have included pre and post surveys documenting teacher beliefs and behavior. Case studies of randomly selected (from within cohort groups) teachers provided excellent insights into the change process, as well as documenting what remained to be accomplished. We also collected some data on student beliefs about mathematics and student plans to study further mathematics. (Both changed positively.) TERC was our evaluator for several years, and we found the evaluation instruments which they and we jointly developed to be quite effective. Boston still uses a pre-NCTM *Standards* standardized test (MAT6), so we did not collect data on student achievement, although we found in city-wide reports that mathematics test scores did improve in each year of the project.

Summary

EM-MAT has been successful in developing a strong group of Leader Teachers, who speak eloquently of their own mathematical empowerment, increased comfort in using technology, and most importantly, their sense of themselves as professional educators who are comfortable teaching their peers. They have made great strides in bringing an awareness of the need to reform mathematics teaching and learning to their schools and colleagues. Unfortunately, this isn't enough. These Leader Teachers were self-motivated, strong teachers when they began EM-MAT and they tell us that the 150 hours of training which they each received only "got them started." How much more is needed to give the large number of elementary teachers the training and support which they need to substantively change their own mathematics instruction. I hope, but wonder if our society is ready for that kind of investment.

Mathematics and Science Enhancement (MASE) Project

Linda Gregg
Clark County School District

The Mathematics and Science Enhancement (MASE) project is a four year leadership program designed to restructure K–6 mathematics and science education in the Clark County School District (CCSD) in Las Vegas, Nevada, a large, growing, multi-faceted district. Project goals are to empower educators to (a) build their capacity to make knowledgeable decisions, (b) develop leaders and change agents committed to restructuring their own mathematics and science programs and sharing that process with others, and (c) ultimately create opportunities for every K–6 student to become scientifically and mathematically literate. As year two draws to a close, it is apparent that Project MASE is having a growing impact within the district, and that there is much yet to do.

Project MASE is a multi-dimensional, child-centered professional development program designed to provide teachers and administrators access to high quality professional development experiences based on the tenets of constructivism. Sessions are thoughtfully designed to respect adults as learners who construct their own knowledge over time from rich experiences and opportunities to reflect on their own learning. Sessions are structured to allow access at multiple entry levels and ideas are revisited over time. Participants are continually challenged to examine their beliefs and instructional practices and to debate ideas in light of current research on how children learn, observations of consultants and expert teachers working with children, work with children in their own classrooms, national standards and current research on how and what to teach children, and their own experiences as active learners in mathematics and science.

Project participants include approximately 150 teacher leaders, 260 site liaisons, and 150 administrators from the 127 CCSD urban and rural elementary schools and teacher leaders from rural Nevada. There are four leadership groups: K–2 mathematics, K–2 science, 3–6 mathematics, and 3–6 science. During the first two years of the project, the teacher leaders actively engaged in over 150 hours of intensive professional development designed to help them restructure how and what they teach and to enhance their own content understanding. Site liaisons and administrators attended sessions designed to develop understanding of research on learning, pedagogy, national standards, and how to shape school cultures to support recommended reform. Site liaisons have also attended up to 60 hours of professional development based on replacement units or science kits.

During the final two years of the project, teachers leaders will continue to enhance their content knowledge and restructure their programs to include performance assessment. As they are ready, they will join mentors in leadership teams to begin sharing the restructuring process with other district teachers in workshops, seminars, and classroom demonstration lessons. Site liaisons will continue to participate in professional development with project consultants and teacher leaders, begin to invite site colleagues into their classrooms to informally share ideas and resources, and continue to work with their site administrators to improve and enhance mathematics and science programs. As leaders emerge among site liaisons, they will join the mentors in the leadership program to continuously expand and replenish the leadership cadre. Workshops for administrators will focus on supervision of inquiry-based learning and programs shaped by constructivism.

Emerging Lessons

The staff and participants in Project MASE are deeply involved with the issues and complexities of deep-level reform of mathematics and science. The following lessons that are emerging from the continuing work to help elementary teachers make informed decisions to improve mathematics and science education may have implications for large-scale teacher change in mathematics instruction.

Mathematics and science are complementary design components. Professional development in one area enlightens practice in both mathematics and science over time. As educators are immersed in doing mathematics or science and have opportunities to interact, they begin to see the natural connections. The philosophical base for reform is the same. The pedagogy is the same. Processes overlap. Mathematics can be used to describe natural phenomena and when appropriate, be integrated with science. Two years into the project, teachers indicate that as they make changes in how and what they teach in their chosen focus area, it becomes clear that the same changes are needed in other areas. It is evident that mathematics reform faces many of the same challenges as science reform, plus the additional barriers created by time-established practices and the threat of traditional assessment.

Internal change is a prerequisite to changing instructional practice. Educators at all levels, as well as those who impact education from outside the system, make decisions based on their belief systems. Beliefs related to how and what students should learn, the role of students and teachers, and what parents, supervisors, and colleagues want shape teachers' behaviors. Beliefs about and experience with mathematics and science color educators' approaches to instruction of each subject. Many participants initially did not view facilitating as teaching. Some teachers talk about teaching and facilitating as if they are two separate acts. Some principals tell teachers they will come back to evaluate them when they are teaching a lesson. Belief systems change over time when examined and discussed in light of research on the brain and how children learn, results from work with children, recommendations in national standards, and the participants' experiences as learners doing mathematics and science. As teachers gain knowledge, expertise, and confidence over time and see student success, they become pro-active and advocate for reform.

Views of mathematics and science need to be reconstructed through experience and dialogue. Most educators, students, and parents have experienced science and mathematics as static bodies of knowledge and procedures to be memorized and transmitted. When they experience both mathematics and science as making conjectures, testing and verifying ideas, and communicating their ideas to others, they begin to view mathematics as a science of pattern and inquiry that reveals and describes order in our world. It is through meaningful experiences over time that learning becomes a process of inquiry, a search for meaning and sense-making that is enhanced by social interaction.

It is increasingly evident that tenets of constructivism apply to adult learners. Learning is a meaning-making process which is personally constructed and impacted by experience, context, and the environment. Teachers need to continuously experience learning through problem solving and inquiry before they can own the process. They need to revisit and debate ideas and know that they will experience states of disequilibrium as a natural part of change. Reflecting on experiences and processes is key to owning and effectively applying recommended practices. Successful reform is contingent on the quality, depth, and duration of professional development and the involvement and commitment of each participant. Steps for most are small, and it is evident that deep-level change is a personal process that takes time, persistence, and patience and is impacted by the culture of the whole system (the nation, the state, the district, and every aspect of classroom life). Telling teachers how to teach children, or colleagues, has little long-term value.

Work with children is emerging as a powerful professional development tool. In one format, a MASE consultant or staff member teaches a full class of students while 10 to 30 teachers and administrators watch the lesson. High levels of engagement and reasoning are evident to observers. In another format, one teacher interviews a small group of students to probe their thinking about specific mathematical or scientific ideas while a second teacher records responses. By learning about the misconceptions that children hold and how children think, educators are increasingly willing to restructure learning experiences in their own classrooms, dialogue about results, and continue to work to improve instructional practices. Work with children is preceded and followed by planning and dialogue sessions with project consultants, staff, and participants. The focus on children positively impacts participants' willingness to implement recommended instructional strategies and resources and to re-examine their own beliefs, assumptions, and practices. Feedback from administrators and teachers indicates that they find work with students to be extremely informative and an impetus for change. The mood shifts from "fixing the teachers" to collaboratively shaping optimal learning experiences for all students. A vision of recommended practice emerges.

Use of hands-on experiences and thematic units in mathematics and science can mask weak programs and create an illusion of reform and student learning. It is much easier to incorporate manipulatives, science kits, and thematic units into the classroom than actually change instructional practice. Use of innovative experiences and materials presented in the traditional telling-teaching mode is too often observed. Some teachers are able to replicate a lesson observed at a workshop but unable to consistently change how they teach because they lack deep understanding of the implications of constructivist theory for the education of the whole child. We observe that teachers' talk changes before their behaviors change. As teachers increase their understanding of how children learn, content, and pedagogy, behaviors begin to align with talk.

Creating common experiences facilitates reform efforts. By saturating a large district with carefully crafted model lessons and selected readings, common reference points develop and meaningful dialogue results within the system. Conflicting definitions and interpretations can be explored and misconceptions minimized. It is a continuous process as learners shape their own meaning.

Professional readings promote dialogue and debate on issues and ideas related to reform of mathematics and science education. Although initially resistant, participants are now asking for readings because they are finding the new knowledge useful when interacting with colleagues and parents. Site-based study groups are emerging that mirror practices established in the leadership project.

Ongoing involvement of nationally recognized experts strengthens and enriches every aspect of reform projects. Consultants bring a level of expertise to a project that enriches and enhances the quality of the program. They have the capacity to be objective about local conditions which impact the success of reform. Outside change agents are free to challenge ideas and practices and offer constructive suggestions from a national perspective. They contribute to the growth and leadership abilities of the project staff as well as project participants. Consultants must model desired practice and be thoughtfully selected. They can help sustain and support reform and move projects to higher levels.

Administrative support is critical to successful reform in mathematics and science. Teachers working with principals who understand constructivism and reform goals are making significant progress toward reform. Informed administrators are able to respond to and communicate with teachers and parents in support of change. Shallow understanding can be eroded by political pressure. When teachers and administrators attend workshops together, they have opportunities to dialogue and plan ways to support reform. Administrators need opportunities to develop supervision strategies that are compatible with child-centered, inquiry-based programs.

Exemplary materials facilitate reform of instruction in mathematics as well as science. There are still too few quality resources and too many inadequate resources available. When purchasing materials, few educators are judging materials based on characteristics that ensure alignment with national standards and current research on learning. Availability, management, and maintenance of tools for learning continue to be barriers to reform. Implementation of inquiry learning is primarily dependent on professional development.

Teacher leadership development is critical to project success. Identifying teacher leaders too early in a project may not result in selection of teachers with the greatest potential for leadership. Being named a leader too soon may actually add a burden of responsibility that inhibits growth. Upon reflection, it seems that offering equal opportunities to all teachers initially and letting leaders emerge would be better practice. Then, as leaders emerge, opportunities for deeper levels of involvement and growth would be made available. After two years of professional development, some site liaisons are emerging as leaders and becoming deeply involved at all levels of the program. We have found that when a spirit of inquiry and continuous learning permeates all aspects of the project and when teachers are not worried about what it means to be a teacher leader, they can focus on reshaping their own philosophy and classroom practice. Then, they have stories to tell and experiences to share about the journey they have begun. In many different but natural ways, these teachers are becoming leaders and change agents.

Leadership development requiring deep level change is proving to be a much longer process than originally anticipated. It is becoming increasingly clear that the vision of what it means to be a teacher leader needs to be reshaped. The vision of the role of teacher leader needs to be changed from a telling to a facilitating model that mirrors the recommended role of the teacher in an inquiry classroom. We observe that teachers do not automatically make connections between facilitating the learning of children and the learning of adults. Teacher leaders at all levels need long-term support. The time required for development needs to be respected. The many different levels and forms of leadership need to be acknowledged and supported. A large group of strong teacher leaders, representative of the diverse teacher population, is needed to provide professional development opportunities for all teachers over time. To reach large, diverse teacher populations, a variety of formats, times, and locations for professional development need to be made available by knowledgeable, experienced leaders in a context that meets the immediate needs of teachers while advancing project goals. This is a long process that leaders are asked to share with others.

Parent support or lack of support impacts reform efforts. Parents have the power to demand or eliminate reform. The more information and experience they have, the more likely they are to understand and support mathematics and science restructuring efforts. Family mathematics and science meetings are proving to be an effective forum for communication.

Several questions are worthy of further discussion to ensure that large-scale teacher change in mathematics and science is institutionalized.

- What level of support will be needed to create opportunities for all students to learn mathematics?
- What systemic elements need to be addressed if restructuring efforts are to be institutionalized
- What process should be used to select leadership candidates?
- What criteria should be used to select project consultants and change agents?
- What criteria should be used to select project evaluators and evaluation tools?

- What criteria should be used to assess student progress?
- What does it take to help administrators, district-level decision makers, and teachers learn to distinguish if resources for mathematics, professional development programs, classroom instructional practices, and methods of assessment are in alignment or misalignment with national standards and reform efforts?

Assessment of student change and teacher change in large-scale projects should be aligned with inquiry learning and the belief that both students and teachers construct knowledge over time. Assessment must communicate what is valued and be consistent with recommended practice and national standards. Students must be asked to reveal their thinking on complex tasks. Teachers and systems must be accountable for making progress toward change that provides all students access to quality, inquiry-based, developmentally appropriate mathematics and science education. Each day that teachers, administrators, and students are held accountable to outdated standards, reform becomes a longer, harder process. If reform is truly the goal, we must assess what is valued. Evaluations of teacher change and student change must be multi-dimensional.

Selection of external project evaluators and evaluation instruments is critical to the success of reform efforts. Evaluators must have deep understanding of inquiry learning, constructivism, and the long-term nature of meaningful change. They need to have a clear vision of best practices in professional development and classroom application. Interaction with project evaluators should strengthen the expertise of project staff while positively impacting the quality of planning and implementation. Evaluation should provide ongoing, interactive, formative feedback and consultation from the beginning of the project. Joint analysis of information should reveal the degree and quality of movement toward deep-level change and, when appropriate, lead to course corrections that shape enhanced plans. The final report should summarize project outcomes and contribute to the field of knowledge on reform.

Internal, ongoing evaluation by project staff through written response, learning logs, classroom visits, student and teacher portfolios, self-assessment, and continuous interaction with all participants helps the project staff maintain a keen awareness of the needs of participants in relation to project goals. The ability of the project staff to constantly assess and adjust the course of the project based on continuous external and internal feedback is essential to maximize reform efforts.

TEAM: Teaching Excellence and Mathematics

Jeane Joyner
North Carolina Department of Public Instruction

The primary purpose of the Team Project was to develop and support leadership in mathematics by elementary teachers. In support of the leadership goal, the TEAM grant was designed to increase the mathematics content knowledge of the participants and to assist them in developing a school improvement plan for mathematics in each of their schools. Evaluation of the project was through documenting the new roles and responsibilities the TEAM teachers undertook, the school mathematics plans which they developed, and the evaluations of workshops they planned and conducted. Increased student achievement was not used as a measure of success of the project, though statements by school system officials who evaluated the project at the end of the third year and again two years later credit the leadership of TEAM teachers with helping test scores to rise in their schools and school systems.

Project Organization

Fifty teachers participated in pairs from the same school system. There were two or more teams in each of the eight educational regions in the state; one team represented private schools statewide. All of the teachers had at least five years experience, and a third had masters degrees. There were three men and 47 women participating with the three North Carolina educators who directed the project. Approximately 20% of the participants were minority teachers. All participants remained with the project through the planned three years and the extended fourth year except one teacher who resigned for personal reasons at the end of the second year. Approximately 20% of the teachers have continued to work toward advanced degrees.

A great deal of flexibility in the way teachers could demonstrate leadership was built into the project. The goal was to expect, nurture, and support leadership rather than to dictate a specific model; to that end, the project had both cognitive and affective features.

For the first two years of the project the 50 teachers were involved in three weeks each summer of content-specific staff development taught by faculty from North Carolina colleges and universities as well as other national leaders. Fall, winter, and spring workshops, 1.5 to 2.5 days each, focused on pedagogy, issues surrounding leadership, and new materials and resources. During the spring meeting with administrators, teams "mapped" out activities and basic plans for the next year.

State Eisenhower moneys supplemented the materials budget provided by NSF. Eisenhower funds also paid for printing and distribution of materials developed by project members (for example, a correlation of the NCTM *Addenda* books to North Carolina's *Standard Course of Study*, three decks of problem-solving cards, and pamphlets for the 100th day of school). With the use of these funds, participants were able to begin personal libraries of professional books and resource materials.

As part of the project, each team was required to plan and conduct at least two mathematics workshops per year in their school systems and to share with their own school faculties in an ongoing manner. Participants were to work with administrators to seek ways to support fellow teachers in implementing the new North Carolina mathematics curriculum and testing program which was initiated during the second year of the project.

In the final two years of the grant, the winter sessions were devoted to planning and preparing materials for statewide staff development led by TEAM members the following summers. A one-week residential staff development was also part of the third and fourth summers. Throughout the project there were numerous communications in writing and by telephone among participants and project leaders.

In the first year, participants were asked to take leadership roles that were not necessarily content-dependent, though many worked with local faculties on the content from the summer staff development. By the end of the third year, TEAM members were working with neighboring school systems as well as their own system, with college and university professors near their homes, and with other projects to implement mathematics staff development. They planned and led workshops for entire school systems in addition to the sessions for their own faculties. TEAM members were being sought by school systems across the state to assist in creating school plans, with curriculum alignment, and with long-range staff development.

Data in the yearly reports and the final project summary illustrate the influence of TEAM members through their staff development and presentations:

1990–91	320 sessions	9,154 participants	1,067 contact hours
1991–92	319 sessions	15,011 participants	1,737 contact hours
1992–93	331 sessions	17,678 participants	2,661 contact hours

While some presentations were to parents, school boards, and civic groups, many of the workshops were presented as series to teachers; the length was often 10 or more contact hours. Accountability within the TEAM project was not ever a problem with one exception. (In that case close contact with the principal and work with the individual proved moderately successful.)

Because student achievement or change was not part of the project design, the evaluation of the TEAM project was based on a number of indicators. Documentation included teachers' personal portfolios and yearly self-evaluations.

- Observations of leadership roles undertaken by participants documented by school system administrators
- Products created by TEAM teachers
- Presentations by TEAM teachers and their evaluations by participants
- Leadership initiatives of TEAM members (for example, starting of local TEAM projects)
- Contributions to statewide efforts such as serving on test development committees, regional textbook review panels, and the state's alternative assessment program in grades 1 and 2

More than half of the TEAM participants started local TEAM projects or helped educators in other systems initiate similar projects. The TEAM teachers, representing 26 school systems in the state (out of 128 at that time), worked with teachers in more than three-fourths of the school systems in North Carolina. They made over 50 presentations at state and regional mathematics conferences, worked with over 20,000 parents in Family Math Nights or Math Carnivals, taught demonstration lessons in more than 300 classrooms, and worked with a dozen pre-service courses at institutions of higher learning on a long-term basis. The TEAM project is frequently used as a model for other initiatives in North Carolina.

Beliefs Resulting from the Project

From the TEAM experience definite opinions about teacher enhancement projects were expressed by participants, observers, and project leaders.

1. *A key component is staff development over time with alternating periods of study, practice, support, reflection, and more study.* The TEAM project was originally funded for 3 years, but participants asked for the fourth year. The TEAM teachers realized how much they did not know as well as how much they had learned and how much they had changed. They placed great value on the expertise they were developing and wanted more time to learn and to share.

2. *The mathematical content should go far beyond that which the teachers will be teaching; but issues of math anxiety cannot be ignored.* Even into the third year when a posttest was administered and project leaders felt confident because of their observations and conversations that responses would demonstrate a greater depth of understanding (even before seeing the results), participants became very "uptight." Affective goals and concerns, though not usually rated very highly in project design, are critical for change to be lasting.

3. *Clear standards related to work, schedules which reflect a professional commitment, and high expectations for performance are also important.* Summer work days included six hours of formal instruction, two to three hours of outside assignments, and opportunities for "choice" activities related to classroom instruction, new materials for mathematics, state initiatives, and special projects.

4. *Participants must become a community of learners as they also become a corps of leaders.* The residential summer program offered added opportunities for working cooperatively and for sharing. TEAM members brought personal resources and planned special "workshops" for each other in the evenings. Networking was fostered throughout the project; personal celebrations and difficult times were shared. There were "team babies," deaths of parents, the death of one son, marriages of children, graduations, and honors celebrated by the group.

5. *Participants need to construct new understandings just as their students do.* The instruction must model the philosophy being espoused. Learners need "buddies" with whom to talk and share. At the beginning of the project there was a very wide range in the mathematics content knowledge among participants, and peer coaching became an important part of the project. Two teachers who had done extensive

work as instructors with peer coaching programs in their system planned special staff development for TEAM members.

6. *Project leaders must value the expertise that participants already have and respect their opinions as they learn together.* Successful projects have leaders who are devoted to and enthusiastic about the project; attention to detail requires that leaders invest themselves emotionally as well as physically in the project.

7. *Participants need opportunities to share their growing expertise.* Since different participants had different strengths, the TEAM project teachers planned together and rehearsed for important presentations. They had increasing success in leading staff development (based on evaluations of every workshop conducted by project teachers), in making presentations to boards and parent groups, in writing materials, and in heading school system committees. Project leaders worked with school systems, the state's Regional Education Centers, and other professional organizations to insure that each TEAM member had some opportunities for leadership activities.

8. *The inclusion of administrators—both principals and central office staff—is critical.* Their awareness and participation in a project set the climate for long-term change. They provide personal support, cheer leading, resources, and opportunities for project teachers to use growing expertise. When the North Carolina Department of Public Instruction renegotiated a new indirect cost for projects and deducted almost 20% more in indirect costs from the project than was in the original project budget, school systems provided more support with substitute moneys, for example, so that project plans could continue.

Looking Ahead to Large-Scale Projects

Successful, large-scale teacher enhancement projects need a tremendous commitment of time and energy by those leading the project. There must be attention to detail, personal availability to and support for project participants, and supportive monitoring of the expectations set forth in the project. Training must be top quality, led by instructors who model what is being taught and who are themselves recognized for their expertise.

Investments of time are critical—time related to participants and time investments of staff. It is unrealistic to believe that lasting change will occur in a year. Summer institutes need the nurturing and continued momentum through seminars during the year. When the TEAM project was first implemented, there were eight Regional Education Centers with consultants who visited TEAM teachers in their classrooms and met with them periodically to talk about what was happening. These contacts were in addition to the four retreats/conferences scheduled as part of the project. Projects of three to four years seem most appropriate to allow participants to incorporate new knowledge into their routine practices and to build confidence that will increase the likelihood that change will become "institutionalized."

Specific expectations should be clear to all involved and assurances should be obtained from school system superintendents as well as principals when a project begins. A very high percentage of the TEAM project teachers experienced changes in administrators throughout the project years, but in every case the new superintendents and principals honored the commitments to the project. Since the investment of a school system was around $8,000 over the three-year project, this commitment was critical to the participation of the teachers.

The design of the selection process can be established to ensure the inclusion of diverse teacher populations. The TEAM project made a commitment to seek out and support minority teachers as a part of this leadership project. When the selection process was designed, guidelines were written which required that a certain percentage of the teachers selected would be African-American or Native American and that teams would be judged within the eight regions rather than statewide. This meant that many teams with extremely high ratings were not chosen to be part of the project. They clustered in areas of North Carolina where professional growth opportunities were easily accessible. One goal of the TEAM project was to include teachers who might not have had the many opportunities to learn and to lead but who were enthusiastic and willing to develop content expertise.

As a personal reflection, for future projects of this nature I would incorporate in the project design broad but more specific ways to document the results of the project. Just as "test" scores alone do not give a complete picture of a student's achievement, a catalog of actions taken does not adequately describe the impact of a leadership project. School system officials from the 26 LEAs all wrote letters of evaluation detailing the impact of the project on their systems, but the variation across those letters made it difficult to compare the impact across the districts. It is clear, however, that the school systems involved in the project are very satisfied, and they feel that the project has made significant contributions to strengthening mathematics education in their systems. Too, other school systems praise the work of TEAM members with their teachers and have repeatedly requested that we repeat the project. In times of shrinking resources, this is a strong statement, since school systems are aware of the financial commitments that were part of the TEAM project.

Mathematics for Tomorrow: Systemically-Embedded Teacher Enhancement

Barbara Scott Nelson
Education Development Center

Mathematics for Tomorrow (MFT) is a four-year, systemically-embedded teacher development and research project based on the premise that many teachers who change their teaching practice in the direction suggested by the NCTM *Standards* need to do more than assimilate new teaching techniques into an existing system of ideas about pedagogy and subject matter knowledge. Rather, they need to examine long-standing beliefs about the nature of knowledge and learning, deepen their mathematics knowledge, and reinvent their classroom practice from within a new conceptual frame. Project work essentially consists of creating rich contexts in which teachers can push beyond the limits of their current knowledge and practice and providing support for the processes of reflection, deeper understanding, and reinvention.

The project is structured in two, two-year phases. There are 26 teacher participants and 14 administrator participants in the first phase of the project, in the second phase there will be about 40 teachers and about 20 administrators. In each phase, school-based teams of K–8 teachers from each of three participating districts attend a three-week institute in each of two summers. In the academic years that follow, they participate in biweekly, district-based "Inquiry Groups" through which they help each other examine and change their instructional practice; attend four day-long workshops; and receive four classroom consultations from project staff and visit other teachers' classrooms. The mathematics supervisor from each district is a regular participant in the program, learning how to support teachers' efforts to change their practice and examining district policies that shape mathematics education. Principals and assistant superintendents of curriculum and instruction participate in parts of the program for teachers. They also have their own "Administrator's Inquiry Group," meeting monthly, in which they examine their own practice with particular attention to the ways in which they define the mathematics curriculum, supervise teachers, build a community of inquiry in the school, and communicate with the external community. Administrators may receive a multi-day "consultation" several times a year on a problem of their choice related to mathematics education.

Psychological and sociological strands of research parallel the teacher development program. In the psychological strand, individual patterns of teacher development are traced, with a particular interest in the role of affect in teacher change. In the sociological strand, the effort is to trace the development of community among teachers in Inquiry Groups and identify and trace changes in the beliefs and practices of participating administrators.

What We Have Learned

Our experience confirms that of colleagues who have provided teachers with the opportunity to change beliefs, deepen subject matter knowledge, and reconstruct their practice (Fennema, et al., 1992; Russell & Corwin, 1993; Schifter, 1996–a, 1996–b; Schifter & Fosnot, 1993; Wood, Cobb, & Yackel, 1991). Specifically, examining one's conceptions of learning, teaching and mathematics and reconstructing one's instructional practice takes time (years, not weeks), requires a small and supportive community in which one's intellectual and practical struggles are sympathetically understood and supported, and consists of an iterative movement between changes in belief and changes in practice. Therefore, work with teachers in their classrooms, as well as in summer institutes and after school settings is highly desirable. As their conceptions of learning and mathematics change, teachers both come to see their classrooms through different eyes and begin to want to interact differently with their students. A knowledgeable and sympathetic colleague can provide the context for reflecting on what happens in the classroom and considering new instructional possibilities. This is not "coaching" or "modeling" in the usual sense of those words, in that the issue is not the modeling of new behaviors that the coach can demonstrate and the teacher can copy. Rather, it is reflecting on and analyzing classroom events and then inventing for oneself the next step. The colleague helps with the observation and reflection processes.

In MFT we have the opportunity to explore the role of the school-based Inquiry Group and the issues raised for administrators.

1. *Inquiry Groups.* We have been finding that a small, school-based group of teachers, working together and with other groups, both in summer institutes and during the school year, can provide a great deal of support for each other in the processes of reflection on practice and

mathematics learning. In the first year of the project, it became clear that the range of ideas offered by the group made richer and deeper the ideas available for consideration by each individual participant. Sharing personal experiences and particular struggles and triumphs in the process of change provided acknowledgment that this hard work is an important part of the process of change and helped teachers see that the process of learning something new has ups and downs for everyone— themselves, their colleagues, and their students. Summer institutes and Inquiry Groups where teachers worked collegially provided a context in which they could be learning to listen to another person's mathematical thinking and to ask the question that helps that person stretch their thinking just a bit. In the second year, the focus of the Inquiry Groups has shifted somewhat, to be more explicitly on investigations into practice. Teachers bring to the Inquiry Group issues from their practice that they wish to think about further, with the help of colleagues. The issue may be a question about students' mathematical thinking, as in the case of the teacher who wants to investigate the mathematical meaning her students are making of a exercise on scale. Or it may be a question about the teacher's own practice, as in the case of a teacher who records and then examines his/her own questioning techniques, looking to see the effects on student response of various types of questions. In the group, all teachers join the investigation, offering alternate interpretations of the data and suggestions of things to try that would yield more information (Hammerman, in press).

The changes in mathematics instruction suggested by the NCTM *Standards* require not only changes on the part of individual teachers, but also the development of a professional and school culture that supports ongoing inquiry into how students' mathematical thinking develops. As inquirers into their own and students' thinking teachers need the freedom to explore, to express doubts and uncertainties, and to engage together in ongoing explorations of students' mathematical thinking. Inquiry Groups are small contexts in which this new culture can begin to grow. In the first stages of the MFT project, project staff lead these groups. In the coming year we will be working with teachers in the current Inquiry Groups on how to help each other, so that the groups can be self-sustaining. We also will identify a few teachers who will become "apprentice" facilitators in the project's second phase, and eventually be able to facilitate groups on their own.

2. *Administrators.* The goals of the strand for administrators are to explore the conditions under which key district administrative personnel can develop a deep understanding of mathematics instruction and can develop the attitudes, orientations, and skills which will permit them to

support and sustain progressive mathematics instruction in their schools and districts over the long term.

If the norms and values embedded in the mathematics education reform movement are to become a permanent part of school life, there will need to be not only a "restructuring" of current school schedules and curricula, but also a "reculturing" of school (Fullan, 1991). That is, not only is it necessary for teachers to reinvent mathematics instruction from within a new conceptual frame, it also is necessary for teachers and administrators together to reinvent school culture from within a new conceptual frame. What is needed is to develop a school culture in which ongoing intellectual curiosity is encouraged for everyone— students, teachers and administrators; in which teachers and administrators develop working relationships that are more like problem-solving partnerships than like hierarchies; and in which all parties share an understanding of the nature of learning and teaching that will occur there and do their part to make it happen.

Administrators—building principals, assistant superintendents of curriculum and instruction—are key actors in this process. And many of the administrators participating in MFT perceive that it is "reculturing" that is at issue. Last spring we asked the 14 administrator-participants how their involvement in MFT could help them do their work. They listed the following, saying that they would like to:

- Participate actively with teachers in all parts of MFT so that they would know the culture of the group and would understand deeply what teachers are doing
- Form new relationships between principals and teachers— relationships of collegiality, through which they can work on issues of mathematics education reform *together*
- Understand the "big ideas" of the mathematics curriculum and be able to sort them from the "extraneous stuff"
- Learn how to spread ideas in a school, encouraging teachers to help their peers
- Develop new criteria and skills for classroom observation and teacher supervision
- Develop the expectation in their districts and among teachers that teacher development is not a one-year process but requires deep understanding of a subject or approach and a long period of experimentation
- Figure out how to fundamentally rethink "what we do and why we do it (we haven't come very far since 1892!)."

We are currently engaged in sustained work with these administrators on these issues. The centerpiece of the activity is an "Administrators' Inquiry Group," in which administrators inquire into their practice in ways analogous to teachers' inquiry into their practice, and a "consultation" in which project staff work with administrators on a short-term basis to help them rethink their approach to a school issue of their choice. These interventions have the same rationale as the project's teacher development project; namely, that conceptual development is a necessary part of the process of change and that that happens according to constructivist principles.

Planning for Large-Scale Teacher Change

Several issues emerge from our work that might inform thinking about the process of "scaling-up." First, the process of teacher development is intense and time-consuming, both in each year of teacher participation and in overall duration. Once teachers have solidly moved into a mode of thought and practice in which they are basing their teaching on what they know about their students' mathematical thought and have the goal of extending the strength of their students' mathematical thinking, their practice will continue to evolve on an ongoing basis. Getting to that point may take two to four years, depending on the teacher. So, the resources necessary for scaling-up need to be thought of not only in terms of the number of teachers one reaches in a given year but also with regard to the capacity to proved supports for those teachers during that year and to stay with those teachers for several years.

Second, because of the need for creating small communities of teachers who can work together with a teacher educator, and because the number of teachers that a teacher educator can work with in this mode is on the order of 10–12, not 20–30, one might have an image of scaling up that is modular. Rather than trying to reach all the teachers in a district by simply adding individual teachers to a project, one by one, creating ever-larger projects, one might think about creating small groups, and then clusters of groups. One needs to keep the basic units small enough, and sufficiently long-term, that teachers can get to know each other well and the teacher educator can get to know each of the teachers well.

Third, since much of what is at issue is the creating of a different intellectual and pedagogical culture in schools, doing work that is school based and includes both school and district administrators is highly desirable.

The limiting factor in scaling up is the number of people who are currently experienced at working with teachers in a mode that supports their conceptual reconstruction of their work. The number is growing all the time, but it is still small. Funding agencies might want to consider funding (a) apprenticeship programs in which teachers who have participated in such programs can learn to facilitate the work of other teachers or (b) collaborations among teacher educators, in which expertise can be shared, in order to expand the field's capacity to work with teachers on a large scale.

Monitoring/Evaluating

Ideally, one would want the monitoring process to follow closely the teacher change process, documenting the conditions that appear to provide support for teachers to fundamentally rethink their beliefs, deepen their mathematics knowledge, and begin to reconstruct their practice. If the monitoring were structured as a research enterprise, rather than as the evaluation of a particular funded project, we might also learn important things that are more general that project evaluations typically provide.

Acknowledgment

The project was supported in part by the National Science Foundation (Grant No. ESI-954479). The opinions expressed are those of the author and do not necessarily reflect the views of the Foundation.

References

Fennema, E., Carpenter, T., Franke, M. L., & Carey, D. A. (1992). Learning to use children's mathematical thinking: A case study. In R. Davis & C. Maher (Eds.), *Relating schools to reality* (pp. 119–34). Boston: Allyn and Bacon.

Fullan, M. G. (1991). *Change forces: Probing the depths of education reform.* New York: Falmer Press.

Hammerman, J. K. (1995). Teacher inquiry groups: Collaborative explorations of changing practice. In B. S. Nelson, (Ed.), *Inquiry and the development of teaching: Working papers on critical issues in the development of mathematics teaching* (pp. 45–55). Newton, MA.: Center for the Development of Teaching, EDC.

Russell, S. J., & Corwin, R. B. (1993). Talking mathematics: "Going slow" and "letting go." *Phi Delta Kappan, 74*(7), 12.

Schifter, D. (Ed.) (1996–a). *What's happening in math class: Envisioning new practices through teacher narratives.* New York: Teachers College Press.

Schifter, D. (Ed.) (1996–b). *What's happening in math class: Reconstructing professional identities.* New York: Teachers College Press.

Schifter, D., & Fosnot, C. T. (1993). Reconstructing mathematics education: Stories of teachers meeting the challenge of reform. New York: Teachers College Press.

Wood, T., Cobb, P., & Yackel, E. (1991). Change in teaching mathematics: A case study. American Educational Research Journal, 28(3), 587–616.

Comprehensive School and District Restructuring of Mathematics: Principles and Caveats

Ruth E. Parker

From 1985 through 1992 the work of the California Mathematics Leadership Program (CMLP) was directly concerned with the question, "What does it take to bring about substantive school-wide restructuring of mathematics programs at the elementary and middle school levels?" Since that time, the principle staff of the former CMLP have directed their efforts to determining what it takes to bring about substantive restructuring of mathematics programs on a district wide level. The goal of our work has been to support the development of children and teachers as knowledgeable, responsible, and reflective decision makers able to use mathematics in powerful ways to interpret information and to make sense of complex situations. Our aim was to help teachers provide a mathematics curriculum that challenges students' intellect and natural curiosity, develops their persistence and flexibility, encourages them to interact around important mathematical ideas, and enables them to use mathematics to make sense of their world. In order for this to occur, teachers would have to become reflective decision makers confident in their understanding of mathematics and responsive to the needs of children. Teachers would need ongoing opportunities to develop an understanding of (a) the nature of mathematics as well as important mathematical ideas, (b) how learners construct mathematical understandings, (c) ways to create a classroom environment that maximizes the doing and learning of mathematics, and (d) more authentic ways of assessing mathematical understanding. We knew that these understandings would develop over time through a process of education not training.

We have experienced first hand the complexity of the task, and offer the following sets of principles and caveats for consideration. The first encompass those that guide the restructuring of the mathematics curriculum and the teaching and learning environment. The second guide the development of teacher leaders able to assist peers and others through the complexities of the restructuring process.

Restructuring the Mathematics Curriculum and the Teaching and Learning Environment

1. *Content and instructional practices of mathematics staff development efforts must be fully consistent with the new paradigm we want teachers to understand.* Constructivism is the learning theory on which all of our work was based. Whether we were addressing theory, mathematical ideas, or learning environment issues, ideas were presented, and teachers were given opportunities to experience the ideas first-hand as learners and then to reflect on their own experiences as learners and the implications for their classrooms.

2. *Teachers cannot teach mathematics differently until they have experienced mathematics differently.* Inservice efforts must involve teachers as active learners. Mathematics for teachers as learners was an essential element of each CMLP inservice session. It should be noted that this practice was not always popular with teachers. As a staff we were quite convinced of the need to help teachers become mathematically confident and competent. We continued to involve teachers in "doing" mathematics even though some teachers argued that they couldn't afford the time. Their preference was that we provide new activities for their classrooms and tell them how to implement the activities. Our experience suggests that over time, teachers come to highly value this process and their own mathematical empowerment. By their third year in the project teachers consistently requested more mathematics for themselves. This is a critical point in time, after which teachers are eager for and open to new experiences, and able to more fully understand and implement ideas encountered.

3. *The full complexity of the change process must be anticipated and acknowledged.* Change of this magnitude will be messy, and will involve levels of discomfort, frustration, and even anger. A natural part of the change process is a long period of time when teachers are dissatisfied with their old practices before they feel competent with their newly developing understandings and methods. During this time of struggle there will be a tendency for many to retreat to a safer place. For a substantial period of time, teachers continue to believe a change agent should be able to provide a detailed scope and sequence and present information in a way that makes the process easy for teachers to implement. This belief is consistent with many staff development efforts teachers have experienced. It is not consistent, however, with a constructivist theory of learning, with the goal of teaching in ways responsive to children, nor with a view of mathematics as a science that involves conjectures, observations, investigations and experiments.

During this period of discomfort, the change agent is the natural target for teachers' frustrations.

4. *A school-wide commitment to restructuring is necessary.* We need to impact the culture and expectations for mathematics education at the school level and create environments where risk taking is valued and change is expected. In addition to providing an environment where teachers are encouraged and supported in their change efforts, school-wide efforts are necessary if children are to have opportunities to develop mathematical power. Essential mathematical ideas develop in complexity over time. While nine months with a teacher who loves mathematics can be beneficial, students don't really have opportunities to develop mathematical power unless there is articulation within a school's mathematics program. Children need consistent opportunities over time to develop their understanding of important mathematical ideas. School staffs need consistent opportunities over time to develop the same understandings before they are able to articulate their mathematics curriculum in meaningful ways.

5. *Principals must be full participants in inservice efforts.* Active participation is necessary if principals are to be knowledgeable of mathematics reform goals, able to distinguish between classroom practices consistent and inconsistent with those goals, understanding of the change process, prepared to support teachers' risk taking and growth through periods of confusion and discouragement, and able to effectively communicate the necessity and goals of mathematics reform efforts to parents and to teachers.

The nature of principal participation seemed to directly affect the level of successful mathematics restructuring at participating schools. It is important to clearly convey the necessity for active principal participation prior to restructuring efforts. Even with prior commitments, principals will interpret "active participation" in diverse ways. It is essential to involve district level decision makers in efforts to ensure high levels of principal participation. We are convinced that where minimal participation occurred it was not a result of lack of interest or support for teachers' restructuring efforts. It seemed instead to be a result of at least two major obstacles: (a) the fact that principals' already have very demanding work loads and (b) conventional beliefs that it is enough for principals to be philosophically aligned with reform goals and unnecessary for them to be deeply knowledgeable of the specifics of what teachers are trying to do. This can become a difficult issue to address once non-participation or minimal participation patterns are established. Districts must find ways to help principals overcome the first obstacle by providing incentives such as monetary support so that principals can hire their own people to act as substitute principals so that they are free to attend project events. This kind of support also results in a dismantling of the second obstacle. Principals who do attend project events are consistently convinced that their participation with their staffs is essential to successful school-wide restructuring.

6. *Long-term support (at least four to five years of intensive workshops and site-based follow up) is needed.* Just as children's understanding of important mathematical ideas develops over time, the same is true for teachers. Change of the magnitude called for by the NCTM *Standards*, necessitates a reexamination and fundamental restructuring of nearly every aspect of mathematics instruction—the content of the curriculum, the learning environment, the role of the teacher, and means of assessment.

It is easier to maintain this level of commitment if decision makers understand that long-term mathematics restructuring efforts result in benefits that extend beyond a school's mathematics program. Learning to teach so that children have opportunities to construct their understanding of essential ideas in mathematics and learning to teach in ways that are responsive to the emergent understandings and interests of children, will cause teachers to reexamine their practices in every other area of the curriculum. Teachers who have participated in these mathematics restructuring efforts over time come to understand the commonalties with reform efforts in other curriculum areas, and embrace those efforts.

7. *Parent education is essential.* Our experience suggests that parents become strong advocates for change if they are kept informed of the need for change and nature of change needed in mathematics education. It can be anticipated that some parents will actively and vocally resist mathematics restructuring efforts. It is unfair to expect teachers to adequately articulate the need for reform or the content of reform efforts to parents before they have had opportunities to experience new practices themselves. Purposeful opportunities for experts to communicate with parents should be built into restructuring efforts.

8. *Teachers should not be encouraged to write mathematics curriculum during restructuring efforts.* The common practice of bringing together good teachers and providing time for them to write curriculum that can be shared with other teachers is often counter-productive. Writing good mathematics curriculum that can be used effectively by others is extremely difficult.

9. *School-wide change efforts must anticipate and respect the diversity of individual teachers' understanding and implementation of desired innovations.* We would caution against being too quick to label teachers or teacher leadership candidates. Some project teachers who

seemed most resistant to suggested changes had, in the long run, great positive impact on their schools. Conversely, some of the teachers identified as leaders or those feeling most confident were unable to reexamine practices and showed little growth. The same was true of teacher leader candidates.

10. *Efforts should be made to develop leadership capacity within participating schools.* Site liaisons can play an important role in supporting ongoing growth during and subsequent to a school's four to five year involvement with an outside change agent. During a school's second year of involvement with CMLP, two site liaisons were identified at each participating school. Attempts were made to identify teachers who had credibility with their staffs and who were also willing to take risks and push for deep level mathematics restructuring in their own classrooms. These two teachers from each site participated with other site liaisons in an extra day a month of inservice designed to support them in implementing deep level restructuring and developing leadership skills. These teachers have played important roles at their sites. They provide informal support to other teachers throughout the school as they talk about their own struggles and successes as they've worked to restructure their mathematics programs; their classrooms become laboratories where the principal and other teachers can observe, first-hand, what it looks like to teach in ways aligned with NCTM *Standards*; and they provide a knowledgeable voice during staff and other meetings and are able to question whether current practices or new ideas are congruent with educational goals established by NCTM and other mathematics reformers.

11. *A school district should be viewed as the unit for mathematics restructuring efforts. School-wide change efforts are essential but not sufficient.* In order to sustain restructuring efforts, district level commitment and support is needed. Unless the issue of teacher and principal turnover is adequately addressed, schools that have gone through restructuring efforts are likely, in relatively few years, to become indistinguishable from those that have not.

Just as school-wide restructuring efforts have multiple and complex systemic implications and effects for schools, the same is true for districts. First, providing long-term mathematics staff development to schools requires a financial commitment from districts that far exceeds the usual practice of providing a collection of unrelated short-term staff development opportunities for interested teachers. In order to commit such resources, district level decision makers must be convinced that efforts are doable and will result in deep-level restructuring aligned with the district's vision and goals for education.

Second, even with such a commitment, a district has multiple demands for limited resources. There is the potential for program personnel from areas other than mathematics to put pressure on district decision makers for their "piece of the pie." Purposeful efforts must be made to convince all players that mathematics reform can provide a lever for reform in other curriculum areas. Teachers and administrators participating in sustained mathematics restructuring aligned with the *Standards* will come to understand constructivism, how the human brain works, performance assessment, what it means to do mathematics rather than learn about mathematics, the kinds of classroom environments that support learning and promote the development of autonomous learners, the value of complex investigations, the necessity to develop dispositions toward persistence and searching for patterns and relationships, the importance of helping children learn to work collaboratively, and the need both to communicate ideas and findings and to consider diverse ideas. All of these are essential characteristics of reform efforts in other curriculum areas. Efforts to have curriculum specialists and teachers from areas other than mathematics participate in mathematics restructuring efforts can result in strong support for those efforts as well as opportunities to understand how mathematics can be integrated within other curriculum areas.

Third, it is important that key players at the district level become intimately knowledgeable of the mathematics reform process, in order to communicate with their constituents and make appropriate ongoing decisions in support of reform efforts. District-level decision makers must be actively involved in a way that gives them first-hand knowledge of, and responsibility for, the change process. If this level of involvement does not occur, it is likely that districts will apply pressure to redirect efforts or prematurely cut back on the level of support needed for deep level restructuring to occur. Fourth, districts must invest in the development of teacher leaders who can facilitate mathematics restructuring efforts in schools throughout the district. Fifth, a process must be put in place to provide substantive and long-term support to new teachers, principals and parents who enter the district over time. Sixth, unless a district is willing to reexamine district level practices that may be at odds with reform efforts, enormous barriers will limit the scope of restructuring efforts.

12. *District and classroom level assessment must be aligned with mathematics reform efforts.* A mathematics program should be dynamic and responsive to the emergent needs and interests of students. As such, restructuring efforts must help teachers learn to observe and assess children's understanding. District assessments must also assess children's ability to do mathematics and their understanding of essential

mathematical ideas. Our experience suggests that standardized testing practices are one of the greatest barriers to teachers risking change while performance based assessment alternatives provide strong motivation and support for restructuring efforts.

13. *External change agents are needed.* Current conventional wisdom does suggest that school improvement efforts should respond to teacher identified needs, but we would like to challenge this notion. When it comes to school mathematics restructuring, there is no way for teachers who have only experienced mathematics traditionally to know what is needed. It takes a long time and many experiences before teachers come to understand important mathematical ideas, what it means to do mathematics, and how to restructure the classroom environment. The goal of mathematics restructuring efforts must be to empower teachers as instructional decision makers. Until these new understandings are developed, however, teachers are unable to design or even request appropriate kinds of mathematics inservice.

14. *It is important that ongoing inservice be provided by the same change agent or a team of change agents working closely together.* Teachers will need coordinated and consistent opportunities to deepen their understandings over time. We feel the common practice of providing a series of short term inservice efforts delivered by unrelated mathematics resource people is unlikely to provide relevant and consistent experiences that support teachers in deep level restructuring. Ongoing inservice efforts must be responsive to teachers' and schools' developing understandings.

15. *Substantial commitments of both financial and time resources are necessary if substantive change is to occur.* Our experience suggests that schools and districts are willing to make such commitments. Principals at participating CMLP schools expressed confidence and felt strongly that their sustained focus on mathematics and how children learn would impact teaching practices in all curriculum areas.

Leadership Development for Mathematics Restructuring

16. *We must invest in the preparation of mathematics change agents who can promote the development of teacher leaders and support district-wide restructuring efforts.* The role of change agent in mathematics restructuring efforts is complex. In order to impact change of the magnitude called for in the NCTM *Standards*, change agents will need credibility on a variety of levels: First, they must have classroom teaching experience aligned with mathematics reform goals. First-hand understanding of what it means to teach mathematics for understanding,

personal anecdotal experiences, and a willingness to teach mathematics in teachers' classrooms are important characteristics for change agents. Teachers have developed a perhaps healthy skepticism of outside experts over the years. Second, ongoing involvement with national mathematics and assessment reform efforts is essential. Teachers, principals, and district decision makers need to see their change agents as experts in their field. Third, change agents must be deeply knowledgeable of the complexities of educational change processes. They must remain firmly committed to providing long-term, high quality support aligned with the goals of mathematics reform in the face of sometimes overwhelming pressure to offer simpler and/or faster solutions.

17. *Mathematics change agents should work in teams with colleagues.* There are two major reasons why change agents should work in teams. First, while many mathematics reform issues relate directly to all levels (primary, intermediate, middle school and high schools), the way those issues play out in specific day-to-day classroom practices varies significantly at those levels. Expertise must be provided at each level while assuring that consistent and compatible practices are promoted overall. Articulation between grade levels and between school levels will become important as districts work to institutionalize powerful mathematics programs. Second, restructuring efforts that result in classrooms, schools and districts aligned with the NCTM *Standards* are long-term, involve many unanticipated surprises, and can often be messy, uncomfortable and frustrating for both participants and change agents. Change agents will need the support that comes from working in teams as they work to understand and communicate with their constituents about the complex dynamics involved in change efforts of this magnitude.

18. *We must invest in the development of teacher leaders prepared to facilitate school-wide mathematics restructuring.* There are insufficient numbers of current leaders available to support school-wide restructuring efforts on a broad scale. The work of the CMLP has demonstrated that teacher leaders can be prepared to successfully facilitate school-wide mathematics restructuring efforts. The complexities of preparing such teacher leaders must not be underestimated. Leaders facilitating school-wide efforts must understand fully what it takes to implement a restructured mathematics program in their own classrooms. They also need to understand the change process and be prepared to challenge current practices and support teachers through times of discomfort and discontent.

19. *Teacher leaders must receive inservice and ongoing support as they work to restructure their own mathematics classrooms in ways*

aligned with the NCTM Standards. Our experience suggests that a minimum of two to three years is necessary for this phase, depending on factors such as the leadership selection process and teacher leaders' previous mathematics education experiences. Unless teacher leaders deeply understand the magnitude of change needed and what it takes to bring about this change in a classroom, they will lack both credibility and self-confidence in their attempts to help teachers and schools bring about these changes.

20. *After restructuring their classrooms, teacher leaders must receive inservice and ongoing support as they work to facilitate school-wide mathematics restructuring efforts.* The job of being a change agent is a difficult one. The change agent is the natural target for vented frustrations during the long and necessary periods of discomfort and confusion that will occur with major change efforts. Teacher leaders will need ongoing opportunities to network with others involved in similar efforts. It is important that teacher leaders working to facilitate school-wide mathematics restructuring do so with a partner. The support is essential and having two perspectives helps in trying to understand the complex dynamics involved in major change efforts.

21. *Our experience suggests that it is very difficult for teacher leaders to be change agents with their own peers.* As such, we would not recommend that teacher leaders work with their own faculties. Although site liaisons provide important support as schools work to restructure their mathematics programs, they should not be given the responsibility of facilitating those efforts.

22. *For many of the same reasons, we suspect that change agents from outside a district might be necessary to district level mathematics restructuring efforts if deep level systemic change is to occur.* Change of this magnitude happening on a district-wide basis results in challenges to many existing structures and practices within a district. Just as the complexity of the change process ensures levels of discomfort, frustration and even periods of anger for teachers, the same is true for districts. We suspect that change agents, working in concert with district decision makers but removed from the internal politics of the district, are necessary to successful restructuring efforts.

A Note to State and Federal Funding Agencies

Purposeful, intensive, and sustained efforts at district level mathematics restructuring must occur on a massive scale if we are to impact the infrastructure of mathematics education throughout this country. Recognition, on the part of funding agencies, of the full complexity of such efforts is essential in order for adequate funding structures to be put in place.

We must invest in the development of leaders able to provide ongoing support to schools and districts working to restructure their mathematics programs. The number of mathematics leaders prepared and available to facilitate district-wide restructuring efforts is woefully inadequate. As demand for sustained mathematics restructuring support for schools and districts increases, there is a need to greatly increase our capacity to provide such support. The complexity and longevity of the task of preparing mathematics leaders should not be underestimated. We do know that teacher leaders can facilitate restructuring efforts that result in deep level changes in the teaching of mathematics at the school level. We also know that the conventional practice of providing short-term trainer-of-trainer models for preparing mathematics leaders must be re-examined. It is unlikely that such models will result in a significant number of leaders with first-hand knowledge of what it takes to align classrooms with mathematics reform goals, and deeply knowledgeable of and prepared for the complex job of providing sustained mathematics restructuring support to schools and districts. It seems essential that state, national and private funding agencies work to leverage efforts to support the development of infrastructures that make leadership development and sustained mathematics restructuring support available to districts on a widespread scale.

The Role of Curriculum in Teacher Development

Susan Jo Russell
TERC

There are several views of curriculum that we, as mathematics educators, often encounter. (In this essay, "we" refers to the group at TERC that has been working through these ideas while developing the K–5 curriculum, *Investigations in Number, Data, and Space*.) One is that teachers, especially elementary teachers, are so under-prepared in mathematics that the curriculum must do everything for them. It must tell them exactly what to do, when to do it, and in what order. Once this was called "teacher-proof" curriculum. Now, of course, that term is no longer fashionable, so teacher-proof-ness, when it is espoused at all, is couched in other terms. For example, a textbook representative recently described to me the lessons in their teacher's guide by saying, "And it's all scripted for the teacher, so that they know what questions to ask." This view of curriculum assumes that there is a Right Way to organize and teach the curriculum, and that, if we have a curriculum that embodies this right way, students will learn mathematics well.

Another view holds that it is only the teacher who knows her students' learning needs well enough to continually modify the classroom environment in response to those needs. Therefore, the teacher must develop her/his own curriculum. Sometimes this view admits that, because teachers are not *yet* adequately prepared to teach mathematics, we may need innovative curricula now—temporarily—*until* we have accomplished the job of large-scale teacher development. This is the view of curriculum as a necessary evil—we don't want it, but we can't yet do without it.

A third view, somewhere between these two, is that of curriculum as reference material. The argument goes something like this. Teachers don't have the time or energy to develop all the curricula for all the subjects they teach. Therefore, they need good reference materials from which they can put together a curriculum of their own. This allows teachers to be creative and to become acquainted with new ideas. The curriculum is a reference library in which teachers browse.

We disagree with all of these positions. Or, perhaps, since all of these have probably been somewhat unjustly characterized, it is more accurate to say that we are trying to find some new ways to articulate what curriculum contributes to the learning and teaching of mathematics. This new articulation is possible, and necessary, because new curricula that are currently being developed are quite different from our traditional notion of what a curriculum is and make possible a different kind of partnership between teacher and curriculum materials.

Perhaps we have been without "good" curricula for so long that we have very low expectations about what curriculum materials can provide. We are used to thinking of a curriculum as something that robs the teacher of her professional judgment and/or does not model mathematical thinking and reasoning as promoted in the NCTM *Standards*. We would like to put forth a new view of what curriculum can be. We believe that curriculum materials, when developed through careful, extended work with diverse students and teachers, when based on sound mathematics and on what we know about how people learn mathematics, are a tool that allows the teacher to do her best work with students. As these new curricula begin to appear, we need new ways to think about the role of curriculum.

We see the best mathematics teaching environment as a partnership between teacher and curriculum. Both teacher and curriculum bring important contributions to this partnership that the other cannot do well. It is not possible for most teachers to write a complete, coherent, mathematically-sound curriculum. It is not insulting to teachers as professionals to admit this. Curriculum development, like teaching mathematics, is a job that requires people and resources; it requires a skilled team of mathematics educators spending many thousands of hours writing, thinking, working in classrooms, and listening to students and teachers. We do not sell teachers short by recognizing that they cannot do this job.

But only the teacher is there in the classroom, observing and trying to understand her students' mathematical thinking. Individual teachers must continually assess and modify their mathematics program for their own classroom. Thus, curriculum is not a recipe or a compendium of what "should" be taught at a particular grade level. Rather, it provides both a coherent mathematics program for students, based on the best thinking available in the field, and material that supports teachers in making better, more thoughtful, more informed decisions about their students' mathematics learning.

The link between curriculum and teacher decision-making is a focus on mathematical reasoning. Neither curriculum nor teacher can fully anticipate the complex and idiosyncratic nature of the mathematical thinking that might go on among thirty students in a single classroom during any one mathematics class. However, both teacher and curriculum contribute to a repertoire of knowledge about student thinking that leads to better mathematics teaching and learning.

How does this work? Each curriculum unit presents a few, related significant mathematical ideas. The curriculum provides four types of information about these ideas: a series of activities for students, explication of aspects of the mathematics content, discussion of students' mathematical thinking in the context of this particular content, and pointers toward issues of pedagogy that arise as students engage with the content. Only the first of these is something provided directly for students; much of what the curriculum provides is for teachers. Curriculum is, in fact, primarily a tool for teacher development. This is a radically different conception of curriculum; it is one that makes it possible for teachers to truly be in partnership with the curriculum rather than simply using it as a guide for sequencing student work.

In order for this partnership to work, curriculum must do its job. What it provides for students is important, but what it provides to support teachers is equally important. Curriculum can only support teachers honestly if it has been developed through intense partnerships with teachers and students. In this kind of development work, curriculum authors are in classrooms *frequently*, each part of the curriculum is thoroughly field-tested in diverse classrooms, and field data are carefully reviewed to inform revision of the materials. This kind of development process results not only in good investigations for the range of students, but also in a wealth of information about how students approach those investigations, what mathematical issues are central to their understanding, what pragmatic and pedagogical issues arise for the teacher, and ways in which teachers can modify and/or extend the investigations to suit their individual class. The curriculum materials must then be designed so that this information is available to the teacher. Let me give an example from a recent episode in a field test classroom of how this works. (Teachers quoted in this essay are participants in an NSF-funded project, Teaching to the Big Ideas, a joint project of EDC, TERC, and Summermath for Teachers at Mt. Holyoke College. Pseudonyms are used.)

Meg, a second-grade field test teacher, is using an activity called "Enough for the Class," in which students consider whether the number of cubes in a bag is enough for each student in the class to have one. If it's not, how many more are needed? If it is, are there extras? Meg thinks of this problem as a subtraction situation and assumes that her students will do something like the following sequence of steps: 1) find out how many cubes are in the bag; 2) remove the number of cubes equal to the number of students in the class; 3) figure out or count how many cubes remain. One day she gives them the following problem: there are 16 blue cubes and 17 red cubes; are there enough for the class? Students quickly decide that there are enough for the class of 26 students and begin figuring out how many extra cubes there will be. Meg is taken by surprise when some of her students solve the problem this way: I can take 10 cubes from the 16 and 10 cubes from the 17, that makes 20. Then I need 6 more cubes, so I take away 6 from the 16. Now I have 26, enough for the class. That leaves just the 7 cubes from the 17, so there are 7 extra. Without ever finding the total, Meg's students have solved the problem. Meg wrote about this episode: "Many children actually did solve the problem the way I expected. Many didn't.... They showed a lovely ability and willingness to take numbers apart and put numbers together. They ... had made sense of what was being asked. But they still didn't figure out how many cubes there were in all! I am not sure what surprises me more—that so many children don't think explicitly about the whole or the total when solving these problems, or that it never occurred to me that they didn't have to."

This is exactly the kind of episode that finds its way into the curriculum itself. We may include a classroom dialogue, based on this episode, to provide teachers with illustrations of the kinds of issues that tend to come up as students talk about their approaches to a mathematical problem. In addition, we would include notes for the teacher about the mathematical issues raised in this episode, in this case, the relationship between addition and subtraction in the structure of this problem and how students' strategies are related to their understanding of the number system. Episodes like this one provide guidance and examples for teachers who may encounter similar mathematical issues in their classrooms. They alert teachers to important mathematical ideas they may have been unaware of, and they provide guidance about engaging students with these ideas. In many ways, each mathematics unit of study, then, becomes a minicourse for teachers about a particular domain of mathematics. As teachers use new curriculum units more than once, they can learn more mathematics and more about their students' mathematical thinking. What they learn from watching and listening to their students will illuminate what they read in the teacher book, while what they read there will alert them to how to better listen and watch. Curriculum must help the teacher assess her students' understanding throughout the year, provide models of mathematical talk that stimulates and supports student thinking, and offer ways for the teacher to learn more about the mathematics she is teaching.

We have often observed that—as part of the old view of curriculum as the RIGHT WAY—when something in a curriculum doesn't work, people consider the curriculum—or the students—to be flawed. Rather, *the curriculum itself must assume that what it suggests won't always work*. No matter how well curriculum materials are tested, no matter how many times they are revised, each school brings its own mix of resources and barriers, each classroom brings its own set of needs, styles, experiences, and interests on the part of both teacher and students, and each day in the classroom brings its own set of issues, catastrophes, and opportunities. We could test and revise endlessly; each classroom test would result in new ideas we might incorporate and raise new questions about pedagogy or content. But at some point we have to decide that the curriculum materials themselves are *good enough*—ready for teachers to use and revise in their own classrooms. Teacher decision-making, therefore, is key, and the curriculum must be designed with this assumption in mind. The teacher's role is to connect the particulars of her classroom and students to investigations in the curriculum.

Taking this role seriously involves making decisions about which mathematical ideas to pursue. Because there are so many connections within the domain of mathematics, issues often emerge from students' thinking that are different from what the teacher—or the curriculum—anticipated. The teacher must decide which mathematical ideas are important to pursue at this time with the whole class, which might be best to pursue with an individual student, and which to put aside. In the following episode, a fifth grade teacher is faced with a choice about whether to move away from the topic on which she expected to focus in order to deal with an unexpected issue that comes to her attention.

Kate watched her students play a number game which involved arranging digits to form 2-digit numbers with a sum as close to 100 as possible. (The game is described in Mokros & Russell, 1995, p. 22.) This game was challenging for many of Kate's poorly prepared students. The game was part of a series of activities focused on developing knowledge about 100, its place in the number system, and its relationships to other numbers. Students scored each round by comparing their sum to 100: a sum lower than 100 was scored as a negative number (e.g., 97 would result in a score of -3); a sum higher than 100 resulted in a positive score (e.g., 101 would result in a score of 1); and a sum of exactly 100 resulted in a score of 0. At the end of several rounds, students added their scores from all rounds; the closer their sum to 0, the better their score. Kate noticed that when students used a number line to compute their total score, they tended to skip zero. She wrote, "The score of 0, which usually meant nothing, was now the highest score ... they decided that if 0 was actually the winning score, it was a pretty important number and really shouldn't be skipped. Usually when they had a score of 0 (for example on a spelling test), it wasn't great. So they had to rethink what 0 meant in this game while they played." As she watched her students, she realized that they were confused about the relationship among positive integers, zero, and negative integers. She devised a problem about owing money to support her students' explorations of these relationships. After some work on these problems, she asked her students to consider what +1 cent, 0 cents, and -1 cent might mean. They decided that +1 meant "a penny you could hold," that 0 meant no money and you don't owe anything, while -1 cents was "a cent that you owe." She concludes, "I'm not sure they understand this, and I hope to work on it some more ... but it did raise a lot of issues." She lists questions she'd like to explore with her students: What is 0? How is 0 used in different ways? Are there numbers that are less than 0? How many numbers can there be that are less than 0?

Curriculum Materials as a Tool for Teacher Development

Decisions like Kate's are complex. Kate needs to consider what mathematics is important for her students, whether a digression from the ideas they are currently pursuing is warranted, and how to create a context and problems that are appropriate for her students. How can teachers like Kate be supported as they use good curriculum materials, try to understand student thinking, and design next steps? It is clear to all of us who have been involved in developing curriculum that any curriculum materials, no matter how well they can be used, can also be used badly and can be misunderstood and distorted. Teachers have not necessarily been prepared, in their own mathematics education, to focus on student thinking or to see their role as partners with the curriculum in the way that we have described this partnership here. The best use of good curriculum materials is in the context of a long-term staff development program which engages teachers in ongoing reflection about students' mathematical thinking and continued work on mathematics content with their peers.

Professional development courses that use innovative curriculum materials as a core can be designed for both preservice and inservice teachers. For inservice work, this professional development/implementation might be composed of two elements: intensive components (e.g., a two-week summer course, or several three-day sessions during the school year) and ongoing, long-term interaction (e.g., a study group of grades 3–4 teachers within a school) that provides a continuing forum for thinking about mathematics content and about students' mathematical thinking. The ongoing school-based component provides the scheduled occasions and communication with peers to stimulate continued thinking and learning as well as help in grappling with the everyday, pragmatic concerns of implementation. However, it is critical that the design of these experiences does not focus on "how to do" the curriculum, but on the development of the teacher's professional expertise—increased experience with mathematics content and with understanding the development of mathematical understanding. This means that teacher leaders who act as facilitators for these ongoing groups need their own support and training so that they can help the teachers in their school or system focus on understanding children's mathematical thinking and developing approaches to best support and extend that thinking. The use of curriculum materials as a core for professional development provides a direct link between teacher enhancement and what actually happens in the classroom. Professional development of this sort has two advantages: (a) the teachers leave the professional development experience with a concrete unit (or units) of instruction—a way to begin implementing what they have learned, and (b) the materials themselves continue to provide information and support to teachers as they teach. They serve as a catalyst for engaging teachers in thinking about children's mathematical thinking—a way of continuing the professional development experience.

Another valuable tool to support this kind of staff development would be classroom episodes, written by teachers, about their own experiences as they used particular curriculum materials. These episodes would describe students' mathematical work, discuss issues about mathematics or children's mathematical thinking that were raised for the teacher by this work, and give examples of decisions made by the teacher based on her observations and reflections. Schifter (this volume) describes some ways that this can happen.

Elsewhere (Russell, Schifter, Bastable, Yaffee, Lester, & Cohen, 1994), we have posited that we can never prepare elementary teachers well enough before they enter the classroom. "In fact, it appears that the new mathematical understandings teachers must develop and the teaching situations they must negotiate are too varied, complex, and context-dependent to be anticipated in one or even several courses. Thus, teachers must become learners in their own classrooms." Teachers must continue to learn mathematics and to learn about students' mathematical thinking as they teach. Curriculum materials that are designed to support ongoing teacher development can be an important tool in this endeavor. As teachers teach a particular curriculum unit—or related units at different grade levels—they meet together regularly. Material for teachers in the curriculum becomes a focus for study and helps the teachers identify areas of mathematics about which they need to know more and questions about children's thinking they need to investigate. These efforts need to be supported by a good facilitator, which may be a teacher who has received special training, as well as writing by other teachers about mathematical issues they have faced in their own classrooms.

Meg and Kate are doing exactly what we want curriculum to orient teachers towards—reflecting on students' thinking, trying to understand it, and then planning the next step. This constant decision-making should be what we expect. It's not a matter of using curriculum or not using curriculum, but of intelligent teachers using intelligent curriculum intelligently.

Acknowledgments

Some of the ideas discussed in this essay are elaborated on in the book, *Beyond Arithmetic: Changing Mathematics in Elementary Classrooms* by Jan Mokros, Susan Jo Russell, and Karen Economopoulos (Palo Alto: Dale Seymour Publications, 1995). The work discussed in this essay was supported in part by the National Science Foundation (Grants MDR-9050210 and ESI-9254393). Opinions are those of the author and do not necessarily represent the views of the Foundation.

References

Mokros, J., & Russell, S. J. (1995). *Investigations in number, data, and space*. Palo Alto: Dale Seymour Publications.

Russell, S. J., Schifter, D., Bastable, V., Yaffee, L., Lester, J. B., & Cohen, S. (1994). Learning mathematics while teaching. In D. Kirshner (Ed.), *Proceedings of the sixteenth annual meeting of the North America Chapter of Psychology of Mathematics Education, 2*, 289–95. Baron Rouge, LA: Louisiana State University.

Attention to Mathematical Thinking:
Teaching to the Big Ideas

Deborah Schifter
Education Development Center

Virginia Bastable
Mount Holyoke College

Susan Jo Russell
TERC

Teaching to the Big Ideas (TBI) is a four-year professional development and research project in which teachers and staff, both collaboratively and in their respective settings, address those central organizing principles of mathematics that emerge in classroom contexts when instruction is organized around and responsive to student thinking. Through our work as mathematics teachers and teacher educators, TBI staff have found that there are particular themes—embodying critical mathematical concepts—that arise time after time with different groups of learners and with which students must wrestle as they confront the limitations of their existing conceptions. It is by listening to students, remarking on common areas of confusion or persistently intriguing questions, and then analyzing underlying issues that these big ideas are identified. Developing a practice oriented toward big ideas would mean giving one's students avenues for confrontation with these basic principles and time to work through their confusions in order to construct new, more inclusive understandings.

At the time of this writing, the TBI project is about to enter its fourth and final year. The project was designed to have a group of 36 elementary teachers work with project staff to identify the mathematical themes that consistently emerge as teachers open up their instruction to student thinking. The first year of the project was devoted to helping teachers begin to think about mathematics in terms of ideas, rather than just facts, procedures, and strategies; learn to listen to and analyze student thinking; and consider the pedagogical implications of committing to helping students become powerful mathematical thinkers. In the second and third years, teachers regularly wrote two- to five-page "classroom episodes" for our seminars, presenting some aspect of the mathematical thinking of a single student or a group of students. The purpose of this exercise was to help teachers to listen carefully (and differently) to the mathematical thinking of their students, to raise mathematical and pedagogical issues that invite discussion and further analysis among colleagues, and to provide a sampling of elementary students' mathematical thinking for TBI teachers and staff to study in the aggregate.

Based on the TBI teachers' writing, the project created a professional development curriculum, to be used with other groups of teachers, called Developing Mathematical Ideas (Schifter, et al., in preparation). At the heart of the curriculum are sets of classroom episodes, illustrating student thinking as described by their teachers. In addition to case discussions, the curriculum is supplemented by a variety of other activities: Teachers share and discuss samples of their students' work; explore mathematics in lessons led by the facilitator; plan, conduct, and analyze mathematics interviews of one of their own students; view and discuss videotapes of mathematics classrooms and mathematics interviews; write their own cases; and read an overview of related research. At the time of this writing, we have developed two modules on the themes of "building a system of tens" and "making meaning for operations."

During the fourth year of the project, TBI teachers will implement school-wide dissemination plans designed collaboratively among teachers, school administrators, and project staff. Many of the TBI teams will be working with their colleagues in seminars based on the Developing Mathematical Ideas curriculum.

What We Have Learned

The TBI project design was based on five principles of teacher development which grew out of our work in previous projects (Russell & Corwin, 1993; Schifter, 1993; Schifter & Fosnot, 1993; Schifter, Russell, & Bastable, in press; Simon & Schifter, 1991).

1. *Just as mathematics instruction must be organized to facilitate construction of mathematical concepts, so should inservice instruction facilitate construction of a new pedagogical theory and practice.* Inservice programs must offer experiences that challenge dominant instructional paradigms, inviting participants to confront and work through such experiences if they wish to develop a more coherent and personally compelling practice for themselves. A corollary: just as students must learn to develop an attitude of inquiry toward

mathematics, so must teachers develop an attitude of inquiry toward their teaching, learning to pose questions about what their students understand and how they achieve that understanding, what kinds of interventions support student learning, etc.

2. *The general level of teachers' mathematical understanding must be raised.* It is well recognized that the mathematics pedagogy in place has not helped teachers develop the mathematical understandings required of the practice they are now being asked to adopt. Thus, teachers themselves must become mathematics learners. When they are challenged at their own levels of competence, are confronted with mathematical concepts and problems they have not encountered before, they both increase their mathematical knowledge and experience a depth of learning that is for many of them unprecedented. Not only must inservice programs provide opportunities for teachers to explore mathematics content, they must also help teachers learn *how to* learn mathematics in the context of their own teaching. This includes learning to pose mathematical questions and to follow, and assess the validity of, student reasoning (Russell, et al., 1994).

3. *Regular school-year follow-up support is an indispensable catalyst for the change process.* While visions of possibility can take shape in an inservice course or summer institute, the bulk of what teachers must learn will necessarily come only in their own classrooms with their own students. The new mathematical understandings they must develop and the teaching situations they will have to negotiate are too varied, complex, and context-dependent to be anticipated in one or even several courses. As teachers begin to change their practice to reflect new insights into the nature of mathematics and mathematics learning, they will be confronted with issues and ideas that could not have been predicted. Some kind of mechanism is required to help teachers learn to pose questions about the issues that arise and to help them learn how to think about those questions. While regular classroom supervision has proved to be effective, it is also labor intensive. A more cost-effective alternative, pursued in one teacher development project, had teachers writing, on a weekly basis, short narratives about events from their own mathematics classrooms. Participants met in small groups to share and discuss their narratives and received written feedback from the course instructor (Schifter, 1994).

4. *Teacher development and curriculum reform must support one another.* The understandings, mathematical and pedagogical, now required of teachers, develop over years rather than weeks or even months. They involve a grasp of connections among mathematical concepts, various modes of representation, and real-world situations, and

knowledge of which concepts and representations, in a given context, are likely to best support student learning. They include an appreciation of how mathematical truth is pursued, validity is established, and the kinds of arguments students are likely to offer and find satisfying. They require an integrated picture of the conceptual logic of the curriculum and ideas for mathematical investigations that will provide opportunities for student engagement. This means that curricular materials must become a vehicle for ongoing teacher development, helping teachers deepen their knowledge of mathematics content, children's mathematical thinking, and pedagogical approaches.

While such curriculum development projects (e.g., Russell, 1994) provide one model for written materials supporting on-going teacher development, writing projects (e.g., Schifter, 1994, 1996–a, 1996–b) offer another. The classroom narratives produced by teachers address issues that confront those working to transform their teaching along the lines proposed by the reforms, providing detailed images of students and teacher engaged in mathematical inquiry. These images, which offer interpretations of a reform agenda which is still foreign to many teachers, support both the development of visions of possibility as well as more fine-grained inquiry into specific aspects of the new pedagogy.

5. *School-wide collaboration is essential to the process of reform.* The workaday experience of most teachers is one of isolation; classroom doors are closed and while the few moments of daily collegial interaction allow for venting frustration over a particular problem student or a new piece of administrative folly, they don't permit serious discussion of instructional issues. In making so little provision for teachers to reflect together on their instruction, school structures support a culture of isolation consistent with traditional practice. But the kind of teaching now proposed, in investing greater instructional responsibility in the teacher, concomitantly entails greater need for collegial cooperation. In the long run, only teachers taking similar risks and experimenting with similar approaches are in a position to support one another. They can, and must, share their reflections on classroom process, help one another plan appropriate lessons, and explore together the mathematics they teach.

Thoughts on "Scaling Up"

The pedagogy proposed by the current reform movement is not about acquiring a set of behavioral routines. Rather, it involves developing a disposition toward inquiry—inquiry into student thinking, into mathematics, and into the kinds of classroom structures and instructional tasks that support students' mathematical understanding. Developing a disposition toward inquiry sharply contrasts with a second aspect of conventional school culture; namely, the assumption that teachers already know all they need to. But, unless this belief is challenged, any large-scale project for teacher change will be severely hampered. Initiating and sustaining a process of transformation among large numbers of teachers requires a changed school culture actively supporting teacher inquiry. Teachers will need to learn how to pose their own questions and will need reassurance that new cultural norms now allow them to freely discuss their own problems. And the school community will need to learn how to cope with the anxiety of leaving questions open long enough to examine them from a variety of perspectives. Whether a particular project begins with a focus on exploring mathematics, examining student thinking, considering alternative assessment, or surveying available resources, conscious attention on the part of project directors must be given to promoting an attitude of inquiry.

Issues of Assessment

There are three common interpretations of the current mathematics education reform movement which, we believe, are especially problematic:

1. Mathematics education reform as the introduction of particular tools, techniques, and strategies leaves basic instructional goals (remembering how to apply particular procedures to specific problem types) essentially unchanged. Many projects that focus on cooperative learning, or use of manipulatives, calculators, or computer technology tend to be of this type.

2. Mathematics education reform as the introduction of problem solving and student engagement abandons the traditional emphasis on memorization and rule-following but does not generate pursuit of such substantial mathematical-conceptual objectives as, say, exploring the structure of the number system or the properties of geometric shapes. While teachers may want to foster (and, at times, succeed in fostering) a "positive attitude toward mathematics," "mathematics" in this case becomes a mere collection of activities without coherence. Their students are left with neither "basic" skills, nor understanding of fundamental mathematical structure, nor the capacity to assess mathematical reasoning.

3. Mathematics education reform as the introduction of "hot" new topics (e.g., fractals, discrete mathematics, probability, algebra in early grades) may also get caught in either of the first two interpretations of reform.

It may be the case that in the context of the current reforms these interpretations can constitute "stages" in teacher development. However, we must be concerned not to reduce the reforms to either of the mis-interpretations cited above. Project directors and staff developers must themselves be aware of the attractions of these reductive interpretations of the reform agenda and the dangers these reductions pose to the success of reform. Assessment procedures should allow identification of those teachers whose instruction enacts these interpretations (Schifter, 1995, 1996–a, 1996–b; Schifter & Simon, 1992).

References

Russell, S. J. (1994). *Explorations in number, data, and space.* Palo Alto, CA: Dale Seymour.

Russell, S. J., & Corwin, R. B. (1993). Talking mathematics: "Going slow" and "letting go." *Phi Delta Kappan, 74*(7), 553–8.

Russell, S. J., Schifter, D., Bastable, V., Yaffee, L., Lester, J., & Cohen, S. (1995). Learning mathematics while teaching. In B. S. Nelson (Ed.), *Inquiry and the development of teaching: Issues in the transformation of mathematics teaching* (pp. 9–16). Newton, MA: Center for the Development of Teaching, Education Development Center, Inc.

Schifter, D. (1993). Mathematics process as mathematics content: A course for teachers. *Journal of Mathematical Behavior, 12*(3), 271–83.

Schifter, D. (1994). *Voicing the new pedagogy: Teachers write about learning and teaching mathematics.* Newton, MA: Center for the Development of Teaching, Education Development Center, Inc.

Schifter, D. (1995). Teachers' changing conceptions of the nature of mathematics: Enactment in the classroom. In B. S. Nelson (Ed.), *Inquiry and the development of teaching: Issues in the transformation of mathematics teaching* (pp. 17–26). Newton, MA: Center for the Development of Teaching, Education Development Center, Inc.

Schifter, D. (Ed.) (1996–a). *What's happening in math class? Volume 1: Envisioning new practices through teacher narratives.* New York: Teachers College Press.

Schifter, D. (Ed.) (1996–b). *What's happening in math class? Volume 2: Reconstructing professional identities.* New York: Teachers College Press.

Schifter, D., & Fosnot, C. T. (1993). *Reconstructing mathematics education: Stories of teachers meeting the challenge of reform.* New York: Teachers College Press.

Schifter, D., Russell, S. J., & Bastable, V. (in press). Teaching to the big ideas. In M. Solomon (Ed.), *Reinventing the classroom.*

Schifter, D., & Simon, M. A. (1992). Assessing teachers' development of a constructivist view of mathematics learning. *Teaching and Teacher Education, 8*(2), 187–97.

Simon, M. A., & Schifter, D. (1991). Towards a constructivist perspective: An intervention study of mathematics teacher development. *Educational Studies in Mathematics, 22,* 309–31.

Schifter, D., Bastable, V., Russell, S. J., Cohen, S., Yaffee, L., & Lester, J. (in preparation). *Developing mathematical ideas: A curriculum for teacher learning.*

The Lead Teacher Program of Virginia's State Systematic Initiative

Robert G. Underhill
Virginia Tech

The Virginia Quality Education in Science and Technology (V-QUEST) initiative is the Commonwealth's long-term plan for systematic reform of mathematics and science education. V-QUEST was begun formally in the fall of 1992, but was preceded by a full year of organizing and start-up activities.

At present, V-QUEST is organized into seven components, which are all overseen by the Project Director, Dr. Joe Exline, who has a 20-year career with the Virginia Department of Education (VDOE) as a science educator. Each component has a coordinator who is *not* in VDOE who works half-time with V-QUEST, a VDOE employee who serves as the Department Liaison, some support staff, and a Steering Committee. The project is aimed at statewide K–14 reform. The V-QUEST Executive Policy Board is chaired by the Secretary of Education and includes her top three executives (Superintendent of Public Instruction, Director of the Community College System, and Director of the State Council for Higher Education). Other members include the Secretary for Economic Development and State Senators and Delegates from the two houses of state government who are key figures on education and economic committees.

The Seven Components and their Long-Term Goals

School-Based Mathematics and Science Lead Teachers: To have two Lead Teachers in every elementary and middle school in the Commonwealth

New Pre-/In-Service Models: To facilitate mathematics and science reform in grades 9–14 and to re-design all mathematics and science teacher education programs

Instructional Materials Reform: To influence the design, marketing and use of all textbooks, software, and other resources for teaching mathematics and science in K–14

Local Educational Leadership/Administrative Support: To inform and gain support for reform from superintendents, principals and other key central administrators

Community Action Campaign: To disseminate the V-QUEST vision and to mobilize numerous constituency groups into supportive action

Communications Technology: To help communicate the V-QUEST mission across the state in all forms of media and to facilitate the use of all appropriate technologies in K-14 mathematics and science instruction

Assessment: To align assessment content and procedures with Project 2061 and the NCTM *Standards*

What Have We Learned?

We have completed our training process for 30 pilot Lead Teachers and 240 Year 1 Lead Teachers. We are about half-way through our program for an additional 240 Year 2 Lead Teachers. By drawing upon the talents of many people across the state and by collecting voluminous amounts of evaluation data from staff and participants, our steering committee has made numerous changes which reflect the best thinking of everyone involved.

Delivery and Participant Selection

1. *A major residential experience is essential.* We have our teachers together for three weeks. Our teachers and staff believe that this is vital for networking and building an *esprit de corps.*

2. *The residential experience needs to be separated into at least two major parts.* We have our teachers together for two weeks on the late summer and then one week after the academic year in late June. Our staff believe that teachers undergo a transformation in self-perception from good teachers to building-level staff developers over this period of time.

3. *Lead Teachers need regular contact over an extended period of time.* During the academic year, we have two regional drive-in conferences (at four different locations), pre-sessions before our state mathematics and science conferences, and a two-day V-QUEST leadership conference. We have developed three special videos (newspapers, gender equity, and assessment); we send a copy to each participating school division with support materials. State-wide television did not work because only high schools have satellite

downlinks. We also have a monthly newsletter and a state-funded electronic mail and bulletin board system.

4. *A cadre of 80 seems to optimize the use of staff and facilities.* We usually have either 40 elementary teachers and 40 middle school teachers at a site or two sets of 40 elementary teachers. This permits us to conduct our sessions in groups of 20, 40, or 80. By running two groups simultaneously, we can use the talents of our staff members more effectively.

5. *A staffing pair of classroom teacher and supervisor or university faculty strengthens the experience base and knowledge base and, thus, the credibility of a program.* Whenever we have 20 mathematics Lead Teachers or 20 science Lead Teachers in a learning session, there are always two staff members who are co-teaching the session.

6. *Staff members need to practice what the program espouses.* Our staff model hands-on, minds-on science and mathematical problem solving environments. Our staff members also use state-of-the-art technology and collaborative learning groups.

7. *Equity needs among staff and Lead Teachers need to be addressed.* Our selection process for school division and Lead Teachers has special requirements and opportunities for traditional underserved and underrepresented populations, especially related to ethnicity and income.

8. *Work with school divisions as the targeted unit of impact in the selection process.* By working with divisions in the application process, we generate awareness, support and commitment at the central administrative/superintendent level.

9. *Once a division is selected, work with four to six schools each year until all are served, as long as there is a good faith effort.* We did this so that we could involve more school divisions in the beginning. It turned out to be a good decision based on two other results: it gives us some leverage in school divisions which are not complying, and it permits a school division to target extra resources to those schools during the year of training.

10. *Require principal participation.* In signing our application, the superintendent asserts that for each school selected, the principal will attend two days of our two-week institutes and one day of our one-week institutes. Principals are also invited to the drive-in regional workshops and receive the monthly newsletter.

11. *Educate key figures in the school division.* After a school division is accepted, we deliver a two-hour on-site presentation for the superintendent, other central administrators, principals and teachers about mathematics and science reform and about V-QUEST.

12. *Train two Lead Teachers for each building.* Our original plan was to have one, but we changed this before we started our pilot. The main

reason was a psychological one: we believe that change agents need strong support mechanisms. The second reason was that it would offer greater strength if *both* could be trained in leadership and integration, but each could specialize in mathematics or science.

13. *Get early resource commitments from school divisions.* As part of our application, we determine such things as how much released time will be granted (usually one day each month), what resources are available for mathematics and science instruction, the availability of e-mail, and so on. In general, the divisions who offer the most are the ones selected.

Content

1. *Every Lead Teacher needs leadership training.* These are good teachers, but they are not necessarily good staff developers. About 25% of our training focuses on adult learners; how to plan, conduct and deliver workshops; how to work with administrators; possible activities and roles for Lead Teachers, etc.

2. *Every Lead Teacher needs to understand connections between mathematics and science.* About 25% of our program focuses on developing conceptual models, creating activities and examining curriculum programs such as AIMS, TIMS, T/S/M, and Mission 21.

3. *Each Lead Teacher needs to be a building-level mathematics or science leader.* About 50% of our program consists of in-depth leadership, content, and pedagogy training in one of these disciplines.

4. *All Lead Teachers need to be able to provide assessment leadership.* Our SSI Assessment Component has developed a video and overheads for use with colleagues. Our Lead Teachers also have at least a half-day session on assessment at our summer institutes.

5. *All Lead Teachers need to be able to provide instructional materials leadership.* Our SSI Instructional Materials Component has formed a 13+ state consortium which has developed criteria for the selection, design and development of textbooks, software, and other instructional materials. Texas, New York and California are among the partners in this consortium.

6. *All Lead Teachers need to be able to interact with the broader community.* Our Community Action Component has developed a video and a handbook for use by Lead Teachers and community leaders. Also, the Lead Teacher Component has developed two speeches with overhead masters and an outline of major points.

7. *Reform needs to be across grades K–14.* Our SSI believes that change can only be systemic when *all* students can experience Project

2061 science and NCTM *Standards* in mathematics in grades 9–14 as well as K–8.

8. *The program needs to focus on teacher empowerment.* We do not tell Lead Teachers what to do. We have a six page, single-spaced list of *possibilities.* We view our role as empowering teachers to be leaders and providing training and ideas through which they operationalize their personal styles according to local needs.

What Implementation Advice Can We Give?

We organized ourselves for a year before we had NSF funding for our SSI. We used VDOE Eisenhower funds to finance a pilot program. We have made many changes along the way, primarily due to conditions which were difficult or impossible to anticipate. Our basic process has served us *exceptionally* well.

1. *Maximize early input.* We had drive-in conferences or discussion days with the university science/science education community, the university mathematics/mathematics education community, community college mathematics and science representatives, the Virginia Science Leadership Association, and the Virginia Council for Mathematics Supervision. Every institution of higher education in the state was extended an invitation to send two or more people.

2. *Appoint a Planning Committee of highly respected members of three major levels: K–8 teachers, supervisors, and higher education.* Since our pilot program was for elementary schools, we chose two elementary teachers who were Presidential Award Winners in mathematics and science, two public school supervisors who had provided leadership in school-based lead teacher training program development and implementation, and two university mathematics and science educators who have long histories of providing leadership in the state. These people designed, developed outcomes for, and implemented the pilot program.

3. *Communicate, communicate, communicate!* We continued to correspond with the community college and university people who attended the invitational meetings and published updates in every newsletter or journal of the four state mathematics and science organizations.

4. *Develop a pilot program.* We selected three school divisions with a total of 15 schools with 30 teachers and 15 principals.

5. *Document the pilot program carefully.* We videotaped all sessions (we used these hardly at all), held staff de-briefing sessions every day,

established comprehensive archives, and collected daily and summative evaluation information from participants.

6. *Revise the program content based on the pilot.* Our Planning Committee revised the outcomes in four categories: leadership, integrated mathematics and science, mathematics, and science. All of these focused on what we wanted *Lead Teachers* to be able to do as building-level staff developers. For each outcome, we prepared institute expectations and a *suggested* set of activities/resources.

7. *Revise the program logistics based on the pilot.* We gave special attention to air conditioning (!), access to suitable technology, and staff selection.

8. *Establish a fair and open staff-selection process for full-scale implementation.* We invited all supervisors and higher education people to attend at one-and-a-half day session on the institutes which was delivered by the planning team. Data were collected from all 45 participants as to which outcomes they felt well-prepared to deliver, teacher and collegial references whom we could contact, a summary of previous work in mathematics and science with elementary teachers, and summer availability. All 45 of these people were also requested to provide names and addresses of outstanding teachers for staff consideration. Data were subsequently collected from all 30 of the pilot teachers and those teachers suggested by the 45 attendees. The Planning Committee made the final selections.

9. *Plan for two-week institute continuity of staffing.* Since many supervisors and higher education faculty are not available for two weeks, we agreed that all staff members who were classroom teachers would be required to be present for the full two weeks, and we decided to use senior staff persons for one week each, whenever possible. We made a deliberate decision to limit our use of one-day consultants, feeling it disrupted continuity too much.

10. *Provide professional development for staff members.* Based on our participant and staff feedback, we ascertained five areas of general weakness in our program. So far we have had two 1 1/2 day staff development sessions on the routine integration of technology in mathematics and science instruction and articulating the leadership aspects of our own work with participants such as planning, determining which resources were appropriate, assessment, determining the sequence of events, and asking questions such as "Why did I say that? Why did I do it that way?"

What Suggestions Do We Have For Monitoring and Evaluating Change?

1. *Develop a set of systemic indicators.* In several days of project team effort over a six-month period, V-QUEST developed a set of indicators which if influenced would imply success of our efforts.

2. *Develop a carefully thought out set of projects.* This was a complicated undertaking. We had a set of 14 major projects for the year, only four of which were the institute experiences for teachers and principals.

3. *For each project, designate a set of activities which will be involved, a time line, success indicators, and an evaluation plan.* For our 14 projects, we had approximately 45 activities which constituted a 90-page work plan for the Lead Teacher Component.

4. *Articulate the relationship between projects/activities and the systemic change indicators: add, delete and modify projects /activities as needed.* This process permitted us to see if too much effort was being expended toward some goals and not enough on others.

5. *Collect, analyze, interpret evaluation data to make changes in all phases of your program in a regular and systematic way.* We view our work as evolutionary. Sensitivity to many diverse aspects of our work is imperative. Constant mid-course corrections and modifications to our work plan are hallmarks of our effort.

Appendix C:
Final Conference Agenda

*Reflecting on Our Work: NSF Teacher
Enhancement in K–6 Mathematics*

Washington, D.C. • November 18–20, 1994

---

*Mathematics teachers develop professionally in the same ways
all other teachers do but with a specific focus of applying
professional knowledge within a meaningful and relevant
mathematical context for the improvement of the mathematical
understanding of children and youth.*

*Professional development takes many forms, but true
professional development, in the sense of resulting in
meaningful and long-lasting qualitative change in a teacher's
thinking and approaches to educating, is an autonomous
activity chosen by a teacher in search of better ways of
knowing and teaching mathematics.*

(Castle, K. and Aichele, D. B., 1994, p. 3)

Friday, November 18

8:30 – 9:15 a.m.   Continental Breakfast (Gallery I)

9:15 – 9:45 a.m.   Introductions (Gallery I)
Overview of conference purpose and
organization
Review newly-revised Agenda for Friday

The purpose of this conference is to organize,
summarize, and discuss what is known about
models of effective teacher enhancement by
addressing the following central question:

> *As a result of research and experience, what do we know about teacher enhancement programs K–6 in mathematics that can inform the design of large-scale teacher enhancement programs with optimal impact?*
>
> (Friel, S. N., NSF Conference Proposal)

9:45 – 10:15 a.m.   Deborah Ball, issues-identification author, reflects on her paper:

Based on additional reflection and/or what you have read, in what ways do you want to expand, highlight, change, redirect, or refocus comments you have made?

10:15 – 10:30 a.m.   Working groups formed (will meet in Gallery I, Rembrandt, Renoir, Rooms 324 or 524) and tasks for working groups clarified

10:30 – 11:00 a.m.   Break (Gallery I)

11:00 – 12:30 p.m.   Working groups meet: each group will identify a facilitator and a recorder (with access to both a computer and easel/chart paper).

Deborah proposes a tentative list of widely held beliefs about teacher learning. In your groups:

1. React to this list, clarifying, revising, expanding, adding, and so on with the goal of developing a tentative list of beliefs about teacher learning from the conference that may be used across different models of professional development.

2. Using the list of beliefs provided (adding any needed updates from your earlier discussion to the beliefs), each person considers his or her involvement in an elementary teacher enhancement project—

either one that is included in one of the response papers or, in a few cases, some other project not discussed in the papers—addressing the following question for *each* of the beliefs:
How did your project take into account this belief?
The first column in the chart provides space for recording reflections and descriptions.

3. The group decides how they want to share the results of individual reflections. For example, the discussion may focus on just one of the nine (or more) beliefs, with each person discussing his or her response. The second column is provided for "after thoughts"—thoughts triggered by the discussions that a person may want to record.

Facilitators will meet with Susan, George, and a few others at lunch so that we can have a single report from the five groups after lunch.

12:30 –1:45 p.m.   Lunch (Buffet in Hotel Restaurant)

If the reforms being espoused [in the Curriculum and Evaluation Standards and the Teaching Standards] are to be implemented in a pervasive manner in all mathematics classrooms, it is vital that models [visions] be developed for staff development that will produce worthwhile and enduring change.

(Jones, G. A., et al., p. 23)

1:45 – 2:15 p.m.   Report back from working groups with open discussion (Gallery I).

2:15 – 3:15 p.m.   Working groups formed (Gallery I, Rembrandt, Renoir, Rooms 324 or 524).

                        Characterizing existing models for professional development and addressing questions of scaling up with respect to these models.

                        Considering the use of curriculum as a vehicle for teacher development.

                        Identifying issues related to capacity-building instead of addressing scaling-up.

                        Identifying issues and/or concerns focused on social, cultural, and community aspects related to professional development.

3:15 – 3:45 p.m.   Break (Gallery I).

3:45 – as needed   Working groups continue as needed.

5:45 – 6:30 p.m.   NSF charge clarified—Margaret Cozzens (Gallery I).

                        What are the parameters of the charge from Congress with respect to professional development? What have been NSF's responses so far? What else does NSF expect to happen in terms of responding to the charge? Where do the guidelines from this conference fit into what NSF is trying to do?

7:00 –9.00 p.m.   Dinner at hotel (Gallery III).

Saturday, November 19

> *The standards in this section are organized around a framework emphasizing the important decisions that a teacher makes in teaching—*
>
> • *Setting goals and selecting or creating mathematical tasks to help students achieve goals:*
>
> • *Stimulating and managing classroom discourse so that both the students and the teacher are clearer about what is being learned.*
>
> • *Creating a classroom environment to support teaching and learning mathematics;*
>
> • *Analyzing student learning, the mathematical tasks, and the environment in order to make ongoing instructional decisions.*
>
> (NCTM, 1991, p. 5)

8:30 – 9:00 a.m. Continental Breakfast (Renoir Room).

9:00 – 9:30 a.m. Clarifying questions for NSF from participants related to discussion of NSF charge provided Friday.

Reflecting on results from our work on Friday: Any questions? Comments?

Clarification of task—Developing a "portfolio" of RFPs:

Part I: Design an RFP for an NSF Program
Develop an outline for an RFP that focuses on scaling up in one of the five areas noted below. As part of the outline, detail a rationale about how scaling up is possible and then what's

essential, what's desirable, and what's variable with respect to the RFP. Do remember to consider the set of beliefs we reviewed Friday.

Part II: Imagine a response to your RFP as a way to "prove" the feasibility of your ideas. Outline the details of this response.

Part III: Identify insights, dilemmas, and so on that emerged during the completion of Parts I and II.

Areas:

1. Capacity building (Bill)

2. Attach scaling up to some other kind of resource(s): video, writing about practice, implementation of curriculum. (Susan Jo)

3. Identify principles of professional development (best practices) from previous teacher enhancement projects and create different framework. (George)

4. Consider scaling up by working within existing institutions, e.g. develop a set of possible ways to respond to the LSI.

9:30 – 11:30 a.m.	Groups work on Part I (take coffee to NSF!)
11:30 – 12:30 p.m.	Groups pair up to present their ideas and receive helpful critiques.
12:30 – 1:45 p.m.	Lunch (Buffet in Hotel Restaurant).
1:45 – 2:15 p.m.	Open discussion (Renoir Room)

		Report on where groups are with task. What are the "tough issues" with which they are struggling?

2:15 – 4:45 p.m.   Return to working groups to finish task

3:45 – 4:15 p.m.   Break Available (Renoir Room—May be brought to NSF?).

Please plan to pick up copies of materials from front desk in hotel at 6:00 p.m. and to have read material for Sunday.

5:00p.m.   Dinner—On your own with reimbursement from Conference ($23.00).

Sunday, November 20

8:30 – 9:00 a.m.   Continental Breakfast (Gallery III).

9:00 – 9:30 a.m.   Individually reviewing notes from Saturday group work.

9:30 – 10:30 a.m.   Discussion of results of our work on Saturday.

Bill, Susan Jo, George, Ann will each provide any additional comments needed and then we will take time for questions, reflections, and suggestions from the larger group.

Next steps: Each group's material will be "smoothed out" by one of the group members (Barbara, Deborah or Susan Jo(?), George, Ann(?)), disk and hard copy returned to Susan by December 2, and mailed out to entire group for comments to be returned by December 19.

10:30 – 10:45 a.m. Break.

10:45 – 11:45 a.m. Surfacing important reminders

(30 minutes) Reflections on monitoring the effects of projects (George Hein).

How best to continue further dialogue (through e-mail ?).

Reflections on addressing issues of equity and diversity (Leo Edwards).

Reflections on addressing the role of technology (Bob Spielvogel).

Reflections on addressing implications for preservice education (Sid Rachlin).

11:45 – 12:00 noon   Next steps

Executive committee will "make sense" of the discussion; distribute synthesis of recommendations to participants for reaction; final recommendations go to NSF by February (and will be included in proceedings).

References

Aichele, D. B., & Coxford, A. F. (Eds.) (1994). *Professional development for teachers of mathematics.* Reston, VA: National Council of Teachers of Mathematics.

Castle, K., & Aichele, D. B. (1994). Professional development and teacher autonomy. In D. B. Aichele & A. F. Coxford (Eds.), *Professional development for teachers of mathematics* (pp. 1–8). Reston, VA: National Council of Teachers of Mathematics.

Jones, G. A., Lubinski, C. A., Swafford, J. O., & Thornton, C. A. (1994). A framework for the professional development of K–12 mathematics teachers. In D. B. Aichele & A. F. Coxford (Eds.), *Professional development for teachers of mathematics* (pp. 23–36). Reston, VA: National Council of Teachers of Mathematics.

National Council of Teachers of Mathematics, (1991). *Professional Standards for Teaching Mathematics.* Reston, VA: Author.

Appendix D
TEACHER RETRAINING:

*Report to the Senate Appropriations Committee
from
The National Science Foundation*

(Senate Report No. 103-97)

*The Committee also directs the Foundation to prepare an assessment of
the proper pace at which the Federal Government should increase teacher
retraining activities so as to reach the ... figure suggested to the
Committee by FCCSET representatives. This outline should be
submitted as part of the 1995 budget request. It should include a
breakdown of the various kinds of retraining activities counted toward
the annual calculation of how many mathematics and science teachers
are reached by Federal assistance.*

Background. The Committee on Education and Human Resources
(CEHR) of the Federal Coordinating Council on Science, Engineering,
and Technology (FCCSET) was established in 1990.[1] During its first
two years, the 16 member research and development (R&D) agencies
generated the first inventory of Federal science, engineering, and
mathematics programs; an education priority framework; and developed
new areas of program emphasis, i.e., public science literacy, educational
technologies, dissemination, and evaluation.[2] With the FY 1994 budget
submission, CEHR submitted *Pathways to Excellence: A Federal
Strategy for Science, Mathematics, Engineering, and Technology
Education*, a five-year framework meant to focus Federal planning and
resources on achieving mathematics and science competence for all
students.

---

[1] Under the Clinton Administration, FCCSET-CEHR has been replaced by
the National Science Technology Council (NSTC) Committee on Education
and Technology (CET).

[2] The 11 key member agencies comprising the FY 1993 CEHR budget
include: Department of Education (ED) and the National Science Foundation
(NSF)—Vice-Chairs; Departments of Agriculture (USDA), Commerce (DOC),
Defense (DOD), Energy (DOE), Health and Human Services (HHS), Interior
(DOI), and the Environmental Protection Agency (EPA); the National
Aeronautics and Space Administration (NASA); and the Smithsonian
Institution (SI).

Defining the Need. National Education Goal #4, that "U.S. Students Should be First in the World in Science and Mathematics by the Year 2000," underlies the framework for the Strategic Plan which sets CEHR objectives and implementation priorities. Throughout its planning, CEHR recognized that immediate upgrading of the teacher workforce held the most promise for making rapid improvements in student performance. The magnitude and nature of the need was identified in a 1988 NSF study which reported that nearly one-half of the nation's 2.2 million mathematics and science teachers, especially those at the elementary level, require extensive upgrading in both disciplinary competency and pedagogical skills.[3]

FCCSET-SEHR Strategy. A cornerstone of the CEHR Strategy, therefore, entailed providing intensive disciplinary and pedagogical training to 600,000 teachers, emphasizing those at the elementary level, from 1993 to 1998. The following table lists milestones initially set forth in the Strategic Plan, as well as a revised delivery schedule:

	CEHR Strategic Plan	NSF	Revised Strategy ED	Others
FY 1993	45,000	46,000	20,000	1,000
FY 1994	68,000	55,000	I	1,000
FY 1995	102,500	60,000	I	1,000
FY 1996	113,000	75,000	128,000	1,000
FY 1997	124,500	95,000	needed	1,000
FY 1998	137,000	115,000	I	1,000
Total	**590,000**	**446,000**	**148,000**	**6,000**

Table 1. FCCSET-CEHR Teacher Enhancement Goals and Distribution Across Agencies Strategic Plan and Current Timetable.

Assumptions Underlying Strategic Plan Milestones. Attainment of the goal was predicated on several factors: (1) all CEHR agencies have a role and responsibility to play in achieving the goal (mission agencies, under direction of DOE, would implement teacher enhancement initiative utilizing Federal laboratory resources; (2) ED

---

[3] See "Course Background Preparation of Science and Mathematics Teachers in the United States," National Science Foundation, 1988.

enhancement initiative utilizing Federal laboratory resources; (2) ED and NSF would necessarily remain the dominant players, most likely accounting for 80–90 percent of the overall figures; (3) ED would seek and attain legislative changes in the Eisenhower Program so as to affect changes in the utilization of these funds to encourage more intensive training of participating teachers;[4] and, (4) the milestone could be achieved only through greater efficiency within existing programs, redirection of resources and/or changes in extant programs, and funding increments.

Defining Intensive Training. The participating agencies, in developing the pre-kindergarten through grade 12 (preK–12) program, defined "intensive disciplinary and pedagogical training" as that which includes experiences that adhere to high content standards, incorporate appropriate pedagogy, and provide sufficient time for learning, practice, and follow-up. The experiences must (1) provide content consistent with national mathematics and science standards, demonstrate pedagogy that reflects current research in teaching and learning, and convey disciplinary knowledge that relates to student environment and experiences; (2) be of appropriate design and duration to constitute a powerful intervention; and (3) ensure enduring benefits that are an integral part of a long-term systemic approach to improving the performance of teachers, schools, and students. See the Appendix of this report for further details on the various kinds of retraining activities.

Meeting the Goals. Under the Plan, NSF and ED share the bulk of the responsibility for providing intensive training to nearly 30 percent of the teacher workforce over the 1993–98 period. The contribution of ED greatly depends on the level of funding for science and mathematics under the Eisenhower Program (there are some plans to broaden its focus to other fields), as well as the leverage that it can exert over use of those funds. Should ED not be able to meet its target numbers, increased pressure will be placed on NSF if milestones are to be met.

---

[4] The distribution of Eisenhower funds is formula driven, reaching States, institutions of higher education, and localities. Much of the training that qualifies as intensive is accomplished under the 25 percent allocation that goes to institutions of higher education.

Definition of Intensive Disciplinary and Pedagogical Training

FCCSET-CEHR Strategic Plan

Intensive disciplinary and pedagogical training provides experiences that adhere to high content standards, incorporate appropriate pedagogy, and provide sufficient time for initial learning, practice, and follow-up. All of the following components of professional development must be included:

1. Identifiable elements in the experiences must include:

    *   Content consistent with the national mathematics and science standards, or with state and district frameworks that are tied to these or comparable standards;
    *   Pedagogy that reflects current research in teaching and learning, e.g., hands-on learning, problem solving, questioning aimed at uncovering misconceptions, on-going assessment of student learning, and cooperative learning; and,
    *   Training that enables teachers to convey disciplinary knowledge that is integrated and connected with students' lives, families, and communities.

2. Experiences must be of appropriate design and duration to constitute a powerful intervention:

    *   Pedagogy used in professional development experiences must be appropriate for experienced adults;
    *   Uninterrupted learning time must be adequate to support the kind of in-depth, inquiry, reflection, and try-out needed to gain mastery of standards-based content and new teaching approaches; and,
    *   Meaningful follow-up should support participants' efforts to effectively apply, adapt, and extend what they have learned.

3. To ensure enduring benefits, the experiences must be designed not as isolated activities but as a component of a long-term systemic approach to improving the performance of teachers, schools, and students.

    *   The experiences should be part of a long-term, coherent individual, school or district plan.

- Whenever possible, teachers (and administrators) should participate as teams rather than individuals; and,
- In addition to an emphasis on individual development, there should be modeling of team efforts by teachers, administrators, supervisors and others who assist systemic reform at the school and district levels.

4. Most importantly, projects should be designed to achieve specific outcomes:

- Acquaint teachers with the content and pedagogy necessary for children to learn mathematics and science to high standards;
- Provide teachers with units of curriculum tied to high standards; and,
- Create positive changes in teaching methods.

Appendix E: Participant List

Deborah Ball	Michigan State University
James Boone	National Science Foundation
John Bradley	National Science Foundation
Peter Braunfeld	University of Illinois
George Bright	University of North Carolina–Greensboro
William Bush	University of Kentucky
Patricia Campbell	University of Maryland–College Park
Rebecca Corwin	TERC
Margaret Cozzens	National Science Foundation
Karen Dameron	E. J. Hayes Elementary, NC
Mary Lee Danielson	Chapel Hill Public Schools, NC
Leo Edwards	Fayetteville State University
Margaret Eisenhart	University of Colorado
Joyce Evans	National Science Foundation
Elizabeth Fennema	University of Wisconsin
Joan Ferrini-Mundi	National Research Council
Susan Friel	University of North Carolina–Chapel Hill
Ann Grady	Humphrey Center, MA
Linda Gregg	Clark County School District, NV
George Hein	Lesley College
Mark St. John	Inverness Research Associates
Jeane Joyner	N.C. Department of Public Instruction
Annie Keith	John Muir Elementary School, WI
Henry Kepner	National Science Foundation
Richard Lesh	Educational Testing Service
Franzie Loepp	Illinois State University
Susan Loucks-Horsley	National Center for Improving Science Education
Barbara Scott Nelson	Educational Development Center, Inc.
Emma Owens	National Science Foundation
Ruth Parker	Consultant
Jerry Pine	CalTech
Sid Rachlin	East Carolina University
Josepha Robles	Rolling Terrace Elementary School, MD
Susan Jo Russell	TERC
Deborah Schifter	Educational Development Center, Inc.
Susan Snyder	National Science Foundation

Robert Spielvogel	Center for Children and Technology
Diane Spresser	National Science Foundation
Joseph Stewart	National Science Foundation
Robert Underhill	Virginia Tech
Jean Vanski	National Science Foundation
Iris Weiss	Horizon Research, Inc.
Karen Worth	Educational Development Center, Inc.

The report of the conference, *Reflecting on Our Work: NSF Teacher Enhancement in K–6 Mathematics*, was prepared with the support of National Science Foundation Grant Number ESI-9452859. Any opinions, findings, conclusions, or recommendations expressed in this publication are those of the editors and the authors and do not necessarily represent the views of the National Science Foundation.

For additional information about this report, contact:

Susan N. Friel
University of North Carolina at Chapel Hill
School of Education
CB #3500, Peabody Hall
Chapel Hill, NC 27599–3500

INSERT COPYRIGHT INFORMATION